LEEK'S GOLDEN YEARS

A portrait of Leek
in Victorian & Edwardian days
with particular reference to
THE SUGDENS,
THE NICHOLSONS,
WILLIAM CHALLINOR,
MATTHEW HENRY MILLER
& WILLIAM KINETON PARKES

Ray Poole

History is the essence of innumerable biographies
Thomas Carlyle (1795-1881) 'On History'

St Edward's Parish church, from Sleigh's 'History'.

An early view of Stockwell Street

CONTENTS

Chapter 1	SPIRITS OF THEIR AGE	p. 11
Chapter 2	NOT FORGETTING THE WOMEN	p. 23
Chapter 3	EARLY VICTORIAN LEEK	p. 29
Chapter 4	LEEK'S VICTORIAN ARCHITECTS	p. 51
Chapter 5	THE LATER SUGDEN YEARS	p. 91
Chapter 6	A FAMILY TRADITION OF SOLICITORS	p. 119
Chapter 7	HEALTH AND WELFARE	p. 135
Chapter 8	THE SHAPING OF THE TOWN	p. 143
Chapter 9	A FLOWERING OF SILK	p. 153
Chapter 10	YORKSHIRE BUSINESS ACUMEN IN LEEK	p. 165
Chapter 11	THE DYNASTY CONTINUES	p. 177
Chapter 12	WORDS WERE HIS BUSINESS	p. 195
Chapter 13	'OLDE LEEKE' AND ALL THAT	p. 213
Chapter 14	A MAN OF MANY PARTS	p. 225
Chapter 15	TIME OFF	p. 247
Chapter 16	FACES IN THE CROWD	p. 275
	POSTSCRIPT	p. 281
	APPENDICES	p. 283

CHURNET VALLEY BOOKS
1 King Street, Leek, Staffordshire. ST13 5NW 01538 399033
www.leekbooks.co.uk
© Ray Poole and Churnet Valley Books 2009
ISBN 9781904546702
All rights reserved. Any use of this book in any form needs the permission of both author and publisher

William Challinor

M.H. Miller

Joshua Nicholson

Mrs Cruso

FOREWORD

This book has been many years a-growing, and it is a very personal book. For as long as I have been interested in local history I have been aware that Leek was a kind of microcosm of the influences which shaped Victorian England, and many of the great movements in industry, commerce and the arts in those years found expression in the town and its people. The Industrial Revolution is here, weaving its way into the development of the silk industry. The Pre-Raphaelites are here, in the fabric designs and art inspired by men like William Morris and Walter Crane. The Arts and Crafts movement is here, in the town's fine Victorian architecture. The drive and energy of empire-building is here, in the men who ran the town's factories, and got themselves involved in local government. The best creative influences in music and drama are here, performed by enthusiastic groups of local folk. And those local folk, who populated the town, dyed the silks, operated the looms, manned the work benches, served in the shops, worked in the market and swept the streets were the life blood of the town.

In attempting to present a picture of Victorian and Edwardian Leek I have chosen to weave the story around the lives, influence and achievements of a group of men who were amongst the movers and shakers of their day. The choice of the leading characters in the story is entirely mine. Another person might have chosen five entirely different personalities, or advanced the argument as to why so-and-so has not been included, for many have a valid right to be here. And why is there no woman in a leading role? All this I accept, but no drama ever succeeds without its supporting cast, and the lives and influence of our main characters touched the lives of many. These were the old days, when the mill owners were still living alongside the people who worked for them and the factories operated under family names rather than the impersonal corporate names which would follow the many take-overs during the next century.

This is a history book, but I would not attempt to pass it off as an academic history, for I am not qualified to write such a book. I have tried to write a portrait of the age, based around some of the outstanding figures of the period. It is meant to be read as a continuous narrative, and for this reason footnotes and numbered references have been omitted, for these would interrupt the flow, and sprinkle the pages like confetti. Nevertheless, there is a wealth of printed and written material, as well as personal memories and newspaper reports, upon which I have voraciously drawn. I am also grateful to those chroniclers of the passing scene who have gone before, and done much of the pioneering work upon which this book is based. All history is judgmental to a certain degree, but I have tried to be impartial, and leave the judgement to others.

Here I must give due acknowledgement to those sources upon which I have drawn, and first and foremost I am sadly aware that during this book's long period of gestation a number of people who were a great inspiration to me have died. I therefore list their names first of all, for in many ways this book is dedicated to their memory.

First, I must mention George Lovenbury, naturalist and local historian. George was probably the first person to recognise the intrinsic value of the work of Sugden and Son, architects. His pioneering work in diligently researching and recording Sugden buildings was published in his little book *The Sugdens of Leek* and in a series of articles in the *Leek Post and Times*. This material provides the basis for others to build upon, and I acknowledge the guidance this has given me. George also took great interest in the lives and achievements of some of Leek's leading citizens, and his booklet *A Certain Group of Men* gave me the title and inspiration for this book. I therefore owe much to the work of the late George Lovenbury, and as he would have been 100 years old in 2007, he provides a direct link back to the times of our story.

Colin Parrack, former secretary of the Leek Civic Society, was another great 'Sugdenarian', and did much to preserve and record Leek's history. His research was always accurate, and his practical skills enabled him to lovingly conserve many features of the Challinor home at Pickwood.

Stuart Hobson was a great collector of all things local, including much Challinor material, and I was privileged to have access to William Challinor's original notebooks. I am grateful to his widow, Barbara, for making this material available.

Mrs Beryl Johnson was the great grand-daughter of William Challinor, and she recorded many family memories in her copious notebooks. Much of this material was published in her modest little book on the history of St Edward Street. Mrs Barbara Priest was also generous with her memories of these times and people.

George Bowyer was a great collector of photographs and postcards, and his extensive knowledge of people from the past is now greatly missed. Harold Bode was passionately keen on Leek's history, and did much to ensure its preservation. His doggedness and persistence were exemplary, and his self-published series of booklets was a fine individual effort. John T. Ellis loved all things local, and had much knowledge of the sculpture of Richard Hassall.

The recording of Leek's history would have been much the poorer without the work of people such as these I have mentioned, and I pay grateful tribute to their memory. Without them, and the memories they have often shared with me, this book could not have been written.

In writing this book I have drawn upon much previously published material, and I give due acknowledgement to this. George Lovenbury's published work has already been mentioned, and the works of Leek's Victorian historians, John Sleigh and MH Miller have been extensively consulted. William Challinor's *Lectures, Verses, Speeches, Reminiscences etc* (1891) yielded many insights into his personality. Local newspapers, *Leek Times* and *Leek Post* have provided much material. Fred Hill's annual journal *Leek News* published during the 1920s and 30s have been a rich source of material, particularly the writings of the Small Boy in the Market Place. *Leek and District Illustrated* (1897) provided much information and many illustrations of Sugden work. Similar valuable source material on the Sugdens was found in the publications *The Builder, The Building News* and *The British Architect*.

Trade directories are always useful, and Leek was blessed in having numerous local examples of these, including White's and Kelly's. The very detailed annual reports of the Leek Improvement Commissioners give very comprehensive accounts of the business of the local government of the day. *Fifty Years of Municipal Government in Leek, 1855 to 1905* continued the story into the time of the Leek Urban District Council. *A History of Trade Unionism in the North Staffordshire Textile Industry* by Frank Burchill and Jim Sweeney (1971) provides a wealth of material on work in the silk mills and the growth of the unions.

More contemporary works of great relevance include: *Sweetness and Light* by Mark Girouard, *Images of Edwardian Leek* edited by Paul Anderton, *Victoria County History of Staffordshire* Vol.7, *The Wardle Story* by Ann Jacques, various issues of 'Chronicles' the occasional journal of the Leek Historical Society, *The History of Leekfrith* by Mary Breeze, *The Nicholson Institute: a study in middle class munificence 1881-1910* by Pauline Smith (1984), *St Edward Street and Broad Street Past and Present* by George Lovenbury, *The Story of a Leek Church* by Henry Woodhouse (1988), *Leek Miscellany* and the three volumes of *Leek Trade Bills* (Churnet Valley Books), Pevsner's *Buildings of England (Staffordshire)* and the fine series of books *The Spirit of Leek* and *Lost Houses of North Staffordshire* by Cathryn Walton and Lindsey Porter (Landmark).

Various organisations and groups have been a great help in providing information and material, and I am happy to list the following: Leek Historical Society, Leek and Moorlands Historical Trust, Leek Field Club, Leek Library, Leek Cricket Club, Keighley Library, Staffordshire Records Office.

There is an army of individuals who have contributed, either directly or indirectly, to the writing of this book, and I acknowledge their great help. I was fortunate, in connection with the Sugdens, to make contact with a Keighley member of the family. Phillipa Blackburn (née Sugden) provided much information on the Sugdens of Keighley and their achievements. A mutual friend, Oliver Gomersal of Buxton, forged the initial contact, and has fed information to me from time to time as I have worked on this book. The late Dr Mike Langham, also of Buxton, contributed particulars of Sugden's 'Red House' in Buxton. Another Sugden link from afar came in the person of Peter Webb of Framlingham, where William Sugden spent his time before coming to Leek. He was able to fill in some of the gaps in Sugden's early years, and gave me photographic evidence of the architectural styles in Framlingham which influenced Sugden's later work. I was also fortunate to make contact with Karen White who owns one of the houses in Hartley's Aintree Model Village.

Then, in April 2008, I met another member of the Sugden family, Mark Sugden of Sydney, Australia, and I was able to show him round the Sugden buildings in Leek.

It is always good to make contact with direct descendents of the person you are writing about, and with regard to Kineton Parkes this came in the person of Mrs Sue Butler-Cole, of Exeter, whose mother, Mrs H Lloyd-Jones, was the grand-daughter of Kineton Parkes. On one memorable occasion the two ladies visited Leek, and sat at the former librarian's desk at Leek Library, surrounded by a selection of his books. *The Socialist History Society's pamphlet on Votes for Women: the struggle for the vote in the Black Country 1900-1918* by George J Barnsby gave me some clues about Mrs Kineton Parkes' activities after leaving Leek.

Many local people have provided help, either directly or indirectly, in a number of ways - the snippet of conversation, the occasional photograph, the original document or map, an article or piece of writing, the odd piece of family history - all these have helped to complete the picture. I therefore list the following, and thank them for what they, sometimes unknowingly, have contributed:

Alan Bednall, John White, Cathryn Walton, Paul Anderton, Robert Milner, Geoffrey Fisher, Basil Jeuda, Robert Cartwright, Edgar Tooth, Anne Senior, Jill Norman, Mrs Keates, Chris Ellis, John Leach, Chris Sheldon, Marion Aldis, Pam Inder, Paul Chaveau, John Newall, Tony Busfield, Geoff Browne, Doug Pickford, Trevor Siggers, Dr Faith Cleverdon, Bud Abbott, Michael Barr, Lindsey Porter, Gerald Mee MBE, George Short, Bill Cawley and the Rev Michael Fisher.

I offer my apologies to any inadvertently omitted from this list.

Finally, a word of sincere thanks to my wife, Dorothy, who manages to live with piles of files, boxes of photographs, books, maps and other documents constantly appearing in various corners of our home. For tolerating these intrusions, I offer many thanks.

Kineton Parkes

Sir Arthur Nicholson

William Sugden

Larner Sugden

One
SPIRITS OF THEIR AGE

A YORKSHIREMAN left his home town of Keighley in 1848 to travel to the moorland town of Leek, in North Staffordshire. The countryside he travelled through was destined later to become a great attraction for the many seeking escape from the smoke and grime of the flourishing industrial towns of Lancashire and South Yorkshire.

This was by no means a pleasure trip for the Yorkshireman, even though, with his solid, middle-class background he would have been able to afford it; rather was it a journey with a mission, and one which would change the shape of his future life and make a lasting mark on the moorland community which beckoned him. He could hardly have anticipated this as he caught his first sight of the town, the only tall building being the tower of the ancient Parish Church of Saint Edward, rising above the simple houses of the townsfolk, and the few small factories and dyeworks where they found employment, for this was a silk town. He could not envisage the changes his subsequent work would make.

As he journeyed south, his mind was firmly on the commission he had been granted, the sole reason for his journey. A qualified architect, he had been assigned the brief to act as the supervising architect for the building of the stations along the line of the Churnet Valley Railway, the latest project of the North Staffordshire Railway Company. The company had been vigorously developing a railway network throughout North Staffordshire and the Potteries towns which now provided a ready means of travel, both for business and pleasure, for thousands of people in the area, as well as transporting products from the factories and coal from the mines. It eventually became known affectionately as the 'Knotty' in deference to the

Staffordshire Knot emblem adopted by the company.

These years between 1845 and 1852 were the age of Railway Mania. The iron highway was spreading its complex network across the land, and by the late 1840s construction of the new line, bringing rail transport to this remote area of North Staffordshire, was nearing completion. The new line would run from Macclesfield through Leek and the Churnet Valley to Uttoxeter, to join with the Trent Valley line at Tamworth, with a line to Stoke-on-Trent and the Potteries, thus linking the industrial North with the Midlands, Derby and London, and establishing the silk town of Leek firmly on the railway map. The advantages of this speedy and efficient form of transport would be clear to the shrewd silk manufacturers and business men of Leek.

The year was 1848. The young Queen Victoria was in the eleventh year of her long reign; the British Prime Minister, in his first term of office, was Earl Russell, a Whig by political persuasion, and Chartism was making its impact on the British political scene. The Second Anglo-Sikh war was being fought in India, the Sikhs being defeated the following year at Chillianwalla and forced to surrender at Rawalpindi. Marx and Engels published the *Communist Manifesto*. The Gold Rush began in California. Charles Dickens was writing *David Copperfield*. The Pre-Raphaelite Brotherhood was in its formative years. The works of Verdi and Wagner were beginning to dominate the world of opera. It was a time of ferment in world affairs, politics and the arts.

As the second half of the 19th Century dawned, the man from Yorkshire, having fulfiled his commission with the railway company, looked around him and decided to settle in Leek. This gritty north midland town, with its persistent rain and its cold winters, bore many similarities to the flourishing mill towns of his native Yorkshire. Leek's practical, down-to-earth people reminded him of the folk back home in Keighley. Hard-headed yet forward-thinking business men and determined members of the professional classes. Several of them served as Improvement

Commissioners, the local government authority of the day.

Here was a decent little town, with a thriving silk industry. With shrewd intuition he could see that trade would be likely to grow swiftly in the coming years. Silk manufacturers would then require new or larger mills, and more workers to operate them. In turn, that increased workforce would demand houses, modest but well-built dwellings to line the new streets that were being laid out around the growing town. Schools, churches and other public buildings would also be necessary. There would surely be an abundance of work here for an ambitious architect.

His family back in Keighley had been architects and builders for many years. Keighley, somewhat larger than Leek, was set in a similar rugged location, with the wild Bronte moorlands close by. The two towns were expanding along similar lines, Leek with silk and dyeing, Keighley, wool and worsted mills.

By 1849, Leek was firmly established on the railway map, and ready to move forward into what might be described as a 'Golden Age' of wealth and achievement. It was the pattern of the times, galvanised by the Imperial progress of Victoria's Empire. Leek's transportation needs were already well served by the Leek Branch of the Caldon Canal, providing a direct link with the Potteries for coal and other goods, but it was a ponderously slow means of transport. Canal boats could not travel faster than the speed of the horses which hauled them, nor carry more than a limited load. The greater efficiency and speed of the railway would, in time, outrun the canal.

It was important that the new Churnet Valley Line should be effective and well-run, with a high standard of architecture in its station buildings. The man from Yorkshire had seen to this, his first commission satisfactorily completed. It was a good, sound Yorkshire maxim that if you raised your standards you would also raise your efficiency, and this would be the hallmark in all the work he would undertake in Leek during the later years of the century. His name was WILLIAM SUGDEN.

ANOTHER YORKSHIREMAN who settled in Leek during the middle years of the 19th century became directly involved in the silk industry. By pure coincidence, he, too, was the son of a builder, but his career took him into the textile industry. He was born in 1812, in the Yorkshire village of Luddenden Foot, between Hebden Bridge and Halifax, and he gained his first experience of the industry in the famous wool town of Bradford. Through the years of his learning, alongside the hard-headed Yorkshire wool merchants, the town of Leek was far from his mind.

During the early years of Queen Victoria's reign the silk industry in Leek showed signs of growth and expansion. The early pioneers saw their numbers increasing as more and more mills were established. Many of them were small scale enterprises, but they were determined to succeed in the burgeoning industry. From the dozen or so button, silk twist and ribbon manufacturers in 1784, there were 17 in 1835 and 46 in White's 1851 Directory of Staffordshire was published.

John Brough had started his first silk 'shade' in 1815 in Stafford Street, just off Stockwell Street (the street was appropriately re-named Silk Street), before moving to a much larger 'shade' in nearby Union Street, on the steep slope which became known as 'Brick Bank'. A weaving shed, or 'shade' was usually a single storey building of a length sufficient to house the long looms. Some 'shades' were located in the attics above the workers' terraced cottages, a 'common' attic often running above several houses. The Parsons and Bradshaw directory of 1818 lists the firm as 'Baddeley and Brough, silk manufacturers, Stockwell Street'. Following the move to Union Street, it became known as 'J and J Brough & Co.' (*Pigot's Directory*, 1835).

As Brough's business developed, it became necessary to seek the services of a commercial traveller to represent the business around the country. A good head for business was called for, as well as drive and initiative, and all the necessary requirements were embodied in this Yorkshireman.

Like most of the local silk manufacturers, Brough's firm had a small, rather modest beginning, and was 'run on very humble lines', as the *Leek and District Illustrated* of 1898 put it. Mr Brough's three sons, Joshua, James and John, were taken into partnership, and following the death of James in 1857, the commercial traveller from Yorkshire, having clearly inspired confidence in the family, became a partner in the firm. His name was JOSHUA NICHOLSON.

A TOWN THAT IS PROSPERING will always find work to support lawyers and solicitors, and Leek was no exception. There were a number of men in the legal profession in Leek in the 17th and 18th centuries, and if there were not the work to keep them, they would not have been there. Early wills and inventories, many of which list clocks and books and mirrors, are sure signs that Leek and district enjoyed a fair level of prosperity at that time; such items were not the possessions of the poor.

An attorney named Thomas Mills was practising in Leek in 1745 when Bonnie Prince Charlie's rebel Highlanders passed through the town on their abortive march south. Another man of distinction, Thomas Parker, the first Earl of Macclesfield, was born here in 1666, in an ancient house near the churchyard. He was the son of Thomas Parker, an attorney, and young Thomas also entered the legal profession, becoming an eminent barrister. He became a Queen's Counsel and Member of Parliament for Derby. He was appointed Lord Chief Justice in 1710, and rose to the high office of Lord Chancellor of Great Britain in 1718, but his illustrious career suffered a severe setback when he was impeached by the House of Lords on charges of corruption, for which he received a heavy fine.

Not all of Leek's lawyers rose to such heights in their profession, nor came to such a sticky end, but they were men of integrity and respected members of the community. As Leek moved into the Victorian age, the prosperity became vested in the growing silk industry. In *White's Directory* of 1834 there were nine firms of attorneys established in Leek, and judging by the workload which passed through their offices they would all have required a large staff of clerks and office workers. By 1851 a number of multiple partnerships had been formed, and the name of one of their number figured prominently in the handling of the affairs of many of the town's leading citizens. A profusion of legal documents carrying the name of his firm bears evidence of this.

He was somewhat Dickensian in character. Indeed, his expertise in chancery law had been drawn upon by Charles Dickens when writing his novel *Bleak House*. He was clearly a man of great energy, for, amidst his heavy professional duties, he also found time to serve as an officer in the Staffordshire Yeomanry, and was a member of the Board of the Leek Improvement Commissioners, being Chairman of the Sanitary Committee. This post brought him into close contact with Robert Farrow, the town's Sanitary Inspector, a diligent and discerning man whose searching reports, as we shall see, revealed much about the social conditions in the town.

In many ways, our lawyer was also was somewhat ahead of his time. A poet in his youth, he demonstrated a great command of the English language, and was possibly a little bold by Victorian standards, as the following poem illustrates.

TO FANNY (On our joint birthday)

Tuneful and piquant, gay and debonair,
My Fanny shines conspicuously fair;
The child of wit and song - her speaking eyes,
Teem with delusive hopes, that sparkling rise,
Till grave sage men, wise in their own conceit,
Made young once more, own something like defeat.
Fate made her Natal Day and mine the same,
And should have wrapped us in a mutual flame,
But I came years too early, she too late,
And fickle hymen did not choose to wait;
Yet still within her heart so form'd to bless,
There is a void - a cave of tenderness,
Oh may the happy man that enters there,
Be nobly worthy of so choice a fair.

His home was Pickwood, a large house with a fine view towards Cheddleton Heath, overlooking a deeply-wooded valley. In this pleasant family home he lived with his wife Elizabeth, who bore him a son and two daughters before dying tragically of cancer at an early age. After his wife's death he remained at Pickwood, where he was looked after by his youngest daughter.

He was a great friend of Leek's Victorian historian, John Sleigh, and was a popular lecturer to local societies. He lectured on subjects as diverse as *Sleigh's History of Leek*, and *The Climate and Natural Productions of Leek*. He was a man of sparkling wit, with a merry twinkle in his eye, his lectures being punctuated with moments of laughter, and he had an ear for a funny story, as this extract in local dialect from one of his lectures illustrates:

The t'other day, my wife were desperate janglesome, and at night she were sittin' at one side o' th' hearth and me at the t'other, an the two cats playin' 'em afore the fire; she says to me, 'How is it you and I canna' be happy and comfortable together, like those two cats?' Says I to her, 'Tie 'em together by th' tail, and then see what they'n do.'

These lecture evenings often included musical items and usually ended with the singing of Auld Lang Syne and the National Anthem. The town had a strong tradition for music, drama and cultural activities. The name of the lawyer who did much to foster this tradition was WILLIAM CHALLINOR.

NEWSPAPERS HAVE ALWAYS BEEN great shapers of public opinion, whether at national or local level. The press is a powerful influence on the life of any community, and the stimulating climate of Victorian Leek provided the ideal conditions for a lively local newspaper to emerge. The success of any newspaper is largely dependent upon its editor, who must be able to present a balanced view of affairs and at the same time be fearless to express opinion in a well-reasoned way. He must represent fairly the views of all shades of public opinion, and yet be able to take a firm stand against any breach in social justice.

To be all things to all men and still hold his council is a secret that must be learned.

To work as correspondent for the *Birmingham Daily Post* for more than four years would surely be sufficient experience for any position, to serve on the outside staff of the *Sentinel* and give local service for the Staffordshire Advertiser was a bonus. The man in question was born in Birmingham on 7 February 1843. He was educated at Severn Street School and was apprenticed to Josiah Allen, printer, of Livery Street. He came to Leek in 1864 to work in the printing business of Robert Nall in Stanley Street - a man who had printers' ink in his blood.

On 30 July 1870 he launched the publication of the *Leek Times* using a partly printed London sheet and printing two pages of Leek news. He managed to persuade local tradesmen to advertise in the paper, and the modest sheet became a success. Its size and price would be adjusted to meet the altered circumstances created by the influx of advertisements.

His fearless criticism of local, county and national affairs soon resulted in the paper gaining a considerable circulation which increased as the years rolled on. He was a keen Liberal, and his democratic sympathies were well known. In local trade disputes the workers were always sure of warm-hearted support. Charitable objectives also found ready support, and the founding of the Cruso Nursing Fund to help working-class folk in times of need was largely due to his enthusiastic support. He was a strong Nonconformist, and gave much support to the local churches.

The *Leek Comet* was another of his ventures. The paper was published each Wednesday and was designed for farmers and others attending Leek Market, where it was on sale. Lack of support brought an untimely end to the publication after a few months - the title proved to be rather prophetic. He turned his attention to local history and began to publish snippets of his gleanings in his newspaper and in books.

He was a founder-member of the Birmingham Press Club, one of the first of its kind in the country, and a member of the

Council of the Institute of Journalists. He was a keen sportsman and a member of Leek Cricket Club. This many-talented man was a humorist and elocutionist and became a member of the Volunteer Theatricals. He took part in the Penny Readings entertainments which enjoyed much popularity at the Temperance Hall in Union Street. His name was MATTHEW HENRY MILLER.

A LOVE OF MUSIC AND THE ARTS was also a strong element in the nature of a Warwickshire man who came to Leek in the later Victorian years. He arrived in 1891 to be head of the School of Art. His life was centred on the Nicholson Institute, where he became its first librarian, the curator of the museum and responsible for the reading room and art gallery. He worked in the town from 1891 to 1912.

He was born at Aston in 1865 and before he came to Leek was living with his parents in Birmingham and working as a merchant's clerk. Articulate and well-educated, he developed a talent as a prolific and versatile author. In addition to a number of non-fiction works on painting and the history of art, he contributed articles to a number of art and literary periodicals, several of which he also edited. His fertile imagination led to several novels, one of which he dedicated to Arnold Bennett who he greatly admired and sought to emulate. Several novels written during his time in Leek had a local setting, rooted in the moorland scene. Notable among these were *Love a la Mode*, *Life's Desert Way*, *Potiphar's Wife* and *Windylow*.

Somewhat Gilbertian in character, this trait was further emphasised by his enthusiasm for the comic operas of those two creative geniuses, William S. Gilbert and Arthur Sullivan. Perhaps in his job as a merchant's clerk he learned how to 'polish up the handle of the big front door'. He was a founder member of the Leek Amateur Operatic Society in 1893, where he played many of the leading character roles, following the tradition established by the original D'Oyly Carte Company in London. To perform these shows in Leek so soon after their original London productions, and to a high degree of excellence in staging them, was an indication of the qualities and enthusiasm of the man. No expense was spared, and the company often ran into debt, in spite of the fact that the productions attracted large audiences.

The operatic society was an enterprise of great style, vision and ambition - perhaps even over-ambition. But this was a man who was obviously strong-willed and single-minded. An example of his cussedness can be seen in one of his letters to Edward Challinor, where, referring to the future plans of the company, he states very firmly:

'These things I will work very hard for, indeed any other things that are likely to lead to something, but I will not spend my time talking and arguing about things which never come to anything. I haven't time or inclination for it.'

Words which could have been spoken by one of Gilbert's own characters! But they were written in the Nicholson Institute office of our Warwickshire man, WILLIAM KINETON PARKES. WILLIAM SUGDEN, JOSHUA NICHOLSON, WILLIAM CHALLINOR, MATTHEW HENRY MILLER and KINETON PARKES were five Victorians whose lives had a great impact on the town of Leek. They were five men of their age, their lives fashioned by the time in which they lived. They were different in birth, character, upbringing, achievement and political beliefs, but they were five men who stamped their image indelibly on Victorian and Edwardian Leek. Their political views ranged from the Tory Challinor, through shades of liberalism, to the socialist Sugden. Their careers followed different courses, but although they never became directly associated in a business, political or social sense, their lives frequently criss-crossed and intertwined like the multi-coloured threads in a piece of the silk fabric for which the town was justly famous.

William Sugden's office in Derby Street stood almost opposite that of the solicitor, William Challinor - their windows faced each other across the street. William Challinor was an

Improvement Commissioner, and the outspoken journalist, Matthew Miller, would fearlessly and comprehensively (sometimes, perhaps controversially) report the meetings and business of the local government of the town. When Joshua Nicholson decided to furnish the town with a building that would house a library, a reading room, an art gallery, a school of art and at the same time provide a meeting place for cultural activities, he commissioned William and Larner Sugden to design the Nicholson Institute. Kineton Parkes became its principal and librarian. Kineton Parkes would come to know Matthew Henry Miller not only as a newspaper man, but also as an entertainer on the local stage - and he lived for a time in a Sugden house in Queen Street. Joshua Nicholson employed Sugden to design his new warehouse and office block in Cross Street, and many of his young designers and technicians received their education at the Nicholson Institute under the direction of Kineton Parkes.

The achievements of these five men, their influence and status, were immense and far-reaching, touching the lives of all classes of the town. This is not to say that they held the entire destiny of Leek in their collective hands, for without the people to work the looms, dye the fabrics, build the houses, and care for the well-being of the growing town, their achievements would have been nullified. The forelock-tuggers, arse-lickers and the people who just stood in the crowd and said 'Rhubarb' all had their part to play, for such as these are to be found in every community of people.

Many influences shaped the direction of the town, not least the growing numbers of workers employed in the burgeoning silk industry, their families requiring education, shops and markets, medical care, churches and leisure activities. Nevertheless, our five men played leading roles in our drama, and around them our story will be woven.

Sugden, Nicholson, Challinor, Miller and Parkes, eminent Victorians to a man, reflected the times in which they lived, and were truly SPIRITS OF THEIR AGE.

A group of Congregational Sunday School Teachers and workers about 1885,
BACK: Wm. Hall, Arthur Lockett, Spencer Warren (with son & daughter), Thos.
Booth, Henry Salt, Mr Phillips, Arthur Nicholson, A. Summerling, Dr JJ Ritchie, John
Jackman, Joseph Lovatt, John Rudkin, Geo. H Bailey, Geo. Brookes, Charles Hancock,
WJ Moorhouse, Joseph Shaw and Gus Carr.
MIDDLE: WH Johnson, Miss Ritchie, Miss Ives, Miss Hankinson, Miss Marsland,
Rev. J Hankinson, Miss Ball, Miss Pollie Ratcliffe, Isaac Heath & Miss L Carr.
FRONT: Miss Overfield, Miss Sugden, Miss Dishley, Miss Singer, Mrs Jackman,
Miss Booth, Miss Lizzie Heath.

Miss Milner's Private School.

Two
NOT FORGETTING THE WOMEN

'Man for the field and woman for the hearth.' Tennyson's words sum up the customary view of the role of women in society at this time, but it would be wrong to give the impression that Victorian and Edwardian Leek was a strictly male preserve. In an age where females were usually subjected to a much more servile role, Leek society was infused with a number of women who made their mark on the town. Indeed, this is another feature of Victorian and Edwardian Leek which in many ways was ahead of the times.

Women had a strong role to play, not only in the homes and factories, but also in public life, for example, the Co-operative Movement. The Leek Women's Co-operative Guild was founded in 1896, chiefly through the efforts of a Mrs Hobson. Miss Coates was its first secretary, and later Leah Provost and her colleagues became the driving force of the Women's Guild, where they discussed matters of social concern and the work of the movement. Harriet Kidd, a silk worker, who was a member of the committee, was a young lady whose name would never figure prominently among the elite of Leek, but she was a pioneer of what women would achieve in the 20th century. An unmarried mother, made pregnant by the unwanted attentions of a factory boss, she took up duties in connection with the work of the Central Committee in London. Disadvantaged and disenfranchised, she is a symbol of what the underprivileged of the town could and did achieve.

Leek was not lacking in feisty females. Working in the silk mills drew them out of their sheltered domestic existence, and the more spirited would no doubt assert themselves in the wider arena. One Elizabeth Phillips, a Sunday School teacher at the Parish Church, in 1842, went to Burslem to support a Chartist demonstration, only to be dismissed from her post for refusing to apologise for her actions!

Textile trade unions began to emerge, and in an industry which relied heavily on women to make up its work-force, the Amalgamated Society of Female Silk Operatives was founded in 1892. This later became the Leek Women Workers' Union, but it always had male secretaries! No doubt feminine voices, in the mould of Harriet Kidd, were heard in meetings of the Union, which became a force to be reckoned with. It was not until the early years of the 20th century that women became fully integrated in the trade unions, by which time the Women Workers' Union was the fastest growing union in the group which would later, in 1919, form, by amalgamation, the Amalgamated Society of Textile Workers and Kindred Trades.

In the 1890s women could take no part in the local government of the town. It would be many years before that came about, but one formidable lady, by the strength of her personality and social standing, coupled with a genuine concern for the welfare of the townspeople, exerted a great influence and commanded much respect in the town. She was Mrs Cruso of Foxlowe, who, it was said, was regarded more highly by Leek folk than 'their own dear Queen'. (By an odd quirk of political 'topsy-turvydom', Foxlowe, home of the Crusos and a symbol of the gentry, a meeting place for the Primrose league and a pillar of the establishment, later became the headquarters of the union, the Amalgamated Society of Textile Workers and Kindred Trades and a workingmen's club!)

Mrs Cruso's generous nature is exemplified by her founding of the Cruso Nursing Association and the Cruso Aid in Sickness Fund, to provide much needed financial help for people who experienced hard times. Originally known as the Cruso Memorial Nursing Association (1898), it had as secretary Edward Challinor. Its main source of income was from subscriptions, and its chief expenditure was the salary and expenses of a full-time nurse. For many years this was Nurse Hall and we should not under-rate the great service given to the community by such nurses. Birth, death and all conditions of health in between came within their scope. They stand amongst the unsung heroines of Victorian and Edwardian Leek.

At the other end of the social scale, Leek was exerting some influence in the field of Victorian art and design, particularly through its connection with William Morris. The work and influence of Elizabeth Wardle should not be underestimated. Founder of the Leek Embroidery Society and leader of the Leek School of Embroidery, Mrs Wardle and her ladies produced many works of embroidery design which were highly regarded both locally and nationally. Mrs Wardle was the wife of Thomas Wardle, and became Lady Wardle when her husband was knighted for his services to the silk industry. The employment she gave to the women and girls who worked on the embroideries gave them a status and a creativity which they would not find in more servile occupations.

The work produced by this group of ladies was varied, and included altar frontals and falls, church vestments and other ecclesiastical items. By far the most ambitious piece of work was the facsimile embroidery of the famous Bayeux Tapestry. 32 ladies worked on this 230 feet long embroidery and it was originally exhibited in the Nicholson Institute in 1886, followed by British and foreign tours. Alas the work did not find a home in Leek. The Improvement Commissioners turned it down and Alderman Hill of Reading stepped in with an offer of £300 that was accepted. The Tapestry is now permanently housed in Reading Museum where it is a major visitor attraction.

Mrs Cruso and Lady Wardle came from very different social backgrounds to women like Leah Provost and Harriet Kidd, but they all have a place in our story of Victorian and Edwardian Leek. The broad canvas of the town, like a Lowry painting, was peopled by many individuals, all contributing to the whole picture. Wives and daughters of the gentry played their part, as did school teachers, nurses and shopkeepers of every kind. But most were silk workers, washerwomen, cooks, dressmakers and household servants, without whom society would grind to a halt.

The importance of the school mistress in Victorian and Edwardian Leek was substantial, although their role is generally poorly acknowledged. They were responsible for the care and education of young children, while their working-class parents toiled long hours in the factories, in the face of poverty and hardship and the associated health problems. Childhood illnesses were rife, attendance was often low, and the teacher had to be mother, nurse and disciplinarian as well.

In the 1860s the children of George Fisher (whom we shall meet later), living in Mill Street, would probably receive their rudimentary education at the Wesleyan day school in West Street where Miss Janet Hay was the school mistress. A small 'ragged' school was started in a cottage in Mill Street and this would develop further when a school and chapel building were erected in 1870 to William Sugden's design.

Schools in other parts of the town in 1868 included an infant school on Compton where Miss Mary Ann Smith was the mistress, and other infants schools at St Luke's (Miss Margaret Thackaberry), Union Street Independent (Miss Ann Barclay), the Wesleyan School in Ball Haye Street (Miss Adams) and the Roman Catholic School in King Street (the Sisters of the Institute of the Blessed Virgin).

The British School in Alsop Street built in 1872 had Miss Annie Brooks in charge of infants. The Congregational School, Union Street, had Miss Hannah Marsland as the girls' mistress and Miss Ruth Gibson teaching the infants. Miss Mary Atkinson was infants' mistress at Ball Haye street School, and the Ragged School in Mill Street was under the care of Miss Jane Kidd. Most of theses ladies were teachers for many years and would see many children from the same families pass through their hands.

This pattern of mainly church schools was the basis for future developments in education and teachers were still overwhelmingly women. By 1896 there was a Girls' High School in Russell Street (Miss E. Brierley, headmistress) and the National School in Britannia Street, built in 1896, with J.W. Scholes as headmaster and Miss Harriet Turner in charge of infants.

For the wealthier and middle class families there were a number of small private schools, or 'dame' schools. They usually only had a few pupils and were often held in private houses. One such was run by Miss Beresford, daughter of the vicar of St Luke's. In 1883 there were also small private schools in Ford Street (Miss Mellor), Queen Street (the Misses Sykes) and King Street (Miss Thomas).

In the Edwardian years the Leek Church High School for Girls was on Clerk Bank with Miss Potts (inevitably and affectionately known as 'Potty') as head mistress. Here the daughters of the more affluent received a sound education before going on to boarding school.

At the extreme opposite end of the social scale children were taught at the Workhouse on Ashbourne Road. In 1888 the school mistress was Miss Elizabeth Lewis who served for at least 10 more years. In 1904 the Matron was Mrs Alice Roberts, and the workhouse Master, Roland Roberts (grandparents of the actor Paul Eddington).

Thus we see that the future citizens of the town received their basic education - and the foundation for their future behaviour - mainly at the hands of a small band of dedicated and devoted women.

Three
EARLY VICTORIAN LEEK

THE LEEK UPON WHICH WILLIAM SUGDEN and his contemporaries were to make their mark is shown very graphically in the plan of the town as it was in 1838 - the year following the accession of Queen Victoria. This map, originally produced by Turner and Co. of Edinburgh, was copied by draughtsman R Ewan in 1899, and appeared in M H Miller's *Olde Leeke* Vol.2 (1900). Ewan made an accurate copy, with a few amendments, so the map gives a good impression of the extent of the town in those early Victorian days when there were no photographers to record the scene.

The medieval pattern of roads and streets around the Market Place and St. Edward's Church was still intact, for this was the ancient heart of Leek and marked the extent of the town in pre-Victorian days. The original Market Place extended to the west, the edge of what is now St Edward Street, thus placing the Parish Church in its traditional location, at the head of the Market Place. Subsequent infill building, in a higgledy-piggledy fashion, brought the Market Place to its present boundary.

This pattern has remained over the ages and is much the same today, in spite of the odd bit of pedestrianisation and road widening here and there, brought about by the demands of the 20th Century - a modern layer, as it were, laid down over its ancient base.

These old streets were largely unmade, often muddy and fouled with open drains. Nevertheless, by the early 19th Century, some improvements had been made, for John Corry in his *1817 History of Macclesfield* included a chapter on Leek, which stated:

Leek though a small town contains thirteen streets and lanes, and according to the population return in 1811, the number of inhabited houses was 832, of families 835, and of inhabitants 3703, of whom 1664 were males, and 2039 females. Of the streets, the Market-place, Spout-street, Derby-street and Stockwell-street, are the most remarkable; they are wide and well paved, several of the shops are large and contain a variety of articles for the elegant accommodation of the community; and some of the private houses inhabited by the silk manufacturers, attornies and surgeons, are equally commodious to the residents, and ornaments to the town. Spout-street extends along the southern declivity of the hill on which the town is situated. It is the principal street, and contains several elegant mansions, belonging to private individuals.

The Market-place is an oblong square containing several shops, inns, and the houses of two private gentlemen. At the southern end, the Town Hall, a small but elegant modern building of stone, is a conspicuous ornament. It is two stories high, one of which is appropriated to public business, and the other is a subscription news room. Derby-street, on the London road, is of considerable extent; it contains the principal inn, a neat modern meeting-house belonging to the Independents, a few handsome mansions, several smaller tenements, and is terminated by a few detached houses and a silk manufactory. Stockwell-street is a wide and clean but short street, containing about thirty good houses. Those built the northern side command an extensive prospect from the gardens in the rear, of the various beauties of hill and dale, woodland and moreland (sic.) *cultivated fields, and lofty barren hills, terminated by the mountains of Derbyshire.*

This description was echoed one year later in the directory by W Parson and T Bradshaw of 1818, which states *'The streets are wide, well paved, and clean; many of the shops large, and several houses of the silk manufacturers, and professional men, are elegant mansions.'* In those days, of course, directories were aimed at boosting trade and business, so it is perhaps not surprising that they often painted a picture with a rosy glow. Nevertheless, affluence and poverty ran side by side, and the former would be reflected in the ethos of the town, whilst the latter impacted on the working classes of the town.

These were the streets trodden by the feet of the monks of Dieulacres Abbey, by Bonnie Prince Charlie's rebel Highlanders in 1745 and by the French Napoleonic prisoners (over 300 were paroled here) in the early years of the 19th Century, as well as by farmers, cattle dealers and townsfolk. The rutted roads rattled to the wheels of stagecoach, carrier's wagon and farm cart, battling against the hazards of winter mud and summer dust.

By 1838 the main roads through the town, turnpiked in the late 18th Century, gave Leek its first real transport links with the rest of the country, putting the town in touch with the wider world. The construction of Mill Street, entering Leek from the north-west, allowed an early type of 'ribbon development' of workers' housing along the entire length of the street. This was the first major development of housing for the growing number of workers in the silk mills, and it led to an enormous increase in the population of that part of the town, as large families were raised in these terraced houses and cottages. Frequently the Improvement Commissioners' reports of births and deaths revealed that the highest birth rate in the town was in Mill Street. For example, in 1869 28 births were recorded, of which three were illegitimate. The nearest to this was the combined total for the streets around the Brough, Nicholson and Hall factory: London Road, Cross, Well, Moorhouse and Grosvenor Streets, where 25 births were recorded for the area.

With the map as our guide, we can walk westwards from the Old Church, to join Mill Street, where the houses were terraced in a higgledy-piggledy fashion, and because of the steepness of the terrain, some were tiered above the level of the road, rising to three or four storeys. There was no uniformity of style or size in the houses, but in all cases the front door opened directly onto the street. When the turnpike road was constructed, it ran through a virtual gorge, and a number of the houses were actually built into the sandstone cliff face, so they stood several storeys high, and had no rear entrances or backyards, and certainly no gardens. If you wished to take the fresh air you would take a chair out of the house and simply sit on the pavement, where you could peel the potatoes, shell the peas and polish the brass (if you were lucky enough to possess any), chat to the neighbours or passers-by), or just sit and doze. All this, of course, after you had cleaned the windows, swept the front pavement, and donkey-stoned the front door step to a clean, whitish-grey finish.

Households rarely kept their doors locked - it was 'open house' to all callers. A regular visitor was the insurance man, who usually did his rounds on Friday evening - pay day. The 'Burial', the 'Co-op' and the friendly societies all had their collectors who would simply open the front door, call out 'Co-op' and enter. He would collect his small contribution from the family, sign the book, perhaps exchange a few words of friendly gossip and then go on his way. It would remain a feature of working class life at least into the 1960s.

Other regular visitors from Edwardian times onwards were 'th' essmen' (the ashbin men) who called to empty the bins. Ashes from the fire, and household waste of every kind - wet or dry - were tipped into the bin, a bin for every purpose. Open access to the backyard was essential so th' essman could hoist the heavy bin on to his broad shoulders and tip the contents into the waiting cart. The full load would eventually be dumped on to the council's open tip.

Along streets like Mill Street, at the beginning and ending of the working day, you would see the moving tide of factory workers - the bold and brassy girls, the loud lads, the men with their cloth caps and pipes and the old women in black frocks and shawls, their backs bent by too many hours at the work bench. Silk dyers like George Fisher would come clumping up the street in their wooden clogs with metal toecaps and heels - the only sensible footwear for the dye-house where water and dyestuffs were liberally spread around. The start and finish of the working day was marked by a cacophony of hooters, sirens and bells, summoning the workers to their place in the factories. Some people could recognise each different call. 'That's Wardle's' or 'That's Brough's' they would say, 'They're all on time today.'

Good time-keeping was always essential. Woebetide the late-comer, whose tardiness rarely went unpunished.

Housing conditions were fairly basic and when the census enumerator visited the area his returns revealed that many of these humble dwellings housed large families, most of them employed in the silk industry. Children were employed in the factories from a very early age as 'half-timers', spending part of the day at school, and part at work. I can recall my own grandmother's vivid memories of working half-time. It was quite common to find a family of parents with three or four children between 10 and 15 all engaged in the silk industry, as well as several younger children. The following extract from the 1861 census is a typical example:

GEORGE FISHER Head	49	Silk dyer
JUDITH FISHER Wife	46	Mangle woman
LEWIS FISHER Son	18	Mill piecer
GEORGE FISHER Son	16	Silk piecer
ROBERT FISHER Son	11	Silk piecer
RICHARD FISHER Son	10	Silk piecer
HARRIET FISHER Daughter	8	Scholar
ELIZA FISHER Daughter	4	Scholar
ELLEN FISHER Daughter	1	Scholar

I have cited the Fisher family because they are part of my own background. They were ordinary working-class folk, of which there were many thousands in Leek, working in the silk industry, keeping the local economy on the rails, while the business of the town was in the hands of the movers and shakers who, by virtue of birth, wealth and privilege were in positions of authority.

George Fisher, like most of his neighbours in Court No 1 towards the bottom of Mill Street, was a silk worker. Judith, his wife worked as a household servant and was born at Warslow. She was 28 when their eldest son Lewis was born, and further children appeared at regular intervals over the next few years.

The older children became 'half-timers', sharing their day into three parts - school, work and sleep. It is interesting to note that this was already the experience of the Fisher family at the time of the 1861 census - the practice was not formalised until the later 1860s, under a new Factory and Workshops Act.

Many children died in infancy, for diseases of childhood were rife, forcing the infant mortality rate to a very high level comparable to the worst figures in third world Africa now. Birth and death were ever present in the lives of the folk who lived on Mill Street, but because of the closely knit nature of the community, there was always someone on hand who would know exactly what to do should either event occur unexpectedly. Usually a mature but active lady, who may possibly have had some nursing experience, she had the expertise to attend a birth before medical help arrived, and was able to 'lay out' a dead body in readiness for the undertaker. She might also be called upon to get rid of unwanted or embarrassing pregnancies, and, as a further service, act as the neighbourhood 'knocker-up', rousing the mill workers from their beds in time for work by tapping on their bedroom windows with a long pole. This versatile, 'unsung heroine' played a vital role in the community.

Mill Street may be regarded as the first workers' community housing development of any size in the town, but there were others, as the 1838 map shows. If we follow Canal Street to King Street, Albion Street and Compton, then on to London Street and Pickwood Road we see many terraced cottages with attic 'shades', where the weaving was done, the families living in the rooms below. Wherever the windows in the top floor of the house are much wider than those below we can assume the presence of an attic 'shade', probably running over three houses, providing a long room to accommodate the looms. The way these houses were built determined the pattern of the working day, the wide attic windows giving the workers the maximum amount of light for the longest hours possible, thus allowing the optimum production.

A number of early silk mills were marked on the 1838 map. Nathan Davenport's mill at the bottom of Mill Street and Hammersley's dye-works in Abbey Green Road were both located near the River Churnet on the north-western edge of town, their workforce being drawn largely from Mill Street. A silk factory was located near the Methodist Chapel on Clerk Bank, and the large factory of Russell and Clowes stood at the top of West Street. The isolated silk shade in Strangmans Walk later became the factory of Thomas Whittles & Co., and streets of terraced houses were developed around it. The area, atop a steep hill approached from the south, was known as Nix Hill.

St Edward Street is, and always has been, a grand street - the grandest street in town - an accolade conferred upon it by Nicholas Pevsner, in the *Buildings of England* series. Its varying width - narrowing, then broadening out to a generous breadth - give it a unique character. The roof line, too, is varied, interposed by stylish chimneys, and the architecture of the buildings covers many styles and periods. Once tree-lined, there was a double pavement on the western side, but these features have now been removed.

What gave St Edward Street a distinct character is the fact that, within its environs, it encompassed the entire social strata of Victorian and Edwardian Leek. On the western side there were the fine houses of the gentry, with extensive gardens at the rear, where lived silk manufacturers and professional people, such as the Sleigh family, Sir Thomas and Lady Wardle and William Allen, lawyer and clerk to the Council. On the eastern side, with one exception, were the much more modest shops, and the courts leading off the street between the shops, to open out into a cobbled yard with a few, perhaps up to ten, small cottages, the homes of the silk workers and their families, with communal washing facilities and privies. Thus you had the employers and the workers living just a stone's throw from each other, across the street. What would a modern sociologist make of this? (An exception on the eastern side is the large, bay-windowed property, entered by a flight of steps, once the home of silk manufacturers, Stephen Goodwin and Andrew Jukes Worthington.)

Turning up King Street and then into Albion Street we find Anthony Ward's Albion Mill, its long history reaching back to 1795. The two separate firms of Carr & Co. and Fynney and Badnall amalgamated in 1808 as Fynney and Carr, and Anthony Ward became a partner in 1814, the trading name became Fynney and Ward, changing again to Anthony Ward & Co. by 1828.

The factory of Gaunt, Wardle and Walmsley stood in New Street, close to Glendinning and Gaunt's California Mill. The twin water tanks in front of Thomas Carr's mill in Fountain Street were marked on the map, and Andrew Jukes Worthington's factory, founded in 1803, stood in Portland Street. Thus, by 1838, a number of Leek's silk pioneers - later household names in Leek - had established their own factory sites, and were ready to face the challenges and opportunities of the new Victorian Era.

Evidence of the prosperity of the town can be seen on the 1838 map in the names of the wealthy landowners who owned land and property around the areas into which the growing town would expand. The Earl of Macclesfield, as might be expected, was a major landowner, as was John Davenport MP, who owned Westwood Hall and much of the land around that part of the town that became known as the West End. Names associated with the silk industry were prominent: John Sleigh, Richard Gaunt, A Ward, J Alsop and S and W Phillips. John Cruso, a lawyer, of Foxlowe, the large Georgian house at the north of the Market Place, owned various parcels of land. Other landowning lawyers were Killmister and Challinor who were in partnership in the early years of the 19th Century. Mrs Grosvenor, of Stockwell Street owned much of the land upon which Southbank Street and its environs were developed - although in 1838 no-one could anticipate this later Victorian and Edwardian development.

Silk, politics, the gentry and the professions were dominant in the landowning classes of early Victorian Leek, but certain areas were designated as Leek Town Lands. The Freeholders of Leek and Lowe were responsible for the management of areas of land comprising Back o' th' Street, Kiln Lane, Nab Hill, Westwood Heath, Woodcroft Heath and Leek Moor. There is no record of how these lands came into the hands of the Freeholders, but in 1848 they were administered by a Committee comprising Messrs Alsop, Brough, Carr, Challinor, Davenport, Hammersley and Russell - names synonymous with Victorian Leek. (A committee of trustees still administers the affairs of Leek Town Lands today.)

The number of inns, taverns and public houses marked on the 1838 map is perhaps surprisingly large for a small town, with a population in 1831 of 6374. There are a number of reasons for this. The fact that Leek was strategically placed on the turnpike road network accounts for the preponderance of hostelries along Church Street, Spout Street, Derby Street and around the Market Place, many of which are coaching inns, or posting houses. Furthermore, Leek, being a traditional market town with regular cattle and livestock sales, saw a great influx of farmers from the surrounding Moorlands on market days. A convivial location in which to meet friends and settle deals over a glass of beer was an essential part of market day. A number of inns also acted as the base for carriers serving the outlying parts of the Moorlands. Thirdly, the growth of the silk industry meant an increasing workforce with prodigious thirsts to quench and money in their pockets on Friday night. I have no doubt that George Fisher was in this category. Innkeeping in Leek in the early Victorian years was a lucrative business, there were many beerhouses where the housewife was able to sell beer by the jug from her front door. Indeed, beer was often considered safer to drink than a town's water supply.

The churches and chapels were clearly marked on the 1838 map. The Anglican Parish Church of St. Edward the Confessor occupied a prominent position, and was the only Church of

England place of worship in town at that time. The Wesleyan Methodist Chapel stood at Mount Pleasant, off Clerk Bank, and there was an Independent Chapel in Union Street. Another Wesleyan Methodist Chapel stood at the corner of Regent Street and Ball Haye Street, and there was a Primitive Methodist Chapel in Fountain Street. The Roman Catholic Church in 1838 was a small building at the junction of Fountain Street and Portland Street. The Calvinist Chapel stood in Derby Street. It is perhaps interesting to note that the old-established Quaker Meeting House is not named on the map.

The old names of some of the roads and streets are very descriptive, for they were directly associated with their surroundings. The appropriately named Canal Street led down to the basin of the Leek Branch of the Caldon Canal. We can imagine the carts trundling up the street, laden with goods for delivery around the town. Similarly, Workhouse Street was so named because it was the location of the town's workhouse. Spout Street had an open ditch running down it, and Custard Street led to the Market Place, its name probably a corruption of the word 'coster', for there would be many costermongers plying their wares there on market days. London Road was the main route through Leek from Manchester to Derby, and thence to London.

Dicky's Gutter is shown on the 1838 map as a narrow route leading down from Stockwell Street to the fishpond at the lower end of the Ball Haye Estate. Narrow and cobbled, with high stone walls on either side, it rarely saw the sun, and was dark, dank and mossy, with a treacherously slippery surface. It was often the scene for dark deeds and had an unsavoury reputation. It was with some trepidation that pedestrians used it as a short cut, particularly after dark.

The Cattle Market was located at the eastern end of Derby Street, where the road widened out, and split between Fountain Street and London Road. Occupying the open space in front of the Talbot, the buying and selling of livestock was not solely confined to this area, for trading spilled over into the surrounding streets. Sheep, pigs and poultry often ran amok, fouling the streets.

The old Cattle Market was also the site upon which the actors of the 'rag and stick' theatres performed they plays. These companies of travelling players came to town and pitched their flat-bodied wagons side by side, set up crude bench seating and covered the structure with a canvas cover, in the manner of a circus tent. Here they would perform their screaming farces and tear-drenched dramas to audiences who could afford the admission charges - Reserved Seats 1/6, Boxes 1/-, Stalls 9d, Pit 6d, Gallery 3d. One of these travelling companies, the Victoria Theatre, declared as its patron the distinguished actor-manager Sir Henry Irving.

A reservoir, marked as 'Fountain' was found at the extreme eastern edge of the map, providing a primitive water supply to the town. This gave its name to Fountain Street, a street which terminates close to the site of the original public baths at the end of Derby Street. The twin reservoirs in front of Messrs Carr's factory were supplied from this source, and the water theme is also reflected in the name of Well Street, leading off Fountain Street. A plentiful supply of water was essential to the silk and dyeing industry, and Leek's climate ensured this.

Located at the very heart of the town was Leek's old Town Hall, at the southern end of the Market Place. This was the headquarters of the local government of the day, the Leek Improvement Commissioners, appointed under the Improvement Act of 1825. It was here, in the upper room, entered by the flight of stone steps outside the building, that the town's magistrates also held their court sessions. There was an old local saying, directed at anyone who had committed a misdemeanour, they would be taken 'up the Town Hall steps' - referring no doubt to these particular steps. There were two cells in the basement, below ground level.

The building also served as the offices of the Leek Savings Bank between 1823 and 1853. Here, when the ground floor was open to the elements like a traditional open market hall, it was used on Wednesdays by the market folk. Later, when windows were installed, the ground floor became a reading room. A great deal of the life of early Victorian Leek was focused in this little building. In 1872 it was deemed inadequate for the needs of the growing town, and following a meeting of the Town Lands Trustees, it was sold for the princely sum of £85. The purchaser was Mr Joseph Flower, who used some of the masonry on his home, Portland House, which stood in Rosebank Street.

The 1838 map outlined the foundation upon which the silk town of Leek was built. If William Sugden had held it in his hands when he arrived in Leek ten years after its publication, he may well have speculated on the possibilities that this network of new streets might yield for an ambitious architect. A canny Yorkshireman, he would perhaps perceive how those open spaces were destined to be filled with houses, shops, schools, churches, factories and other public buildings.

What exciting plans were to find fulfilment as men of vision stamped their mark on the growing town! This was the stage upon which many dramas of progress and development would be played out.

If the 1838 map provides the back-cloth for our drama, then its cast of supporting characters may well be found in a publication of 1834. *White's Directory of Staffordshire* for 1834 tells us that the population of the township of Leek and Lowe at the census of 1831 was 6372, and points out that in 1821 it was 4855, in 1811 it was 3703, and in 1801 it was 3489, a gradual growth due almost entirely to the burgeoning silk industry.

In 1825 an Act of Parliament was obtained for lighting, watching and improving the town, under the authority of Improvement Commissioners. Prior to this Act the streets, highways and roads were managed by Highway Surveyors and Parish officers appointed at vestry meetings. The Gas Works was established in 1826, and there were 103 street lamps.

The police force consisted of four constables, a surveyor, a scavenger and a few watchmen. The police station was then at the top of the densely populated Mill Street, strategically placed, it may be said, in view of the teeming life of the area.

The Earl of Macclesfield was the proprietor of the waterworks, the supply coming from the springs on Leek Moor where there were two reservoirs.

The Court Leet was held yearly in October, at the Red Lion Inn, under John Cruso, Steward of the Earl of Macclesfield. Officers of the court were a constable and deputy, a head borough and deputy, two market-lookers, and a beagle, bang-beggar and pinner. These men collectively were the administrators of the local government of the day.

White's 1834 Directory was the first to attempt to be fully comprehensive. The directory includes the following interesting piece of social comment:

In the silk trade many large fortunes have been made by the late and present manufacturers; and some of their weavers and other workmen have been enabled, by industry and economy, to build convenient houses for their own occupation; but unfortunately a large portion of the operatives here lack that providence and sobriety which are so much wanted in all other manufacturing towns.

IMAGES OF VICTORIAN LEEK

Cottages in Mill Street.

The Old Town Hall, Market Place

THE HUB OF LEEK

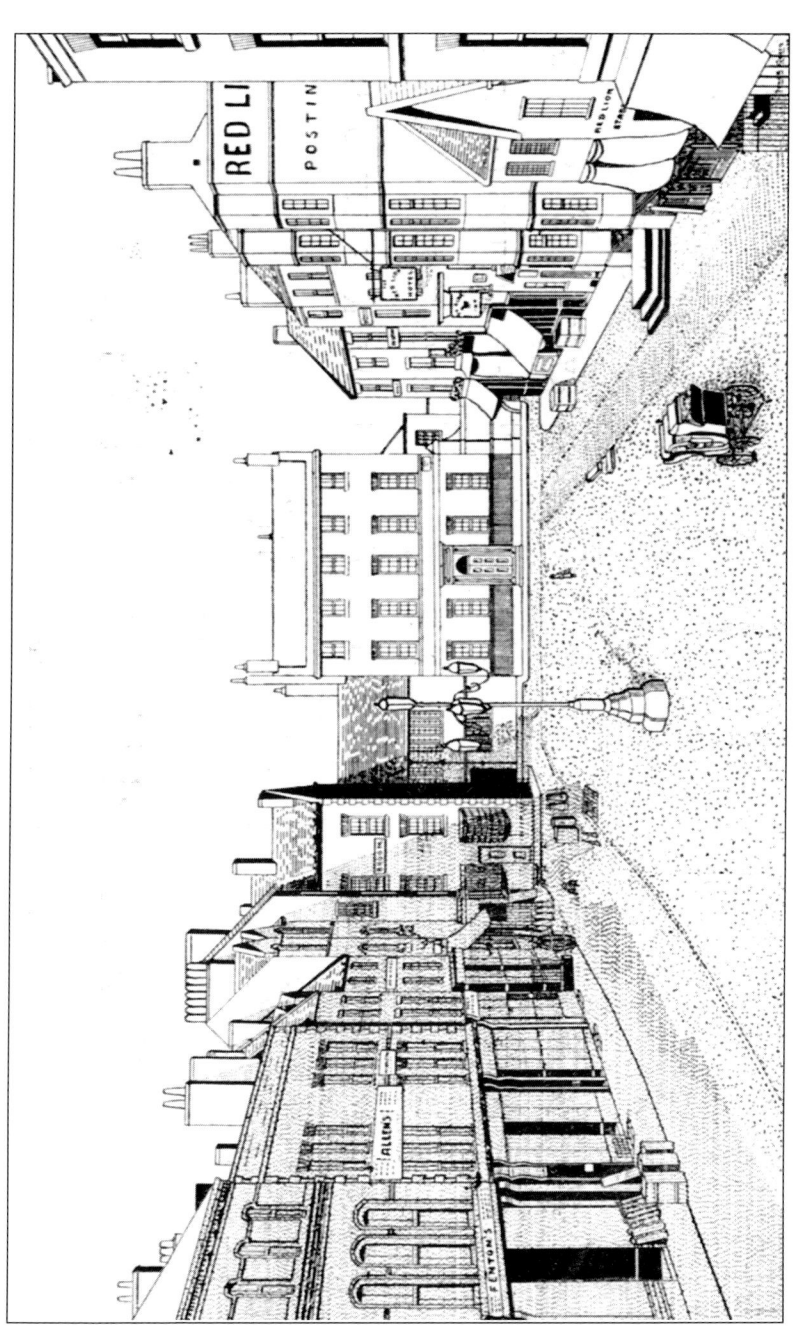

Dr. Jim McClew	Mrs. Underwood	Miss McRobie
Mr. C. T. Gwynne	Dr. J. M. Johnson	Mr. Arthur H. Shaw
Mrs. C. T. Gwynne	Mr. W. Tipper	Mr. Wm. Tatton
Mrs. Wm. Tatton	Dr. John McClew	The Rev. T. H. B. Fearon
An Assistant of Dr. Burnett's	Mrs. John McClew	Mr. Henry Salt
Dr. J. J. Ritchie	Mrs P. J. Worthington	Miss Salt
Dr. R. Burnett	Capt. Smith	Mr. Thomas Shaw
Mrs. J. M. Johnson	Mr. John Hall	Mr. William Carr

THE above group was taken at the Cottage Hospital on the 7th July, 1898, when an influencial gathering assembled to witness the dedication of a piece of ground to the north side of the Hospital.

Miss Carr, who performed the ceremony, can be seen in the centre of the group. On her right is the late Mr. John Robinson, of Westwood, and on her left (standing) is Mr. William Carr— two very generous benefactors to whom Leek owes much.

A GATHERING OF IMPORTANT PEOPLE AT THE COTTAGE HOSPITAL
RE-VISITED IN THE LEEK NEWS OF 1932.

Dr. A. Somerville	Mr. Sumerling	Mr. John Robinson
Miss Shaw	Mr. R. Farrow	Miss Carr
Mr. Isaac Heath	Mr. S. Blades	Sir Thomas Wardle
	Mrs. John Hall	Mrs. Arthur Shaw
Mr. R. S. Milner	Mrs. B. B. Nixon	Mrs. S. Gibson
Mrs. Sumerling	Mrs. E. Gailey	Mrs. Sugden
Mr. Joseph Challinor	Miss Robinson	Mrs. Cartwright
Miss Rayner	Mrs. Fearon	Mrs. S. Blades.

The land then dedicated was comprised of three lots. The first lot contained 487 square yards and was purchased for £150 4s. 0d., of which Miss Carr gave £33 8s. 7d., the balance being raised by subscriptions. The second piece, which cost £77 14s. 0d., was purchased and given to the Hospital by Mr. John Robinson, who also defrayed the cost (£44 10s. 0d.) of the West fence. The third plot was purchased for £95 0s. 0d. and given by Mr. William Carr.

It is a particularly interesting group in which can be seen many who were prominent in the public life of the town at the end of last century.

Waterloo Mill

Wellington Mill

Leek's Golden Years 47

St Edward Street, looking South.

St Edward Street, looking North.

Market Place, pre Buttermarket.

Mills seen from Park Road.

Mill Street.

Stanley Street, formerly Custard Street.

Leek The Congregational Church

Four
LEEK'S VICTORIAN ARCHITECTS

WILLIAM SUGDEN WAS BORN on 16th June, 1821 at Keighley. He was the son of William Sugden, whose family firm of architects, builders and contractors had been working in Keighley for many years. Young William served his articles of apprenticeship with Mr Samuel Fruer, of Framlingham, Suffolk, before taking up the post of managing clerk with the firm of Andrews and Pepper in Bradford.

He married Elizabeth Larner, of Stoke Ferry, Norfolk in 1846, and in 1848 came to Leek with a commission to supervise the building of the stations on the Churnet Valley Line of the North Staffordshire Railway which was under construction at that time. Several buildings in Framlingham designed by the architect Fruer show many similarities with Sugden buildings in Leek. Clearly William learned a great deal from his master and this inspired knowledge found expression in many of his future designs.

William and Elizabeth made their home in Leek, and soon William established himself in business as an architect. His skills were quickly employed in the fast-developing town, where the silk industry was entering a period of great expansion. One of William's early commissions in Leek was to replace the little half-timbered inn at the southern end of the Market Place, the old Black's Head, sometime known as the Blackamoor's Head, with a much larger, more imposing building. The new Black's Head rose impressively, three storeys above street level, its huge facade dominating the south end of the Market Place, but in perfect proportion to the broad expanse of the square. A little-seen feature of the building is the row of carved heads and stone bosses just along the eaves, below the roof line, probably the work of the local sculptor, Richard Hassall. So, by the early 1850s, William had already shown that he was not afraid to make a bold, ambitious statement in his architectural style - a trait that would become more and more apparent as other buildings materialised from the drawing board.

Sugden again collaborated with the sculptor Richard Hassall in 1862, with additional work on the Gothic-style chapel in Leek Cemetery. This small church is embellished with stone bosses, many of which are in the form of carved heads, similar to those on the New Black's Head, typical of Hassall's style. Richard Hassall (1831-68) was born in the Leekfrith parish, at Pheasant's Clough farm in the shadow of the rocky face of the Roches, an imposing gritstone escarpment to the north of Leek. A natural craftsman, he honed his early skills by carving on farm buildings around his home before entering Macclesfield School of Art. He went on to further education at South Kensington Museum in London. A fine example of his work can be seen in Meerbrook Churchyard, where an elaborately carved angel embellishes the headstone of the grave of his father, situated to the right of the main path leading to the church door.

Richard Hassall's life was tragically short. He died in 1868, at the age of 37, long before he had achieved his full potential. Had he lived, there could have been a very creative partnership between Hassall and the Sugdens, and he would surely have achieved the recognition he deserved.

William Sugden had completed the building of the Cemetery Chapel in 1858 at a cost of £1073. The report of the Leek Improvement Commissioners Cemetery Committee states: *'the principal works such as fencing, laying out the ground, and building the Chapels, have been brought to a close. They* (the Committee) *feel great pleasure in recording that the plans selected, both as to the Grounds and the Chapels, have met with general approval. They have also equal pleasure in stating, that the whole works have been carried out with a degree of unanimity, rapidity, and substantiability, the retrospect of which is especially gratifying.'*

According to the Cemetery Committee's report of 1861 the Chapel suffered storm damage when two of the pinnacles of the spire were blown down and other incidental damage occurred. Extensive repair work was therefore necessary after the severe winter of 1860-61, and it was at that time that Richard Hassall carved the heads and bosses around the chapel. The Committee's report states: *'Last summer the bosses of the Chapels were carved into various devices in a very masterly manner by Mr Hassall, and now contribute much to the finish and architectural effect of the building.'*

These early years of Sugden's work in Leek could be described as his 'Gothic period' for they also saw the building of Brunswick Methodist Church (1856), the Roman Catholic School in King Street (1863) and the Congregational Church (1863), as well as the 1856 'mini-Gothic' tomb to Richard Cutting in St. Edward's Churchyard. Cutting worked in the local silk industry. He was one of Leek's Improvement Commissioners and an officer in the Staffordshire Yeomanry. Although buried in an Anglican churchyard he was a prominent Methodist, being the Superintendent of West Street Sunday School for 48 years from 1808 until his death in 1856. A good musician, he was the conductor of the hymn singing at the annual Sunday School Festival ('Club Day') during those years.

This outbreak of Nonconformist Gothic in Leek was part of a distinct trend in Victorian architecture, where growing affluence allowed the free churches to strive to emulate the traditional architecture of their Anglican brethren, where spires and towers were prevalent, and this would appeal to William Sugden's principles.

It was at this time, in 1868, that Sugden was commissioned to carry out the adaption and alteration of an old flour mill back in Framlingham, for use as a People's Hall with reading room, library and lecture hall - similar to the earlier Mechanics Institute in Leek. Built in red and white brick it had a staircase tower and arched windows. It became a Wesleyan chapel and is now a United Free Church. A 1990s extension has been added in very sympathetic style.

William Sugden built his first houses in the 1850s, his earliest probably being three houses in Queen Street - Nos. 49, 51 and 53 - for George Salt, in 1856. He completed more work in Queen Street two years later, with the construction in 1858 of Nos. 4, 6, 8 and 10 for W B Nixon. In 1857 he built Rosebank House for James Johnson, a house on Ball Haye Green for T Shenton and two houses in Brunswick Street for Joseph Hall. 1859 saw the building of six houses in Park Road for Isaac Middleton, and a house in Westwood Terrace for a Mr Needham. Sugden houses began to make their appearance in those undeveloped streets shown on the 1838 town map.

William and Mary's first son, William Larner Sugden, was born in Leek on October 5th, 1850. Maintaining the family's Yorkshire connection, Larner was educated at Leeds Grammar School, and returned to Leek in 1867, to become articled to his father, working in the Leek office. He entered into partnership with his father in 1881, when the firm became known as William Sugden and Son, Architects.

Back in Keighley, William Sugden's younger brother, John, continued to run the family firm until his death in 1871 at the age of 49. His eldest son, William Hampden Sugden, was born on December 15th, 1849. He appears, for some reason, to have been known as 'Walter' to the family, and he served his articles of apprenticeship with his uncle William at the offices in Leek. So, for a while, there were three members of the Sugden family working as architects in Leek - William and his son Larner, and Larner's cousin, William Hampden Sugden.

William Hampden Sugden afterwards returned to Yorkshire, to join George Smith, a well-known Bradford architect, as chief assistant. In 1882 he began business on his own account, and his younger brother, Arthur Sugden, went into partnership with him in 1893. He died at Keighley on December 19th 1920, and is buried in Keighley Cemetery. There is therefore some considerable Sugden influence on the Victorian architecture of Keighley. Indeed, it was while William Hampden

Sugden was working in Leek that the firm drew up plans for the Cavendish Street United Methodist Church, now demolished. But perhaps the most significant contribution of the Leek office to the architecture of Keighley was Dalton Mills, built for J and J Craven and Co, worsted spinners. This massive construction was built in stages during the late 1860s and 1870s. The size and style of the new buildings attracted comment from the beginning, and in 1871 *The Builder* praised the designs, describing the style as Roman-Italian and naming the architect as Mr Sugden of Leek. The distinctive Sugden influence was also evident in other Keighley buildings - Laurel Mount, St. Barnabas Church, Keighley Technical Institute extensions - and, in France, the Keighley Hall at Poix-du-Nord.

Larner Sugden also had a French connection. In 1894 the Vicomte du Parc appointed him surveyor for the proposed canalisation of the River Bourne, in the mountainous region of the French departments of Drome and Isere, the purpose of which was to provide light and motive power to a large district extending from Grenoble in the north to Valence in the south, a commission which Larner carried out successfully. And of course, Larner's wife was French - Mlle Marie Josephine Bucquoy, of Paris, whom he married on March 2nd 1875. The marriage was childless.

The offices of Sugden and Son in Leek were established in a fine 1789 building in Derby Street, set back from street level and fronted by a shrub garden bounded by iron railings, and it was in this somewhat unpretentious building that much of the work of the firm was produced. The property came on the market in the 1870s when the following advert appeared in the Leek Times of November 19th:

> *'Valuable freehold and genteel residence with garden, stable, coach house and other premises to be sold by auction by Messrs Fergyson and Son.... No 13 Derby Street... lately occupied by J.H. Hacker Esq. deceased.'*

William Sugden was the purchaser and with his son Larner now working in the Leek office, the firm was set for a bright future. Unfortunately, developments during the early years of the 20th Century destroyed the splendid Georgian doorway and ground floor, when shops were built in front of the main house. The property is now occupied by Boots the Chemist. Only the upper floors of the original building remain, and can still be seen above and behind the modern shop which occupies the site today. Larner Sugden himself supervised the conversion of the frontage to shops in 1900. It was one of the last things he did for he died in 1901.

The great prosperity that Leek was enjoying during those middle and later Victorian years meant that competition in the field of architecture was very fierce. John Thomas Brealey, a local architect and surveyor with an office in Stockwell Street, was a great contender for business, and much of his work complements that of the Sugdens, displaying many similarities of style. In addition, a London firm, F H Francis, was tendering for much of the work for the Leek Improvement Commissioners, including a new town hall. Francis also won the contract for the new St. Luke's Church.

Other local architects in competition with the Sugdens included C Littler (1851), Uriah Hudson (1872) and John William Critchlow (1892), who also worked as the Earl of Macclesfield's agent. Later came James Gosling Smith and George H Chappell. It may fairly be said that Sugden was the trendsetter and other architects had to strive to match his standards. This was good for the architectural image of Leek and left the town with many fine Victorian buildings.

Architects of national renown also came on the scene when silk manufacturer Hugh Sleigh engaged Richard Norman Shaw to build the Tudor style Spout Hall in St. Edward Street for him, and George Edmund Street won the contract for the Victorian chancel at St. Edward's Church. Norman Shaw was also responsible for the splendid All Saints Church, highly regarded by the late Poet Laureate, Sir John Betjeman, its stature now recognised by its status as a Grade I Listed Building. Leek was very much in the forefront of all that was best in Victorian architecture, and it was in this highly refined environment that the Sugdens did much of their best work.

An important public building in Leek, designed by William Sugden, was the Mechanics Institute in Russell Street. The Leek Literary and Mechanics Institute was founded in 1837 in a cottage building which was replaced in 1862 by the more substantial Sugden building. The names of some of the men who founded and managed the Institute reads like a roll-call of the 'movers and shakers' of Victorian Leek: James Alsop, Joshua and John Brough, Dr Ritchie, Thomas Wardle, John Cruso, William Challinor, Rev John Sneyd, Joseph Challinor, Richard Place, Rev J Hankinson, William Sugden, Rev R Goshawk, W S Brough, Rev W P Bourne, Edwin Brough, C T Gwynne, Rev Carr Smith, M H Miller, R S Milner, J G Beckett, Thomas Shaw, John Robinson, Thomas Carr, A J Worthington, W D Badnall, H Bermingham, John Ward, Robert Farrow, John Sleigh and many others. (It will be seen that most of our cast of leading players are there!)

Originally lit by candles (there is a bill in 1842 for 'new snuffers'), it later changed to gas. In the early days newspapers were provided only occasionally, and fiction was never in the library. All this changed in 1860 when an Art School was established. The study of science and technology was introduced. A debating society, chess club and musical classes were formed. Regular lectures, concerts, recitals and dramatic entertainments were given, to a very high standard. As an early example of adult education, the Leek Mechanics Institute was exemplary.

The new building in Russell Street, to Sugden's design, was opened in 1862. It cost £869, the money was raised by donations, life memberships, bazaars and fetes - one such being held at Alton Towers, when local manufacturers closed their mills to allow their workers to attend. By 1867 the Institute was free from debt, and there was a balance of £40 in the building society. There was a well-lit reading room with papers and magazines to suit all tastes, a well-stocked library and the billiards and games room was much used.

Sugden's design for the building displayed many of the features which were becoming hallmarks of his style: the blend of different building materials, brick, tile, stone and terracotta, ornamental and decorative features, curved windows and usually a date stone, which helps to date Sugden buildings.

William Sugden returned to industrial architecture in 1864, when he built Alexandra Mill in Earl Street. A typical Victorian factory structure, its grimness is relieved by decorative window features and ornate work on the upper gables. Also in 1864 Sugden designed a fine shop at No. 7 Derby Street for H G Carr, a building also rich in the features that distinguished Sugden's architecture.

Sugden's next major industrial building in 1865 was the warehouse and offices in Cross Street and Well Street for Brough, Nicholson and Hall Ltd. This imposing curved frontage again displays all the Sugden hallmarks. The name of the company is displayed on a large stone high on the outer wall, which also carries the date 1815 - the date of the founding of the firm by J J Brough in Silk Street.

The later 1860s saw many commissions, small and large, pouring into the Sugden offices. Industrial and commercial work was uppermost, with extensions to the Leek Foundry by the canal and a factory in Weston Street, and alterations to Howard's hardware shop in the Market Place in 1866. Wooliscroft's shop at No. 12 Derby Street was also built in 1866.

By 1867 Stockwell House was owned by Joshua Nicholson, and he commissioned Sugden to carry out some alterations. A silk shade was also built in Bath Street for the firm of Price and Fynney. The frontage of Peter Magnier's shop at 15 Derby Street was substantially altered in 1868. This was again altered in 1885 and later became a bank.

Two major Sugden buildings appeared in 1869 - the Alsop Memorial Cottage Hospital in Stockwell Street and Carding's Corn Stores on the corner of Bath Street and Derby Street. The town now had its own cottage hospital, where minor operations could be carried out, enhancing the health care facilities of the town, much needed in view of the growing population.

1870 was a busy year, with the building of the Cemetery Chapels and more church work for the Methodists - the Wesleyan Chapel and Ragged School on Mill Street. Set in the middle of its teeming population, this provided not only a place of worship but a school where the children of the area could receive a rudimentary education. Sugden also built four houses in Grosvenor Street for Isaac Heath, and carried out alterations on Compton House for Joseph Challinor.

St. Luke's School in Earl Street was built by Sugden in 1871, followed by extensions to his earlier Roman Catholic School in King Street. The Temperance Hall in Union Street also came in for some Sugden treatment, and a building long-demolished was the boiler house and chimney of the Broad Street brewery of George Walker and Co. The Congregational Church was enlarged by the addition of a lecture hall and schoolroom in Russell Street.

Bath Street is a fine example of Victorian town houses in contrasting styles. Two fine houses in Bath Street, Nos. 29 and 31 were built by Sugden for Richard Lovatt in 1872. These were followed in 1880 by two houses, Nos. 33 and 35 for Mr Rider. These are richly embellished, displaying all the hallmarks of the Sugden style. Compare these with the row of much simpler Sugden houses beyond Ford Street, which were enhanced by some delicate tile work around the doorways.

The late 1870s continued to see much Sugden work appearing on the streets of Leek. In 1876 the building known as Haywood Mill was built in Haywood Street for the agricultural agent, H D Bayley. The building is distinguished by his initials, HDB, and the date in the brickwork on the face of the mill. The major restoration of Mount Pleasant Methodist Chapel was carried out in 1877, and two years later Sugden built two houses in Portland Street North for John Naden, distinguished by their interesting chimneys.

W.S. Brough commissioned Sugden in 1880 to build 'Littlehales' on Buxton Road. A fine detached house, it is a typical gentleman's residence of its time. More domestic architecture, Nos. 6 and 8 Hugo Street, appeared that same year.

The Sugdens continued to make their mark on the architecture of Victorian Leek, and in turn were influenced by the wider movements in contemporary art and design. When William Morris visited Leek in the 1870s, on his forays into Thomas Wardle's Hencroft Dyeworks in his relentless search for perfection in the colours for his fabrics, it was inevitable that he would come into contact with the Sugdens.

Perhaps he saw, on his way down Mill Street to Abbey Green Road where Wardle's works were situated, the massive 'Big Mill', with its impressive Italianate style, built only a few years previously for Lovatt and Gould in 1860, and admired its architectural style. Industrial buildings of this calibre were in line with Morris' ideas of what the working-class environment should be. But its high brick wall and huge iron gates separated the workplace from the freedom of the street and the workers' home environment. One can imagine that its awesome, fortress-like appearance would be viewed with wonder and respect mixed with a measure of dread by people like George Fisher and his family. Once you were through that gate you were under the authority of the factory-master and human nature being what it is, not all were blessed with altruistic feelings.

William Morris had much in common with Larner Sugden, and these fellow-feelings found common ground in the Society for the Protection of Ancient Buildings. Indeed, it may be fairly said that, although this society exerted national influence, there was a strong Leek input into its foundation and composition. It was founded in 1877 - the period during which William Morris was visiting Leek - and Thomas Wardle and Larner Sugden served on its committee. Some of its first members were prominent Leek citizens, William Challinor, Edwin and William Spooner Brough and George and Henry Davenport.

The 'anti-scrape' movement was gaining support in Victorian England, as more and more people became concerned about the fate of old buildings, not wishing to see insensitive repair work being carried out for mere cosmetic reasons. The movement found official recognition in the founding of the S.P.A.B. It expressed a philosophy about buildings and architecture that was close to that of the Sugdens - certainly Larner Sugden.

It was this great principle that ensured the preservation of the 17th century house 'Greystones' on Stockwell Street. This was formerly the home of Joshua Nicholson, and when he generously decided to provide Leek with public building that would house a library, reading room, art gallery and school of art, as well as meeting rooms for cultural activities the idea of the Nicholson Institute was born, and the Sugdens were commissioned to build it. Nicholson had the land available, but 'Greystones' stood in the way of allowing the new institute to have its imposing facade fronting directly on to Stockwell Street, so Nicholson's extensive land at the rear of Greystones provided the actual site for the Institute. Thus it may be said that Joshua Nicholson built the grandest 'garden shed' in the land! The S.P.A.B. ensured that 'Greystones' should be preserved, and the two buildings co-exist, which they do, in a harmony not always possible with buildings from two different centuries. That this harmony was feasible is a tribute to the genius of the Sugdens.

The Nicholson Institute was probably one of the first buildings upon which Larner Sugden had been given his head since joining his father as a partner. Certainly his principles and beliefs about architecture are well displayed in this fine building, in the Queen Anne style - a somewhat revolutionary movement amongst the more forward-thinking Victorian artists and designers, embodying much of the philosophy of the Pre-

Raphaelites, thus providing a further link with William Morris. Did Morris ever see it? We do not know, but if he did he would have loved it, and endorsed all it stood for.

The main contractor for the building work was Messrs H and R Inskip, of Longton, with the Leek firm of Edwin Phillips in charge of the plumbing and painting. Many other local firms contributed to the work; Minton, Hollins and Co. of Stoke-on-Trent, the tile floors, D Cartwright and Sons, many of the metal fittings and bronze door-handles. Much of the furniture was supplied by Overfields of Leek, and local builders, Mackrell, Nixons, and P Tomkinson also contributed. It was truly a combined operation, drawing upon the talents of many different people.

Mark Girouard, in his book *Sweetness and Light*, a fine treatise on the Queen Anne movement 1860-1900 (Yale University Press 1977) describes the Nicholson Institute in glowing terms:

.....rich with broken pediments, huge windows of many lights and busts of famous men, with a great red-brick Flemish gable at one end and a Wren-like tower capped by a green copper dome at the other, it still dominates the skyline at Leek - a secular church dedicated to the new religions of culture, art and education.

And so it was - a testimony to Sugden's architectural philosophy and Nicholson's Liberal non-conformist beliefs.

If the Nicholson Institute displayed the Queen Anne movement on the grand scale, some finer, small-scale elements can be seen in other Sugden buildings. Take, for example, the sunflower motif. The sunflower was given great prominence by the Pre-Raphaelites, where it is seen in the works of Morris, Rossetti and Burne-Jones. It is also featured in their writings by other Victorian poets like Tennyson and Blake. It is not surprising, therefore, that it finds its way into Sugden's work, where it graces the outer wall, above the coal shute, of a pair of houses in Bath Street and is seen blossoming in a flowerpot in the brickwork above the side-by-side front doors of houses in Portland Street.

Images in relief on the face of buildings are another distinctive feature of the work of the Sugdens. It was used to good effect on the Nicholson Institute, where the busts of famous men - Shakespeare, representing drama and literature, Newton for science, Reynolds for art, and Tennyson, poetry - epitomise not only the purposes for which the building was intended, but also four centuries of cultural development. These effigies are carved in high relief in stone, from models by Stephen Webb. And crowning them is the Milton quotation: 'A good book is the precious life-blood of a master spirit.' It was reported that the first book to be issued by the new library was to Mrs Cruso.

The adjoining buildings, Larner Sugden's Technical Schools, 1899/1900, have some fine plaster relief work over the windows. Modelled by A. Broadbent, these images depict art, commerce, industry and agriculture, a summary of the subjects taught at the school. The cornerstone of the building was laid by Millicent, Duchess of Sutherland on 24 July 1899, and the opening ceremony took place twelve months later, on 28 July 1900, and was performed by HRH the Duchess of York. At the same time, the Duke of York laid the foundation stone of the nearby Carr Gymnasium, another Sugden building. The royal couple were to make a return visit to Leek, as King George V and Queen Mary in 1913.

There was a fine clock above the inner door, surrounded by a painted design with Pre-Raphaelite imagery, bearing on its face the phrase 'I mark time, dost thou?' - a rather timely reminder for a school clock! The design also incorporated the phrase 'Old time is a'flying.'

Larner Sugden again used relief plasterwork to good effect in 1899 in his design for the new building for the Leek and Moorlands Co-operative Society on Ashbourne Road. This is a commission that would appeal to his Socialist principles, with the emphasis of the movement being on workers' co-operatives. The panels below the seven windows of the upper floor echo the industries, trade and commerce of the Moorlands, and are surmounted by a large, impressive pediment, the theme of which reflects the co-operative principle of prosperity through diligent industry and prudent saving. The panel incorporates an image of the Leek halfpenny, a reminder of the days when workers were paid in local coinage.

The Sugdens had already used an image of the Leek halfpenny, in stained glass, in a window of the new branch at Leek for the Manchester and Liverpool District Banking Company, built just before the Nicholson Institute, in 1882. The impressive gable, with its fine Venetian windows, has some elaborate decorative plasterwork, modelled by Messrs Collinson and Lock, from designs by Stephen Webb. The builders were Messrs Isaac Massey and Son, of Alderley Edge.

The interior of the bank was as impressive as its exterior. Windows of stained glass illuminated the arcaded walls, with bands of marble and white marble concrete, with moulded parts in scagliola, a polished imitation marble made up of ground gypsum bonded with glue. American walnut was used for the wainscoting of the walls, and the fine panelled ceiling was American whitewood, walnut and seasoned pitch-pine.

The 1880s were the peak years of achievement for the Sugdens as a father and son team, much of their best work appearing during those years. By 1881 Larner was in partnership with his father, and his enthusiasm for decoration and light found full expression. It was a decade of change nationally. Gladstone had formed as new government in 1880 and major reforms were introduced, beginning with compulsory education in 1880. The Employers' Liability Act of 1881 was something of a revolution for the doctrine of common employment, and Parliamentary Reform was inaugurated in 1884, followed by the Home Rule Bill in 1886. There was unrest in Ireland, and the rumblings of trouble with the Boers in the Transvaal. The British army was fully occupied in Egypt and the Sudan, culminating in the fall of Khartoum and the death of General Gordon in 1885. Queen Victoria's long and eventful reign reached a landmark with the celebration of the Jubilee in 1887.

Against all this Leek was enjoying a period of prosperity, as the silk industry was flourishing. Most of the major factories were well established by this time, and were employing increasing numbers of people. To accommodate larger numbers of pupils, an extension to West Street School was necessary in 1881. The original Sugden building of 1854 was now inadequate, for the catchment area served by the school now had many factories surrounded by streets of terraced houses for the workers, where large families were growing up. St. John's Mission Church and School in Mill Street was also built in 1881 as an extension of the work of St. Edward's Parish Church. By this time, Mill Street had become virtually a self-contained community, with churches, schools, shops and pubs.

1881 also saw the building of Fynney's Mill in Market Street, which became the offices of the *Leek Times* newspaper, the editor of which was Matthew Henry Miller. This was substantially altered in 1898 by Larner Sugden, and later became the Liberal Club. This would have pleased Larner, and today the club has a meeting room called 'The Sugden Room'.

By 1890 a new police station was also required. The little old police house at the top of Mill Street was redundant, as the number of officers was to be increased. Staffordshire County Council invited tenders from local architects and Sugden's plan was accepted. The new building was to be sited in Leonard Street, near the Cattle Market, and the accommodation was for a superintendent, a married sergeant, a single sergeant and twelve police constables, the superintendent being housed in separate building at the upper end of the site. The purpose-built station would also include an administrative block, offices, charge room and six cells, as well as domestic accommodation for the resident officers. Thus, with the entire force living on the site, it was virtually a police barracks.

This military aspect was further enhanced by the architectural style employed by the Sugdens. Sometimes described as 'Scottish Baronial', this gave the building a distinct military aspect, further enhanced by the corbelled turrets at each end. These were not merely ornamental features, but they had a functional purpose, providing a look-out over the surrounding streets. Within the site was a parade yard, plus stabling and coach house and an exercise yard for the prisoners. The building was completed in 1891. It was one of the last major buildings that the father and son Sugden partnership worked on together.

William Sugden died in 1892. In the 43 years that had passed since he arrived in 1849 the town of Leek had been transformed. Public buildings, schools, churches, factories and houses had filled out the streets that were hardly laid out at the time of his arrival, and Sugden architecture was strongly in evidence. The firm's domestic architecture was much in demand by many of the town's leading citizens, but perhaps this is seen at its best in the houses which the Sugdens built for themselves in Queen Street. If you are a successful architect, with a business that is doing well and your services in great demand, and you wish to build a house for yourself, it is perfectly natural that you will build well, and indulge yourself with all the characteristics that are the hallmark of your work. So it was with the Sugdens. William had already made his mark on Queen Street with the building of a fine row of houses, numbers 4 to 10, in 1858. On the opposite side of Queen Street a large site invited development and it was here that William and Larner built the houses which they were to occupy themselves. Prior to this, according to the Leek Commercial Directory of 1876, Larner had been living at Holyoake Cottage, Gratton.

Numbers 29, 29A and 29B Queen Street display lavishly all the features held dear by the Sugdens - the use of different building materials, brick, stone, tiles and terracotta, arched and curved windows, some with stained glass, decorated porches, doorways, chimney stacks and ridge tiles, elaborately carved barge boards and iron railings - all are here in abundance, a veritable riot of 'Sugdenalia'. Larner's house, number 29, incorporates in brickwork the initials of his French wife, JMBS (Josephine Marie Bucquoy Sugden) and his own, WLS.

William Sugden, the father, lived in the house next door, and these comfortable Victorian villas, lovingly built and maintained by the family, stand as a testament to the work of the creative partnership which ended with William's death in 1892.

Larner had then but a brief time left to continue the work, his creative genius being cut short by his untimely death in 1901. Ten very productive years during which Larner's style edged towards the 20th century, with the greater use of wood and glass in his buildings. Examples of this trend are Overfield's Showrooms, Russell Street (1895), the Co-operative Society central premises on Ashbourne Road (1899), Picton Street Co-op (1895) and the Technical Schools (1900). Had he lived, and been spared to make his mark on the new century, Leek would undoubtedly have had an even richer heritage of fine architecture.

Brunswick Methodist Church, Market Street (1856).

Leek's Golden Years 69

Rosebank House (1857).

Cemetery Chapel (1858).

70 Leek's Golden Years

Detail of the Richard Cutting tomb, St Edward's churchyard (1856).

Carved heads and window, Cemetery Chapel (1858).

Carved heads, Cemetery Chapel (1858).

Mechanics Institute, Russell Street (1862).

Mechanics Institute, detail between windows.

Alexandra Mills, Earl Street, Davidson & Myatts factory (1864).

West Street School (1854), extended 1881.

Congregational Church 'Frog' (1863). A small detail typical of Sugden architecture.

Brough, Nicholson & Hall, Cross Street (1865).

H.G. Carr, 7 Derby Street (1864).

BELOW
Ragged School, Mill Street (1870)

Houses in Bath Street (1869).

Shirley's Buildings (1875). Stone Lion.

Leek's Golden Years 77

Cottage Hospital (1871).

Houses in Bath Street (1880)

78 Leek's Golden Years

Manchester & Liverpool District Bank (1882). A Sugden drawing.

Detail above door of the bank (1882).

M & L District Bank, gable.

M & L District Bank, window.

Nicholson Institute (1884). Greystones in front.

Leek's Golden Years

The Nicholson Institute (1884).

82   Leek's Golden Years

Nicholson Institute (1884). Busts of famous men.

Nicholson Institute, Queen Anne style gable.

Nicholson Institute, Main entrance (1884).

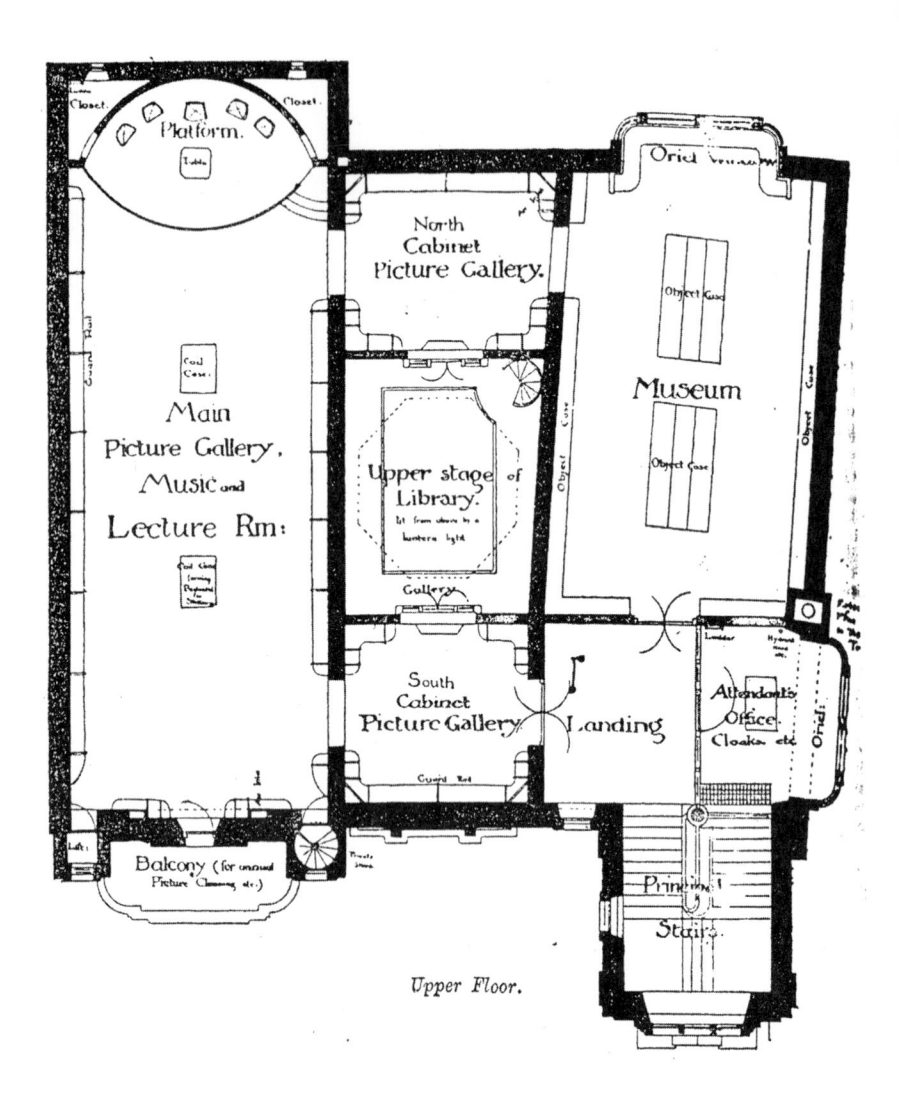

Nicholson Institute (1884). Sugden plan of upper floor.

Nicholson Institute, Milton quotation.

Nicholson Institute, Art Gallery.

Sgt. Major John Allen's tombstone, Leek Cemetery (1894).

Boat House.
Rudyard Lake

Planned extension to
Leek Town Hall.

88   Leek's Golden Years

Hartley's Model Village.

Alterations to Woodcroft Hall.

Secular Hall, Leicester (1879).

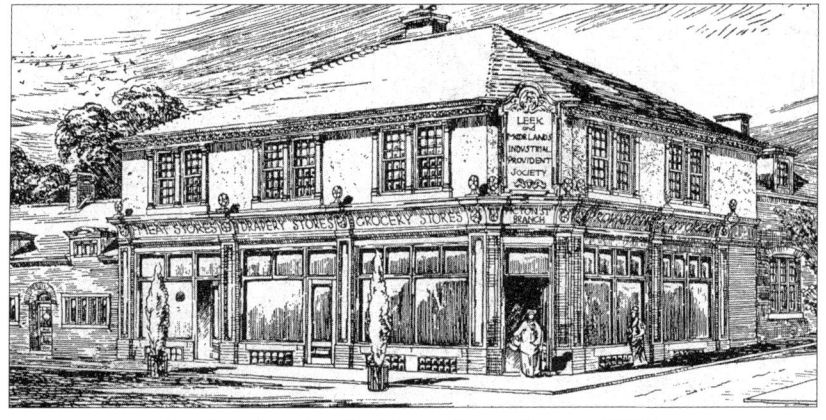

Sugden drawing for Picton Street Co-op, (1895).

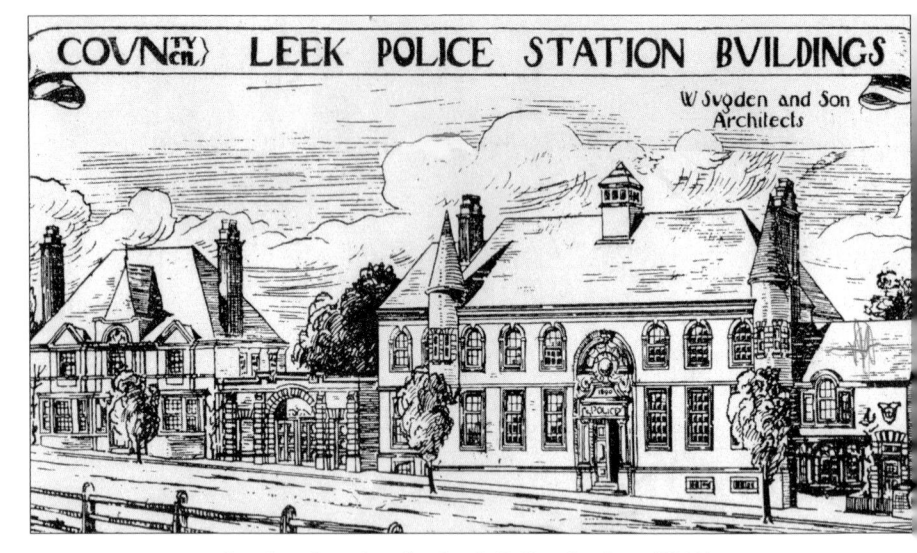

Sugden drawing for Leek Police Station, (1891).

The Inspector's House, Leek Police Station. 1891

Five
THE LATER SUGDEN YEARS

WHEN WILLIAM SUGDEN DIED on 24th September 1892, in his seventy-second year, the Leek Times was euphoric in its tribute:

There is now a void in the body politic that can only be filled when his memory shall cease to be green... Professionally he has left his mark on Leek for all time; politically he was argumentative and sturdy; religiously, earnest and true; and socially he has left no-one more beloved. Leek can ill spare one of her most distinguished and least pretentious citizens. A memorial service was held at the Congregational Church, where William had been a deacon, at which the Rev J Hankinson said: 'If we look around there are, in the public buildings and improved dwellings of the town, many monuments which will serve to keep his memory green for many coming years. But while men think of his skill as an architect, they will turn their thoughts with still greater interest to the man he was - so quiet in demeanour, and in determination also, his quietness sometimes adding strength to his purposes. No one could doubt his integrity and uprightness'.

Following the death of his father Larner took sole charge of the business and there was still much work to do, much to achieve. Only 42 years old at the time of his father's death, he had barely ten more years to live, but such thoughts were far from his mind as he applied himself to the task of running the business without his father - and commissions kept rolling in.

None of William's other sons entered the business, their careers taking them in other directions. The family house in Queen Street continued to be the home of Frederick Larner Sugden who was in the silk business. In partnership with Joseph Lovatt and trading as Sugden and Lovatt, the business was transferred to William Milner and Sons in 1907 when Lovatt retired. The three directors were Robert Schofield Milner, Arthur Fogg and Frederick Larner Sugden. The factory was in Union Street and Frederick Larner Sugden was in charge of the firm's operations in Ireland. He ran a silk factory in Dublin which suffered a disastrous fire in 1913. His son, Mark Sugden, was born in Leek, and educated at Denstone College and Dublin University. He became an international rugby union half-back for Ireland, making 28 appearances between 1925 and 1931, and captain for several matches. A teacher by profession, he was for many years a master at the Royal Naval College at Dartmouth.

William also had a daughter, Mary, his first child, who married Dr J.J. Ritchie, Medical Officer of Health for Leek. She was his second wife, but he died within a year. William's third child was Frank Larner, and his last child was Harry L. Sugden who worked for Brough, Nicholson & Hall.

William Sugden's house in Queen Street was later owned by a man for whose company the architects had worked in the past - Alfred H Moore was a director of Brough, Nicholson and Hall Ltd. His sister, Lavinia B Moore, remained in the house until the 1930s. The houses have remained largely unaltered to the present day.

During the father and son partnership years it was usually Larner who took responsibility for domestic architecture designs. His feeling for houses of both style and substance is apparent in all his work and many examples still remain in the old streets of Leek. In 1880 Larner was commissioned to build a pair of houses on the corner of Bath Street and Ford Street (numbers 33 and 35) for Sam Rider. These are built of local red brick, with stone dressings and red terracotta, roofed in brown Broseley tiles. Some of the brickwork is carved, incorporating the owner's initials, and the familiar sunflower design. The date is embodied in the decorated barge boards. In accordance with Sugden's instructions, the external painting was to be done in peacock blue and white.

On the opposite corner of Bath Street is a row of four

terraced houses, numbers 25 to 31, dating from a little earlier. These are much simpler in design, probably built for the middle management class in the textile industry. Nevertheless, they have some fine small coloured tile designs around the doorways, all different, and have splendid interiors, with some splendid woodwork.

Another of Larner's projects in the same year, 1880, was a house for W S Brough, on Buxton Road, Leek. An old stone cottage formerly stood on the site, and the architect cleverly incorporated this into his larger design, as kitchen and scullery, with servant's bedroom and a bathroom above. Again, local red bricks were used, and the house has some timber framing. The house was built by local builders, Messrs. Knowles and Henry and Micah Carding. A few years later, in 1885, Larner designed a house named Wyndyate for Mr Brough, at Scalby Bridge, Scarborough.

The reputation of Sugden and Son in the field of house building was recognised far beyond Leek. One Ash, a large house with wide gables and ancillary buildings was erected at Woodthorpe near Loughborough in 1894. In the following year, Larner turned his attention to the grand Queen Anne style Hillmorton House, Rugby. The Keighley connection was maintained with the building of Strong Close House, in the Yorkshire town.

Larner Sugden's services were called upon by most of Leek's leading citizens from time to time. Socially he enjoyed a high standing amongst the town's citizens. The work varied, from the actual building of new property to alterations and additions to the old, as well as occasionally designing pieces of furniture. Thus, in 1891, William Prince, a local silk manufacturer, engaged Larner to design elaborate extensions to his home, Woodcroft Hall. These included highly stylized, elaborate gables, and a corner tower capped by an eastern minaret. It is doubtful if the extensions were ever completed and the hall has now been demolished.

In complete contrast, a fine piece of furniture was designed for Edward Challinor in 1886. This was an elaborate oak buffet, made by Sam Walwyn, a local cabinet maker. This large piece had bronze lion-head handles and other special metalwork by Messrs Elgood of Leicester. The wood carving was done by a Mr Millson of Manchester.

The student of domestic architecture of the Victorian period will find much substance in the work of the Sugdens. The firm never took on the task of planning an entire estate in Leek, or even an entire road or avenue, preferring to let their work stand beside that of others. And this is its strength, for there is not one jarring note in any of the Sugdens' work; nothing is out of place, and there is a harmony of style everywhere. The houses on Bath Street sit nicely against others by Brealey, and the various Queen Street properties are in tune with their neighbours. Much the same can be said for other terraced houses in Broad Street (76 & 78), and Hugo Street (Glenochil House and Athlone House, a Scottish theme). There is something of a surprise, however, with the two houses in Portland Street South, which, surrounded by factory buildings, assert themselves in an almost impudent manner, making, with their wallflower brickwork and unusual corner chimneystacks, a bold statement on the street scene.

An example of the rivalry between Brealey and Sugden can be seen in the circumstances surrounding the building of Leek's Butter Market and Fire Station in 1895. Local government at the time was going through a period of transition. Under the terms of the Local Government Act of 1894 the work of the Leek Improvement Commissioners, in operation since 1855, was to pass into the hands of the Leek Urban District Council. The first election of councillors under the new act took place on 17th December, 1894, when there were 53 candidates for the 24 seats. The result proved to be very much a victory for the 'old guard', as 15 of the old Commissioners were elected to the new council.

One of the first tasks of the new authority was the provision of a covered Butter Market. Three shops at the north-eastern end of the Market Place had already been purchased, together with property adjoining Stockwell Street, with land at the rear. In order to provide a frontage and main entrance from the Market Place the council bought the Red Lion and stables. There was a great public protest regarding the cost of the proposals and the loss of the Red Lion. Eventually the hotel and stables were resold and architects were invited to submit plans for a covered market and fire station on the corner site. William Sugden had died in 1892 and Larner collaborated in this project with another architect, Abraham Mosley, whose family came from Kingsley. (Mosley went to America in 1904, where he had a distinguished career as an architect. He was acknowledged as the pioneer of the English collegiate school of architecture, and was responsible for many large-scale projects including public buildings, halls and churches in Kansas City, Suffolk, Virginia and other towns and cities along the Mohawk River. He died in Albany, having lived in America for over 40 years.)

In an attempt to keep the competition fair, the plans were to be entered under a pseudonym, and the Sugden plan was submitted in the name of 'Bon Marche'. This was placed second, and when the Chairman of the Council, Councillor John Brealey, announced the winner as 'Butterfly' it turned out to be the plan submitted by his nephew, John Thomas Brealey.

Outside Leek, Larner Sugden made a significant contribution to the architecture of Victorian Buxton when in 1897 he built the Red House, a large house standing in extensive grounds on the Manchester road out of Buxton. Built mainly of red brick, with large bays and broad gables, and a wide balcony across the entire front, the Red House has a flavour of the Scottish Baronial style, with massive corbelled turrets at each end - the style he adopted for Leek Police Station. The Red House was demolished in the 1980s and a block of residential flats now stands on the site.

The Sugdens were never involved in estate planning on a large scale in Leek, but there is a notable exception to this rule outside Leek. During the later Victorian years, as business and commerce prospered, there was a trend amongst the more enlightened entrepreneurs to develop 'industrial garden villages' for their workers. Thus, the soap manufacturer WH Lever founded Port Sunlight, Sir Titus Salt founded Saltaire, there was Robert Gardner's settlement at Barrow Bridge, Price's Candles at Bromborough Pool Village, and of course, George and Richard Cadbury's Bournville. The name of Sugden found a place in this distinguished company in the planning in 1888 of Hartley's Model Village at Aintree, Liverpool, for WP Hartley, in which substantial villas are laid out in formal avenues around a central square, situated near the preserves factory, for whose workers the housing was intended. Architects were in competition for the scheme, and plans had to be submitted anonymously, Sugden choosing the pseudonym 'Sweet Auburn'.

The Builder 25 Aug 1888 said this of the Sugden plans for the Aintree Model Village:

The architects have endeavoured to obtain a certain degree of picturesque effect without eccentricity, and have designed the cottages in conformity with the old domestic buildings indigenous to the district, and avoiding all flimsy and supposed "picturesque" ornamental additions - for which they are entirely to be commended.

These comments could readily be applied to most of Sugden's domestic architecture in Leek

After William Sugden's death, Larner became more and more involved with public bodies and institutions. His political leanings led to an influx of work for the Leek and Moorlands Co-operative Society. As the local workforce expanded so did the influence of the Co-op movement and new branch shops were opened where the people were. Picton Street, in the heart of a network of streets of terraced houses, got its shop in 1895. The Society opened its Ashbourne Road (then London Road) shop and bakery in 1880, and in 1899 purchased adjoining land. Larner Sugden was then commissioned to design extensions, including doubling the size of the bakery. The new shop on Ashbourne

Road also included stabling for delivery vehicles, and a hall above the shop where meetings and functions could be held. There was a penny savings bank, to encourage thrift, and the buildings were known as the Central Premises. This is the building with the fine decorated plaster work on the facade, recently restored to its former glory and appropriately named Penny Bank House.

Derby Street has a number of Sugden shops and shop alterations, and the block on the corner of Haywood Street, Sanders Buildings (1894), has many typical Sugden features, although the chimneys are rather stark and plain, which is unusual for Sugden. A similar corner block stands on the junction of St. Edward Street with Sheepmarket. Shirley's Buildings (1875) was originally owned by E Shirley and Co, corn, seed , guano, wool and cheese merchants, who also traded in Longnor. It later became a cheese factors and grocery shop, trading as Bastin and Co, followed by E Green. The property was later occupied by Boots, chemists and lending library. During World War II it was a 'comfort station' providing recreation and refreshment facilities for the American servicemen billeted in Leek, when it became known as the 'Doughnut Dugout'. Its role changed yet again after the war, when it became the local National Insurance office. It is currently an Indian restaurant, and of all the Sugden buildings in Leek, this one has changed its role more than most.

A departure from the usual Sugden style was seen in Larner's 1895 design of the furniture warehouse and emporium for Overfields in Russell Street. Here wood and glass have largely replaced brick and stone, the large windows giving a light and airy feel to this large building, a sharp contrast with the Gothic Congregational Church opposite and the much earlier Mechanics Institute, classical Sugden, just above.

During the 1890s Larner Sugden became increasingly involved with local authorities. The old family link with Keighley was still strong, for, in open competition in 1890, plans for new municipal buildings in Sheffield were submitted in the names of W. Sugden and Son, Leek, and W L Sugden, Keighley - but there was no W L Sugden in Keighley at the time. Perhaps Sugden exploited his Yorkshire roots in seeking Yorkshire business. The ambitious design was a departure for Sugden, being somewhat French Renaissance in character.

In 1893 Larner submitted, in limited competition, a design for a Town Hall and Library in Cheadle. Strict economy was urged upon the competitors, to keep costs down. Larner's estimate was £2487.10s including fixtures and decoration, and this would incorporate a large hall. At about the same time he submitted designs for an elaborate extension to Leek Town Hall, on the Silk Street side, but this work was not carried out.

Larner Sugden was appointed architect and surveyor to Stoke-on-Trent Rural District Council, and in the course of this work he drew up plans for a land drainage and sewerage scheme at Bucknall, with a new stable and cart shed on the pumping station site. These buildings were purely functional, with none of the usual Sugden embellishments. In the 1890s Larner had an office in Hanley at Miles Bank Chambers.

Sugden on the grand scale was seen in 1893, however, with his design for the new County Lunatic Asylum at Cheddleton. Staffordshire County Council had been seeking a site for its new mental hospital, and eventually Cheddleton was chosen. Tenders were invited from architects, and, as with the earlier Leek Buttermarket scheme, Larner Sugden again collaborated with Abraham Mosley in submitting plans for an ambitious scheme. Again, the plans were submitted under a pseudonym, Sugden choosing the name 'Sunbeam'. This clever design made the best use of light and air, envisaging a continuous arterial corridor running round three sides of a triangle, with a central block comprising stores, kitchen and a large dining and recreation hall, the whole being linked by the continuous corridors. The various specialist wards led off the outer corridors, making them isolated, but at the same time there was ready access between all parts of the hospital complex. Clever though Sugden's very symmetrical design was, it was not accepted by the hospital authority, and the contract was awarded to Giles, Gough and Trollope, of London. Nevertheless, Larner Sugden's name was now recognised and respected by local authorities and statutory bodies, which would enhance his already high reputation still further. His plans were not always accepted. Perhaps he had a tendency to be a little over-ambitious. But then, Larner Sugden was always a bold architect and was never afraid to step out of line. Had he, one wonders, become too bold? Had his genius outgrown the small town of Leek.

His nonconformity was further expressed in his political convictions. He was a socialist in the William Morris mould, and was passionately opposed to the Boer War, and his intense feelings were deeply stirred by the sufferings of women and children in the conflict. This led him to work passionately for their cause by raising funds for their relief, a campaign in which he was still engaged at the time of his death.

One of Larner Sugden's last commissions in 1900 was some work for himself, namely the conversion of the firm's old offices at 13-13a Derby Street, building two shops on to the frontage. His health was beginning to fail, and it was almost as if he wanted to ensure that the future of the site was secure commercially. It was not possible to preserve the fine Georgian doorway but by making the two shops single storey he managed to keep the upper floors which can still be seen today One wonders what his feelings were as this work was done.

On March 2nd 1901, his 26th wedding anniversary, Larner left Leek with his French wife, to spend a holiday in Littlehampton. He had not been well for some time, and was unable to complete the journey. He spent several weeks in Hampstead, under medical care, and a slight improvement allowed him to return to Leek on April 26. His condition continued to improve after his return home, but he suffered a relapse and died on June 18 1901.

At his own request, Larner Sugden was cremated at the

Manchester Crematorium on Friday, june 21st, 1901. The ceremony was attended by a few immediate family and friends, and a number of his business and professional associates, although many people turned out in Leek, as his coffin was taken to Leek Railway Station. Leek's librarian, Kineton Parkes, actor and elocutionist, recited a few verses from Shelley's *Adonais*, and the funeral oration, full of Victorian hyperbole and ostentation, was given by J. Bruce Glasier, chairman of the Independent Labour Party. In parts of his address, he said:

'Larner Sugden was one of the rarer human spirits of our time. He was refined in temperament to a high degree, and his mind was very beautifully poised. He was high above the order of men who live merely to prosper their own interests in the world... He possessed the rare quality of civic courage - rare in these days when the world is chiefly intolerant of any earnestness or devotion that is calculated to disturb the smoothness of commercial and social self-advancement... The spirit of beauty and craftsmanship which inspired Ruskin and William Morris dwelt in him; and he has by his hand touched with permanent beauty his native town and innumerable places far and near. He died undaunted in his faith in Socialism and in Peace... There are not, I venture to say, many things in England in these latter days more prophetic of the greatness of our England that is to be, than is this brief episode in its history - the life and work of Larner Sugden, of Leek... He departs from us leaving behind him, not a sunset, but a morning glow of affection and fame, which will for ever linger in our hearts.'

After the cremation, to the accompaniment of Beethoven's Funeral March, a further tribute was given by Mr Raymond Unwin, who then read the following sonnet, written by Kineton Parkes:

> *Now after months of pain comes gentle peace,*
> *The body crumbles into dust, the soul*
> *Aspiring ever, fighting to be free,*
> *Escapes its fetters, finds at length its goal,*
> *Inexorable as the stern decree*
> *That claims the body for its pain's surcease;*

Yet 'tis but reason that it so should be;
Perish the clay but keep the spirit whole!
So on the day when Death comes down to earth,
When sombre-winged he hovers over all,
Calling the spirit to its second birth,
We tremble near, resenting the low call.
While in our hearts we, selfish, feel the dearth;
There yet is mixed some honey with the gall.

The Cremation Service was very reverent, but avoided any traditional Christian sentiments, for Larner Sugden was not a churchman. His deeply held beliefs were more humanitarian. His faith in Socialism and in Peace have been seen in his abhorrence of the Boer War. The benediction at the end of the service reflected his humanist beliefs: *'May the blessing of all those who love their fellow-men be with him and his memory now and for evermore.'*

In the year of the death of William Morris, 1896, the Leek Labour supporters took over the 1697 Quaker Meeting House on Overton Bank and established the William Morris Labour Church. Dedicated to the principles of humanitarian Socialism, where art, life and religion are one, it perfectly suited Larner Sugden's outlook and beliefs, and he became deeply involved in its organisation and work. (See Footnote)

It was therefore perfectly appropriate that a Memorial Service should be held there on the Sunday following his funeral, when the Labour Church was crowded. Giving the memorial oration was the famous figure of the Socialist MP Keir Hardy. Extracts from his speech are as follows:

'Larner Sugden was no ordinary man. Trained to a profession in which all his worldly prospects and interests were bound up in keeping on good terms with the respectable and the rich and the well-to-do elements of society, he appeared to have gone out of his way to give offence, and yet he did not require to say that he had any pleasure in running counter to the wishes of others or had any desire to give pain, but such was his great large-hearted human sympathy... The human element

within him was so highly developed that he could do no other. His sympathy was neither with nationality nor creed, nor class, nor caste, nor profession. Wherever there was human suffering he felt a desire to mitigate it and relieve it... He looked upon life with the eye of an artist. He saw how the conventionalities in politics, in religion, in commerce were clothing the nation with hideousness, deforming and degrading, and demoralising humanity. He did not agree with the system upheld and supported by the Church and State, a system which mankind would one day look back upon and wonder that a nation calling itself civilised could have allowed in its midst, and seeing these things he forgot self interest... The one thing wanted in religion or business, in civil life and in domestic life, was manhood - courage, honesty and integrity. Larner Sugden possessed all those things. He was, in every sense of the word, a man. Might I presume to convey to the relatives, the sympathy not only of myself or the more intimate of his friends, but of the thousands and tens of thousands who never saw him, but who were inspired by his courage and his devotion to the work of uplifting of humanity. It was a glorious record... Larner Sugden was honest, earnest, sincere and true, and if his worldly prospects suffered because of his opinions, he had shown devotion and love for those who were endeavouring as best they could to leave the world brighter than they found it'.

A series of annual Larner Sugden Memorial Lectures was planned, at which nationally famous personalities in the Labour movement came to Leek, to speak on contemporary issues in the fields of politics and the arts. Speakers included Keir Hardy, Philip Snowden, J Bruce Glasier, G K Chesterton and J W Mackail, the biographer of William Morris. The lectures were a fitting tribute, of which Larner Sugden would no doubt have approved.

FOOTNOTE on the William Morris Labour Church:

The Labour Church movement was established *'to give expression to the religion and general principles of Socialism. It is not theological, each individual's personal convictions upon such matters being respected.'* The Leek Labour Church was transformed from its austere appearance when used by the Quakers to a richly decorated interior, the walls being lacquered a rich red with stencil ornaments which were the work of Walter Crane.

The book of the Opening of the William Morris Labour Church in Leek (1897) continues:

The ceiling and overhead beams are being finished (as also the barred sash windows) in pure white and the woodwork (upright high-back pews etc) painted in translucent green. The west and south windows will be draped with Morris blue velvet fabric, and the gaslighting is to be incandescent, with pink shades etc. The decorations by J. Ratcliffe are under the general direction of Messrs Sugden and Son, and Mr Craigmile and George Rigby (as well as Mr Crane) are giving valuable help.

The interior must have been a colourful sight indeed - a bold statement of the design principles of its founders. The involvement of Walter Crane is a further example of the way in which Victorian Leek was able to attract eminent figures from national life to the town. Crane was well known as an illustrator of children's books, and his farmyard and railway alphabets were enormously successful, selling many thousands. He was a Socialist in the William Morris mould, hence his enthusiastic response to contribute designs to the Leek Labour Church, which was dedicated to the memory of Morris.

Walter Crane was an important figure in the decorative arts of the time, and his work included book illustrations, nursery wallpaper, wall hangings and stained glass. He was a prolific illustrator of books, and his work extended beyond the toy books for which he was famous to include illustrations for adult books published by the Kelmscott Press of William Morris. Much of his work was anonymous. He was principal of the Royal College of Art for a time, and became a strong influence on the Leek School of Art. He died in 1915.

The interior decorations of the Labour Church included Morris blue velvet fabrics for the windows and silk banners with Morris quotations, designed by Stephen Webb, one of the founders of the Arts and Crafts movement, and associated with William Morris at South Kensington. Larner Sugden would have been perfectly at home here!

Police Station (1891).

Cast-iron lion on gate post.

Leek's Golden Years 105

Police Station, chimneys and turret, Scottish baronial style.

Police Station yard, Leonard Street (1891)

Littlehales, Buxton Road, 1860. Sugden drawing.

St John's Mission Church, Mill Street, 1870. Sugden drawing.

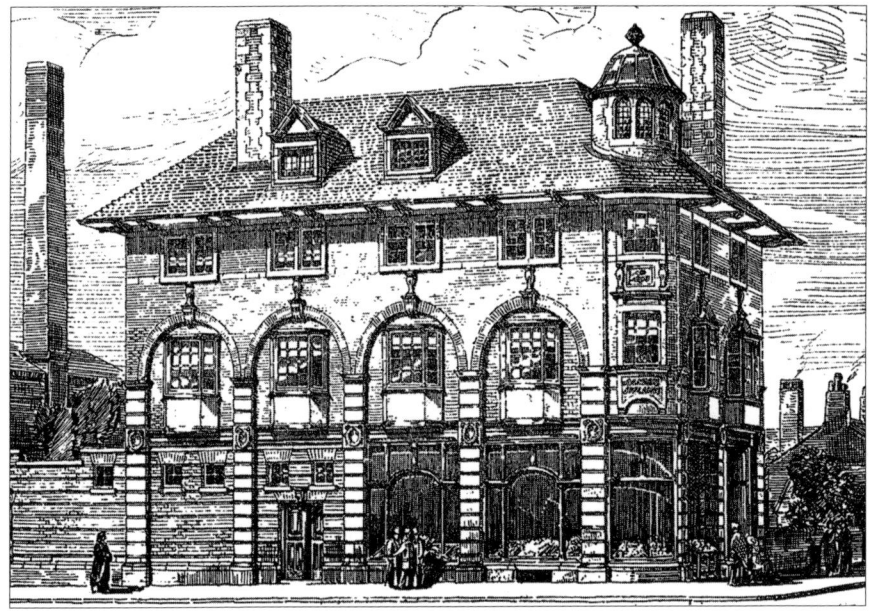

Sanders Building (1894).
Sugden's drawing which stated 'Anchor Buildings for Mr William Sanders'.

Sanders Buildings (1894).

Sanders Building (1894).

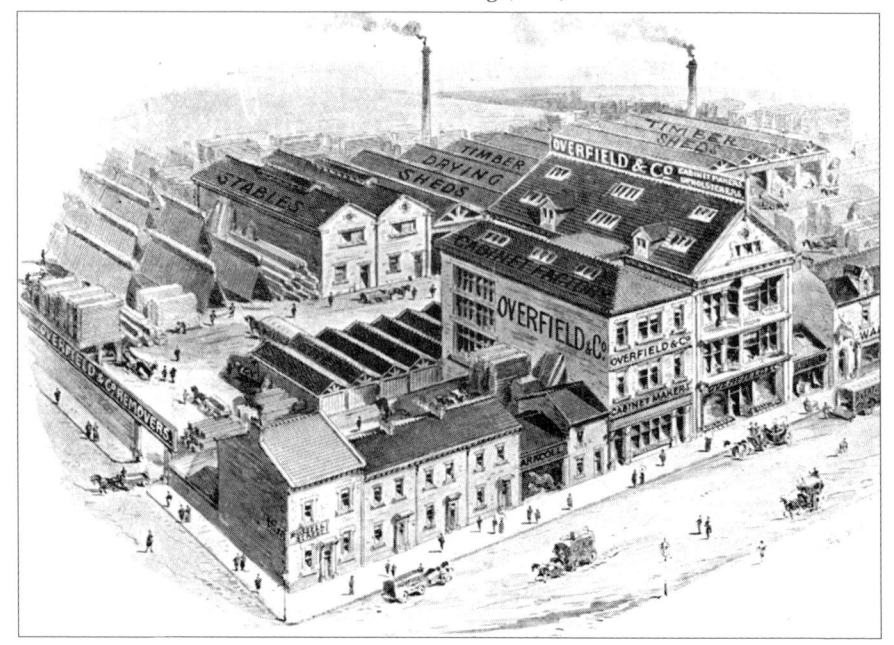

Impressionistic drawing of Overfield's furniture warehouse, Russell Street (1895).

Overfield's warehouse, Russell Street (1895).

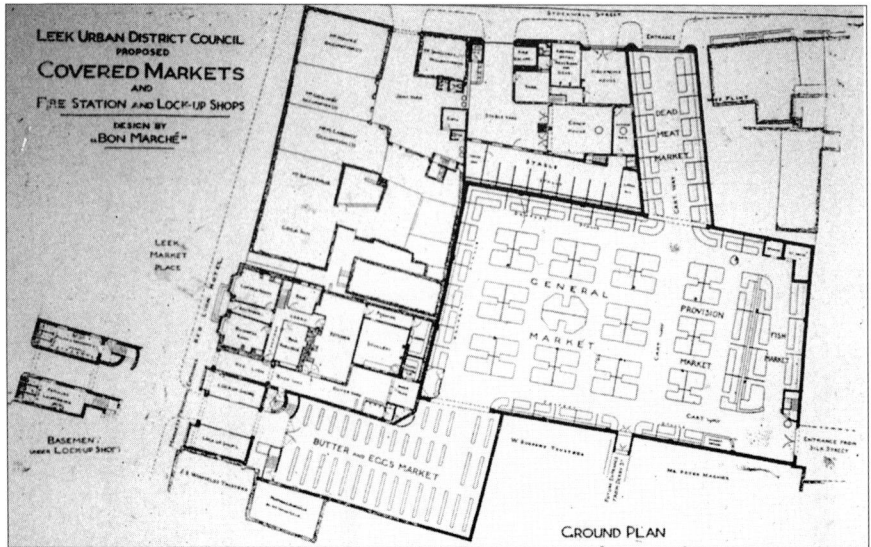

Larner Sugden's plan for the proposed Butter Market, which was not accepted (1895).

The Co-op Central premises (1899).

Le Pont de la Goule Noire, Gorges de la Bourne. Larner Sugden's canal scheme in France (1894).

BELOW:
The clock in the Technical Schools.

Leek's Golden Years 113

The Sugden houses in Queen Street.

The Sugden offices in Derby Street.

Houses demolished for the building of the Leek Technical Schools.

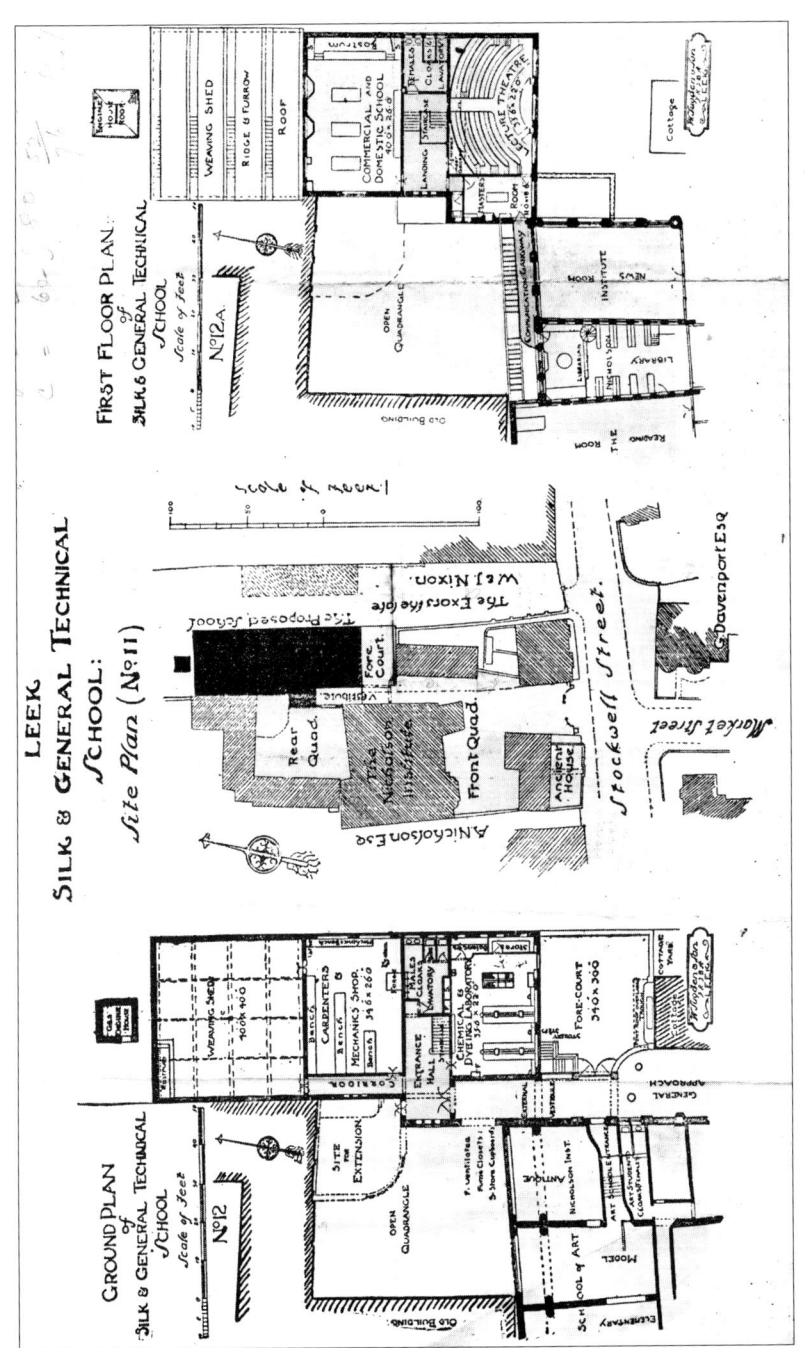

Leek's Golden Years 115

Larner Sugden's plans for the Leek Technical Schools.

WORKMEN INVOLVED IN BUILDING LEEK TECHNICAL SCHOOLS (1900).

Top Row
1 J. Eliner
2 Tom Oliver
3 G. Sales
4 J. Haywood
5
6 H. Birkenhead
7 E. Sherrat
8 H. Atkinson
9 J. O'Hara
10 H. Biddulph
11 H. Grace
12 A. Woodings
13 J. Jones
14 A. James
15

Second Row
1
2 W. Salt
3 H. Ball
4 F. Bradley
5 T. Goldstraw
6 T. Salt
7 J. Goldstraw
8 C. Mason
9 A. Wright
10 P. Wright
11 W. Merritt
12 R. Cowell
13 T. Lindop
14 R. Sorrell
15
16
17

Third Row
1 A. Grace, stand'g
2
3 H. Slater
4 W. Wood
5
6 J. Nixon
7 J. W. Ward
8
9 J. Horne
10 H. Brown
11 J. Brooks
12 J. Billing
13 R. Horne
14 J. Simpson
15 E. Evans
16 H. Smith
17 J. Bowcock

Fourth Row
1 — Scholes
2
3 P. Plant
4 J. Lowe
5 J. Turner

Leek's Golden Years

LARNER SUGDEN SEATED FRONT ROW 6TH FROM LEFT IN A WHITE SUIT.

6	18 J. Deakin	8 D. Wilmer	**Sixth Row**	12
7 Ernest Birch	19 E. Bullen	9	1 H. Grace	13 F. D. Galton
8 J. Curtis	20 H. Birchenough	10 David Hibbert	2 J. Carding	14 W. H. Galton
9 Edward Birch		11 C. Stretch	3 M. Carding	15 R. Walwyn
10 M. Minton	**Fifth Row**	12 H. Hammond	4 K. Parkes	16 — Porter
11 H. Hobson	1	13 G. Mollatt	5 T. Grace	J. Grace (seated
12 Walter Lay	2 J. Condlyffe	14 Will Carding	6 Larner Sugden	in front)
13 Vinct. Robinson	3 H. Porter	15 R. J. Wragg	7 G. Wood	
14 T. Vickerstaff	4 T. Carpenter	16 Geo. Hocknell	8 — Broadbent	
15 E. Bendall	5 Edgar Wilmer	17 Geo. Trafford	9 A. Carding	
16 E. Sheldon	6 A. Vass	18 A. Pegg	10 W. A. Overfield	
17 J. Fallows	7 E. Spare	19 T. White	11 H. Sugden	

The Challinor Fountain on its original site in the Market Place.

The Challinor Fountain re-sited in Brough Park.

Six

A FAMILY TRADITION OF SOLICITORS

'GOOD MORNING, MESTER CHALLINOR.' Such might be the greeting from the townsfolk of Leek, rich and poor, upper or working class, as they met in the street, this smart, somewhat Dickensian Victorian gentleman in his black frock coat and bow tie, as he went about his business in the town. Such was the status of William Challinor, solicitor and Improvement Commissioner, whose life and work touched many, and whose remarkable influence on Leek we shall now explore.

Almost directly opposite to the Derby Street offices of the architects, William Sugden and Son, another fine Georgian building graces the street scene. The upper windows of the two buildings face each other across the thoroughfare, as the townsfolk and market people hurry by on their routine business of the day, for Leek is a working town, and Derby Street lies at its commercial heart. The busy passer-by, if he has time to stop and look, will see the stone above the splendid doorway bearing the date 1760. In 1818 this fine building was the offices of Killmister and Challinor, one of seven firms of lawyers in Leek at that time. In White's Directory of 1851 the firm is listed as Challinor, Badnall and Challinor, also with an office in Stockwell Street. The name Challinor has been ever-present, and for more than 100 years No 10 Derby Street has served as the offices of Challinors and Shaw, solicitors.

The first William Challinor (1752-1800) was a Leek solicitor, who took over the practice of John Davenport of Ball Haye Hall. He made a success of his career, and was an excellent horseman. His eldest son, William, born on 5th August 1783, continued the practice in partnership with George Ridgway Killmister, his late father's partner, whom he joined in 1807. Killmister had been running the firm himself since the older William's death in 1800. After the younger William joined Killmister seven years after his father's death, the firm became known as Killmister and Challinor.

The second William Challinor was educated at Ashbourne and Derby. He served in the Leek Company of Volunteers, and was one of the first Leek Improvement Commissioners appointed in 1829. Like his father, he was a keen horseman. His other interest was farming. He died at the Derby Street house in 1839, and of his five sons, two became solicitors. Joseph had an independent practice at Compton House, and William (the third William) continued in the Derby Street practice after his father's death. It was this William who made his indelible mark on Victorian Leek. He was born at Pickwood on 10th March, 1821.

Pickwood is a fine house on the south-eastern edge of town, commanding a splendid view over a deep valley towards Ballington Wood. A small brook runs down the valley from Lowe Hill to join the stream near the Lady of the Dale Well where the old drive to Pickwood from the south was located. It was the Challinor family home for many years, and under their occupation it underwent many changes. An extra wing was added, and some of the work was done by Sugden.

William Challinor III (1821-1896) was educated at Leek Grammar School on Clerk Bank, and at King William's College, Isle of Man. He was admitted a solicitor in Trinity Term 1842, subsequently taking first his BA and then his MA at Trinity College, Dublin. He studied for the Bar, but was not called, and completed his legal training under Judge Baylis, who was then an eminent barrister in Chambers. There was a warm friendship between tutor and pupil. During his studies he found the energy to lend his support for the North Staffordshire Railway's scheme for a line to connect Macclesfield with Derby. He also joined the troops of the Queen's Own Royal Yeomanry, and held the rank of Cornet but retired before attaining higher rank.

He returned to Leek following the death of his father, to join the family practice. Miss Ferriar, daughter of Dr John Ferriar, of Manchester, was a great friend of William. They never married, she being much older than William, but she worked as his housekeeper at Pickwood, which he had taken over from Edward Challinor.

Jane Catherine Ferriar (1788-1864) was the only daughter of John Ferriar, MD who became Senior Physician at Manchester Infirmary. Besides having a distinguished career as reformer and innovator in the medical profession, Dr Ferriar was an eminent man of letters. His commentary and essays on the works of Sterne were held in high regard in the literary world. He had an encyclopedic knowledge of the classics and his poetical writings had many classical allusions. He had an extensive library, a portion of which came into the possession of William Challinor by the bequest of Miss Ferriar, following her death in 1864. She is buried in Leek Cemetery.

William Challinor married Elizabeth Mary Pemberton, third daughter of Thomas Pemberton of Warstone House, Warwickshire in 1851. Her sister Sarah married Andrew Jukes Worthington, a silk manufacturer of Leek. They set up home at Pickwood, but William was not to have two ladies looking after after him at Pickwood, for Miss Ferriar then moved out. However, she remained a good friend, as is evidenced by her bequest of some of her father's precious books to William.

The Challinor marriage produced one son, William Edward, and two daughters, Mary Katherine, who died at the age of three, and Mary Edith (1858-1898). Elizabeth died of cancer at an early age, on 7th November, 1880, and Mary Edith remained at Pickwood to look after her father, with the help of a housekeeper Mary Provost and two domestic servants. In 1884 Challinor's daughter married Charles Watson, JP of Leek but died at the age of 40, on 2nd January, 1898.

William's son, William Edward (1852-1926) did not follow the family tradition of becoming a solicitor. In the 1881 Census his occupation was stated as earthenware manufacturer, and his home was Haregate Hall. However, the law touched his life in that he was a JP, and he married Catherine, daughter of William Allen, a prominent Leek solicitor, whose firm, Hacker and Allen had offices in St. Edward Street. William Challinor IV suffered from asthma and, unlike his father, did not get involved in public affairs.

William Challinor III was a man of boundless energy, deeply involved with the public business of the town, besides handling the legal affairs of countless clients. He was very active, and his accounts reveal a great annual expenditure in shoes and shoe repairs and tack for his horses! One can picture him travelling on foot to visit his town clients, and on horseback for his country business, being frequently stopped and diverted on his way by the many who inevitably wanted a word with him! He always had time for people.

The workload of the firm was immense, and must have employed the services of many clerks, all records being handwritten, in those days before typewriters and word processors. Huge, leather-bound ledgers lined the office walls, and the vaults were stacked high with books, files, portfolios, documents, plans, correspondence, bills and strong boxes. William Challinor was running a highly successful business. Challinor & Co. became Challinors and Shaw in the 1890s, after Thomas Shaw joined the practice - a name by which Leek people know it to the present day, even though it has become a member of a group practice.

Records suggest that William Challinor was a very generous and public spirited man. He enjoyed a privileged position in society, and was able to use this in creating for himself a position of power and influence in the town. There were few families or business enterprises in Leek that he was not involved with in some way, which enabled him to gain an intimate insight into many confidential matters. Nevertheless, there is no evidence to suggest that he ever abused his power in an underhand way. He was generous with both his time and his money, and did not stint himself in his public service. He had boundless energy and clearly had the ability to organise his time in order to carry out all his many commitments, and indulge his various interests. His hand-written notebooks reveal much about his character. He would use his oilskin-bound notebook to write down random thoughts, odd facts and notes about events in the form of an occasional diary. Much of this material he later included in his published *Lectures, Verses, Speeches, Reminiscences &c.* in 1891.

His humanity and his sense of humour are illustrated in an incident in December 1878, where he recalls visiting one of his old clerks, a Mr Hallowes, who was seriously ill at home, and although the man was dying they had a long conversation in which *'he said he well remembered some of the old times between 30 and 40 years ago, when I took part in the debates at the Mechanics Institute, and especially one, when there was a discussion on the subject of dancing, which Mr Burgess, an ironmonger, and some of the extreme dissenters disapproved of taking place, as it sometimes did after some of the Institute entertainments. Someone remarked that dancing was not disapproved of in the Scriptures. Mr Burgess remarked that it was said David danced before the Ark, but this was evidently not mixed dancing, upon which Mr Hallowes said I came down upon him like lightning with the remark, 'Ay, but it is further said 'In the midst were the damsels playing on the timbrels,' and this seemed for a moment to settle the question.'*

Another amusing incident, recorded in one of his notebooks, states:

'Went to tea at Mr. Fynney's. Afterwards had a game at whist. A coincidence in one of the games that is perfectly true, but which I never remember being equalled. Mr Fynney dealt and turned up the Ten of Clubs. Afterwards I dealt and turned up the Ten of Clubs. Miss Anne Fynney then dealt and to our astonishment turned up the Ten of Clubs. I saw well if Miss M Fynney who was playing with me turned up the same I should think it a marvellous business. She then dealt, and turned up, I think, a small Club, but immediately flung the cards down for some reason, and then claimed to deal again. She accordingly dealt, and lo, she turned up the Ten of Clubs!... True!'

In another incident he recalls something his father told him:

'I remember my father telling me he had a clerk named Prime, a very handsome man, but not the sharpest. My father once spoke to him about some business. 'Man,' he said, 'why don't you think?' 'Mester,' he replied, 'I am na' paid for thinking.' My father also once said he had been asked whether he would rather be rich with little or no appetite, or poor with a good one. He replied that he much preferred the latter.'

In May 1899 he writes philosophically about the nesting of rooks, and at the same time gives us an impression of the setting and solitude of Pickwood, and a little vignette of its natural history:

'One rook built a nest at Pickwood about 10th of March last year, in a high beech tree not far from the house. This year more rooks commenced building, and have continued to do so through March and April, until by the 4th of May there are no less than 17 rooks' nests, all in beech trees, except one in a larch tree. This is the first time rooks have been known to build here, though there have been old oaks in a wood here for generations, probably from very ancient times as the place was called Pickwood (as appears from the deeds I have) as far back as the time of Philip (sic) and Mary. When watching these rooks build and carrying sticks to form their nests which are all at the very tops of the trees, supported generally by a branch of perhaps the thickness of the wrist only, and liable to sway about in the wind, though apparently firmly fixed, I wondered whether they had always built in the same manner from the Dawn of Creation, or whether their instinct or constructive power in this respect had been improved or developed by time.'

These recollections are perhaps trivial but they give a good insight into the character and personality of William Challinor. He led a very busy public and professional life, but he had time to visit a sick employee, time for a game of whist and time to watch the rooks at Pickwood. His notes also form a picture of life in Victorian Leek, which was rarely dull!

An example of William Challinor's generosity is seen in his gift to the town of the Pickwood Recreation Ground. The occasion was Queen Victoria's Silver Jubilee in 1887. The celebrations included a great procession through the streets of Leek to the Recreation Ground, where Challinor formally handed over to the Chairman of the Commissioners the Deed of Conveyance of the land. The children were then presented with a commemorative mug, which carried the inscription:

> QUEEN VICTORIA ASCENDED THE THRONE 1837
> JUBILEE FESTIVAL LEEK JUNE 21st 1887
> GOD SAVE THE QUEEN
> 5000 SCHOLARS ENTERTAINED WITH TEA
> ON THE PICKWOOD RECREATION GROUND
> PRESENTED TO THE TOWN BY WM. CHALLINOR Esq.
> AND OPENED THIS DAY

One of the 5000 children present at the event contributed his personal memory in the 1926 edition of *Leek News*. He was a seven-year-old boy at the time and remembered leaving the Cattle Market where a ceremony had been held, then marching up Grosvenor Street to the new Recreation Ground where he received a bag containing a pie and an assortment of cakes, together with the souvenir mug. His only other recollection is of a huge bonfire at the top end of the Recreation Ground, and there was a display of fireworks later in the evening. By that time the boy was back at home safely tucked up in bed. (It is likely that he was William Warrington, who contributed several articles to *Leek News* under the pen-name of the Small Boy in the Market Place.)

To further mark the occasion Challinor's colleagues, the Leek Improvement Commissioners, presented to him a letter of appreciation. Couched in effusive and somewhat flowery language, typical of the times, the document read as follows:

To William Challinor Esquire, Pickwood, Leek.
In accepting your gift of the Pickwood Recreation Ground which you have presented as a memorial of the blessings, National and Local, enjoyed by all classes during the 50 years of the reign of Her Majesty Queen Victoria, whose jubilee is celebrated today, your fellow

Commissioners, acting under 'The Leek Improvement Act, 1855', desire to record their sense of the important services which you have, during the greater portion of that period, rendered to the town. Not only have you been a Promoter of the above Act, under which Leek has grown and prospered, taking an active and prominent part in carrying out its provisions, and in securing that which was one of its chief purposes - an abundant supply of pure water, so necessary to the health and comfort of the people - but you have been Chairman of the Board for several years, as well as of the Sanitary Committee for 25 years, whose labours, supported by the co-operation of the Inhabitants, have resulted in improved health, prolongation of life, and substantial progress on all sides. In your support of Educational, Sanitary and other agencies, having for their object the advancement and welfare of the Inhabitants, you have also been very studious. These services are now supplemented by your gift of the Pickwood Recreation Ground formally opened today, for the benefit of your fellow Townsmen, and especially the young; the Commissioners therefore, on behalf of themselves and the Inhabitants generally, hereby testify their most cordial thanks, and express the hope that you may be long spared to witness the enjoyment by those for whose use it is intended.

Dated this 21st June, 1887

The document was signed by all the Improvement Commissioners who clearly desired to keep on the right side of such a powerful man, whilst at the same time, expressing genuine appreciation of his efforts.

There can be no doubt that Challinor loved Pickwood and wanted to make the best of its potential, both for himself and the town in general. On one occasion, in June 1873, he invited the North Staffordshire Naturalists' Field Club to spend a day at Pickwood. The party travelled to Leek by train, walked from the station to Pickwood, where Challinor provided luncheon. The members then spent the afternoon walking through the woods.

Challinor farmed the land around Pickwood, growing hay and other crops. The Recreation Ground was formerly a hay field, as his journal for July 4th 1887 states:

'New Recreation Ground opened on 21st of June. We got the hay in that field before the opening, a moderate crop. Since then we have got the hay from the seed field, and also at two mornings from the meadow behind the house, and strange to say for the first time in my experience without any of the hay being at all rained upon. We concluded getting the hay into the barns today, and immediately after we had done so the rain came.'

William Challinor started to write poetry at an early age, and some of his verses written in his youth reveal a high level of maturity. His long poem *On a visit to the Isle of Man* (where he received some of his education) concludes:

> *And now my song has ceased - the tiny spring,*
> *That gush'd forth into numbers, and did fling,*
> *Its warblings o'er the way, has ceased to be.*
> *Hushed is the fountain of its minstrelsy,*
> *For ever hush'd - and thou fair Poesy,*
> *Bright goddess of the heart and soul to me;*
> *Thou dost refuse from out thine ample store,*
> *To this unworthy wreath, one single floweret more.*

This was written at the age of 18, when the memory of his schooldays would be fresh, and his love poems are penned with great wit and feeling. His *Valentine to Maria* has the verse:

> *The flowers diversified and strange,*
> *Are various in their scent and hue,*
> *All lovely things are given to change,*
> *Then why not fair Maria too?*

Whether 'Maria' was a real person or a wistful figment of his imagination is not known! And another short poem ends with the verse:

> *Love rules the captain bold, the courtier fine,*
> *The well read Lawyer and the grave Divine,*
> *Nor can the Doctor heal with all his art,*
> *His secret ill, affection of the heart.*

The new Electric Telegraph clearly excited Challinor's interest. A poem which sings its praises begins with the verse:

> *'Tis done, and through the ocean,*
> *Connecting thought with thought,*
> *The swift electric motion,*
> *Sets distance now at nought.*

The poem ends:
> *But mind to mind it linketh,*
> *From furthest shore to shore,*
> *Till space for what man thinketh,*
> *And distance are no more.*

These are verses that might have been written by John Betjeman a century or so later - their style is 'Betjeman-esque'.

Challinor included a number of his verses in his published *Lectures etc.* (1891), and this appears to be his sole venture into print with his poetry. He was an inveterate scribbler, and it is likely that he wrote much more that did not get beyond the pages of his notebooks.

Not so with his writings on Chancery Reform, on which he was an acknowledged expert, having devoted much time and study to the subject. In 1848 he published a short pamphlet, advocating a much needed review and reform of the Court of Chancery. This was circulated widely, and a copy was received in the House of Commons by Joseph Hume, MP, who was a member of the committee set up to examine the whole question of fees and the Court of Chancery.

Challinor met Hume in London, and was given copies of the files containing all the evidence taken before the House of Commons Committee, which he undertook to study, and assimilate into an enlarged version of his original pamphlet. He was also given the opportunity to make suggestions for a reform of the unsatisfactory state of affairs in the Court of Chancery - an opportunity which he grasped with enthusiasm.

He completed the work in 1849, and Hume distributed copies of the revised pamphlet amongst his fellow Members of Parliament. The Leek lawyer had thus made a significant contribution to a much needed reform of this aspect of English law. As a result, Challinor received many letters of appreciation from leading barristers, and prominent members of the legal profession, including Sir Robert Peel, Lord John Russell, Lord Langdale, Lord Denman, Lord Langdale, Purton Cooper, QC, John Bright, and the great reformer, Richard Cobden, who had been a founder member of the Anti-Corn Law League, and a champion of free trade. Thus it is seen that Challinor's views won the respect and support of many of the leading reformers of the Victorian age.

His views on Chancery Reform also brought him into direct contact with Charles Dickens. At the time, Dickens was writing *Bleak House*, a substantial part of which is devoted to the case of Gridley in the Court of Chancery. Dickens was concerned about the monstrous wrongs perpetrated under the laws of Chancery, and Challinor's pamphlet was a Godsend to him, and he was able to draw many points from it, which he incorporated in the book. Dickens sent a warm, if brief, note of acknowledgement to Challinor:

Mr Charles Dickens presents his compliments to Mr. Challinor, and begs with many thanks to acknowledge the receipt of his pamphlet and obliging note.

Tavistock House,
Tavistock Square, London.
Eleventh March, 1852

Dickens quoted from Challinor's pamphlet in the novel, and acknowledged his source in the preface: 'I *mention here that everything set forth in these pages concerning the Court of Chancery is substantially true, and within the truth. The case of Gridley is in no essential altered from one of actual occurrence, and made public by a disinterested person who was professionally acquainted with the whole of the monstrous wrong from beginning to end.*'

The newspapers of the day devoted much space to the debate which Challinor's views on Chancery Law had provoked.

Challinor himself wrote at some length to the Editor of the *Evening Sun* in December 1851, and the subsequent editorial picked up Challinor's point *'that there is no necessity for retaining the Courts of Chancery as a separate jurisdiction from the courts of common law; and that, in fact, the law of the country may be more beneficially and cheaply administered by one tribunal.'* The editorial refers to Challinor as *'a veteran reformer, to whose able productions on the inherent defects of our so-called equitable tribunals we have already had the pleasure of directing public notice.'* Challinor himself was proud to be a champion, as he put it, of the *'great cause of Humanity v. Chancery.'*

Another of William Challinor's gifts to the town of Leek which will forever bear his name is the Challinor Fountain. As chairman of the local Sanitary Committee, it had long been Challinor's wish to erect a fountain in Leek to mark the Improvement Commissioners' success in their long negotiations with Churnet and Dove mill owners and Sir John Crewe to secure a water supply for Leek from *'those beautiful and abundant springs... beneath the rocks, and from amid the moors and heather'* around Upperhulme and the Roches. He originally imagined *'a neat granite fountain, of a smaller and simpler character'*, but on a visit to London he saw the bronze part of the fountain on exhibition at the Royal Academy. Being a man for whom only the best was good enough, it was, as he would say later, *'a case of love at first sight'*, and he successfully negotiated for the purchase of it from the Royal Academy.

The ornamental part of the fountain was designed by the sculptor, Joseph Durham, ARA, and it was highly regarded by art experts of the day. Indeed, the secretary of the London Drinking Fountain Association expressed his regrets that the fountain was leaving London. Sir Francis Grant, president of the Royal Academy, had said that it was *'the best yet'*. The Art Journal described it in glowing terms: *'A double drinking fountain, cast in bronze, showing two nude children gambolling among the water-flags, until one detects a frog and recoils with childlike horror, while the one on the other side continues his laughter and his game. Nothing could be more appropriate and naive than this.'* The base of the fountain was an octagonally shaped pillar, around which was the highly appropriate quotation, the second line of which is the first line of *Endymion* Book I by John Keats: *'From limpet springs beneath the rocks and heather, a thing of beauty is a joy for ever.'* The circular basin around the base of the fountain was of red polished granite from the quarries at Peterhead, north of Aberdeen, and was worked by Robertsons of Aberdeen. The actual fountain was a single jet of water rising from the centre three feet in height.

The townsfolk watched with interest as the fountain was erected in the Market Place, on the site of the old Town Hall, towards the southern end. William Sugden, in association with the sculptor had approved the site as being the most suitable. The work of assembly took about a month.

On Saturday, December 9th 1876, the official ceremony of handing over the Challinor Fountain took place at half past noon. Although the event took place in the depth of a Leek winter a good crowd turned out. The sculptor, Joseph Durham, was present, in spite of suffering a heavy cold, together with several Improvement Commissioners, with the Chairman, Joshua Brough. Also present at the ceremony were the following leading citizens of the town: J W Sneyd, H Sleigh, J Ward, Joshua Nicholson, Dr J J Ritchie, A Nicholson and P Worthington. A large crowd of townsfolk turned out, which surprised the organisers, who were expecting only a few. However, in spite of it being winter, it was a fine day, and Leek people have never been ones to miss an event like this. William Challinor gave an address, speaking of the work of the Sanitary and Water Committees over the past twenty years in carrying out sanitary, drainage and water supply arrangements, most of which were out of sight. The new fountain would be a visible testimony to this work.

The ceremony in the Market Place came to a conclusion in typical Victorian panache and theatricality. The sculptor, Mr

Durham, made a short speech, which could scarcely be heard, in which he approved of the chosen site for his fountain. Then, with a flourish, Miss Edith Challinor unveiled the bronze upper part of the fountain, to the applause of the onlookers. Mr Joshua Brough acknowledged the gift in fine ceremonial style by drinking the health of those present in a tin cup full of ice cold water from the fountain. Speeches by J J Ritchie, the town's Medical Officer, and Joshua Nicholson brought the ceremony to a conclusion, and the officials sought the warmth and hospitality of the Red Lion.

The fountain remained on its Market Place site until 1924. It was then removed to a somewhat greener location in Brough Park, when the park was opened to the public. There it remained until the late 1980s, when, following local government reorganisation, a large new office block was built in Stockwell Street to house the new local authority, Staffordshire Moorlands District Council. The fountain was then moved to a new site within a few hundred yards of its original position, in the forecourt of the new district council offices, where water was restored to it, its gentle, tinkling spray fulfilling its original function as a fountain.

Towards the end of his life, William Challinor was invited to present the prizes to the Leek Church High School for Girls, on 28th July 1893. His speech to the girls, although it abounds in Victorian platitudes, is a testimony to William Challinor, the man, and further illustrates his sense of humour and understanding of human nature. This is what he said:

I have been requested by Mr Maude to present the school prizes today and am glad to observe from the report that the scholars who numbered 22 in 1889 when the school commenced have now (including 27 Kindergarten pupils) reached 61, which we consider a very prosperous state of things doing much credit to Miss White and her assistants. I can only say I wish I were young again that I might have a share of Miss White's attention. The poet Pope says, speaking of the value of education:

> *'Tis education forms the common mind,*
> *Just as the twig is bent the tree's inclined,'*

and as you all know, in a fruit garden, unless the fruit trees are carefully trained against the wall, there will be a lack of fruit. I only hope that the pupils here present may be well trained and bear good fruit. I recollect once being asked at a party, which on the whole we thought gave most pleasure, eating or reading. Some answered the one and some the other. My late wife who was a great reader used to say she was 'never less alone than when alone.' In my early days, children, like tops, were considered to go best when well whipped, and no doubt this was the case in Shakespeare's time, who describes the schoolboy as 'creeping like snail unwillingly to school'. A stupid boy, who was always at the bottom of his class, once told his father he had been at the top. 'No', said the father, 'you were at the bottom'. 'Well', said the boy, 'that's the top of one end'. Another boy used to say when he went to school he generally took two steps backward for one forward. On being asked how then he got to the school, he said, 'I turned my back on it'. Sir Walter Scott in, his journal, speaks of a schoolmaster who said he loved his boys' heads too much to spoil them in order to save their opposite extremity, Well, in the case of little girls, I suppose it never comes to extremities. I have been much pleased that the Kindergarten system has been adopted here, which in fact being in some respects half play, interests the children and gives them instruction in a pleasant way. Teaching in the morning of life should be like the morning sun, bright but not oppressive.

How much this little bit of homespun philosophy would be appreciated by today's young students is open to question, but Challinor's words were a model for the typical prize-giving speech of the day, and even then, with an audience of shy Victorian maidens, one can imagine a certain amount of giggling behind handkerchiefs.

William Challinor died in March 1896, just 11 days before his 75th birthday. He had been suffering from diabetes for some time, and his health gradually deteriorated. In spite of this, he continued in his public and business duties until the last few days of his life, when he was confined to the house. The respect which the people of Leek had for him was evidenced by the fact that flags on many public buildings and churches flew at half mast, and in true Victorian tradition, blinds were drawn at a number of private houses.

William Challinor took his public duties very seriously, serving as one of the Leek Improvement Commissioners for many years. It was a position which placed him at the centre of the town's affairs, a unique advantage for a solicitor handling most of the legal business of the town's citizens. Ever diligent, as in all things, he maintained a record of very regular attendance at meetings. The story of his public life in the local government of the day opens up a new chapter on his influence on the town of Leek, and is typical of the Victorian paternalism so rife at the time. It was his work as Chairman of the Sanitary Committee which gave rise to his association with Leek's Sanitary Inspector at the time - Robert Farrow, from whose work we learn much about the social conditions in Leek at that time.

The Jubilee Mug.

Seven
HEALTH AND WELFARE

HOW HEALTHY WAS VICTORIAN LEEK? What were the social conditions? The town was thriving, and building projects were proceeding apace, as existing factories expanded and new ones were built. Alongside this growth, the population was increasing, for the silk industry was taking more and more people into employment. Housing was needed for the young, often large, families who were finding work in the town. Where did they live and in what conditions? The answer to these questions is to be found in the records of the administration of the Leek Improvement Commissioners and in particular, the influence of the Sanitary Committee, with its Chairman, William Challinor, and Sanitary and Workshops Inspector, Robert Farrow.

Robert Farrow was born at Eye, in Suffolk, in 1822. He married Eliza Rodwell, of Sturston, Norfolk, in 1843, and their family comprised one son and two daughters. He was appointed Sanitary and Workshops Inspector by the Leek Improvement Commissioners in 1866, and along with this office he had the responsibility for the supervision of the markets. The family home was in Ford Street, Leek.

His appointment in Leek bridged the transition of local government from the Improvement Commissioners to the Leek Urban District Council, for he worked until he was 82 years old, retiring in January 1905. He died just 12 months later, on January 22nd, 1906 at the age of 83, his wife having pre-deceased him.

In many ways, Robert Farrow was a man ahead of his times. He had a keen sense of social justice, and his work placed him in a unique position to observe the living conditions of the working classes in the town at that time. He was diligent and searching in his examination of particular cases, often having to work in nauseating and foul conditions. Little escaped his keen eye. A big man, with a full beard and a strong constitution, his imposing figure carried an air of authority wherever he went. At the time of his death, the *Leek Post and Times*, in its obituary, said this:

Singularly attached to his not over pleasant duties of Sanitary Inspector, he made no enemies: indeed, we know of no one who had a greater hold upon his adopted town than he whose death we mourn. He was, in addition, an important figure in the sanitary world, and was generally esteemed an expert, the remark being frequently made that what he did not know was not worth knowing.

The newspaper also made reference to the great strides made in the improvement of the sanitary conditions in Leek during his tenure of office. *'Any measure that had for its object the increase of the value of the lives of the population had his most strenuous support.'*

His meticulous, enquiring mind enabled him to produce some searching and very detailed annual reports, which stand as models of their kind. He studied the techniques of statistical science and record keeping under Dr. Farr at Somerset House, and this knowledge enabled him preserve a vast amount of valuable information in his tidy record books. In his early days in Leek he attended the chemistry classes at the Mechanics' Institute, and the *Post and Times* added the comment that many *'heard him describe the experiments which were made at the expense of the sparrows roosting among the ivy clinging to the gable in front of the old vicarage.'* Apparently at the time there was some concern about the condition of the churchyard, the general opinion being that it should no longer be used for burials. The paper went on to state that the experiments *'proved that the emanations from the burial ground were prejudicial to the health of the community.'*

In all his duties for the Improvement Commissioners, Farrow worked closely with William Challinor, chairman of the Sanitary Committee. Indeed, the two men shared the same views and ideas, and each wanted to see living and working conditions in Leek established on a sound, wholesome basis. In

1870 Farrow published an eight-page booklet which was a review of the living conditions of the local population within the limits of the Leek Improvement Act for the 19 years from 1850 to 1869. This included the inmates of the Leek Union Workhouse. The booklet was printed in Leek by James Rider and sold for one penny.

Farrow's report reveals some interesting facts. During the 19 years in question, with a rising population, the average number of persons in each occupied house had decreased from 5.1 to 4.4. From 1850 to 1859 the total number of deaths was 2819, an average annual rate of 29 in the 1000, the average age of death being 24.8 years. From 1860 to 1869, total deaths was 2248, average rate 24 in the 1000, and average age at death 32.5 years. The total number of working days lost to sickness in Leek was considerably less than the projected national figure. Farrow translated his statistics into cash terms, and stated:

Assuming the average total loss attending each case of sickness to amount to 5 shillings per week, (which is a very low estimate) it would follow, during the last 9 years, that £12,688 has been saved under this head. Of the 50,752 weeks' sickness prevented, 16,917 weeks is the proportion due to persons between the ages of 15 and 55 years, who are supposed to be the producers; and assuming a male person's earnings to average 10 shillings and a female's 5 shillings per week, this represents a saving of £6343-17-6, in addition to this there are the 492 deaths prevented; supposing the average funeral expenses in connexion with each death to amount to 5, we have here £2,460; clearly making the total direct money saving effected (mainly from the decrease of Zymotic disease) during the last 9 years, into no less a sum than £21,491-17-6, to say nothing of the great increase effected in the value of life, and the moral and social improvements which always attend such increased values.

Robert Farrow was clearly a statistician of the very highest order, and his interpretation of the figures gives a fascinating insight into the living conditions of Victorian Leek. Indeed, his work has been used as a basis for studies in this field today.

Farrow was not afraid to express his thoughts and opinions most forcibly in his annual reports. In 1879 he concluded his report with the following paragraph:

As the exact determination of the worst evils is the first step towards their remedies, it may be well to repeat the fact that if classes of people drink alcohol to excess, if they consume polluted water, if they breathe impure air, if they herd in rookeries and lead idle, vagabond lives, they soon perish.

Farrow's first priority was to address the social problems of the day, and his views were shared by his chairman, William Challinor, who, in 1881, said:

Crime, for instance, has been ascertained not so much to depend on low wages, but is often to be found most constant in ill-drained localities, in closely-crowded houses, and in those places where body and mind are least cared for. It has, indeed, been proved in Leek as well as other places, that it is disease that is expensive, and health that is cheap.

On another occasion, Challinor expressed his firm belief in the old adage that 'prevention is better than cure', and both he and Farrow held to that view throughout their service to the Leek Improvement Commissioners.

In addition to his professional duties, arduous enough in themselves, Robert Farrow found time to act as secretary to the Leek Fire Brigade, a task in which his knowledge of the layout of the streets of the town, its houses and its water supply, would be most useful. In the early days, the Fire Engine House was located on the old Cattle Market site, between the Talbot (formerly Spread Eagle) and Cattle Market inns. The fire engine was a horse-drawn vehicle known as a Firefly Manual, a popular and efficient model in its day. There were often several members of the same family in the Brigade, and the names Foster, Carding and Hall recur several times over the years.

Robert Farrow was also involved with another organisation in which his knowledge of the living conditions in Leek would prove most useful. This was the Poor Children's Dinner Committee, which during the 1890s provided nourishing hot meals for the needy children of the town. The Chairman of the committee was William Walker, and its members included Robert Farrow, J A Ind, W Knowles, J C Clemesha, W Garner, W J Govier, M Carding, A Crompton, E Lownds, W H Hudson, A Fogg, W Tomlinson and G Ratcliffe. It is perhaps significant that many of the prominent business and professional men in Leek at the time did not appear to serve on this committee. Politically, it was unlikely to appeal to their inclinations, but they would no doubt be called upon to contribute to its funds. Later, W Allen, H Brunt, M H Miller and C Robinson were invited to join the committee.

At a meeting at the George Hotel on Monday 5th January 1891 Farrow suggested that the town be divided into districts, and the children to be fed were to be selected from the districts in rotation. Miss Ives of the Coffee Tavern had informed the committee that she could supply *'a good bowl of lobscouse and a slice of bread'* at 2d per head, and she could feed 100 children twice a week. (Lobscouse was a local dish consisting of a thick soup with meat and pearl barley.) Robert Farrow was given the responsibility of distributing the tickets, and his professional duties would enable him to highlight areas of need. Apart from doctors and perhaps clergymen, Farrow was one of the few Leek men whose job gave him the right to enter homes, for he was also the school attendance officer.

The Poor Children's Dinner Fund was entirely non-sectarian, and the committee's minute book recorded that *'no Clergymen or Ministers of Religion be invited to or allowed to take part in selecting the guests or feeding them.'* Miss Ives was able to supply the dinners on Tuesdays and Fridays, and in order to allow her to make a small profit she was paid at the rate of 2d per head. Children under 4 years of age were given a bun.

The meals were only supplied during extremely cold weather, and on 19th February 1891 it was resolved that they be discontinued for the time being. Farrow presented the following report of dinners supplied:

SCHOOL	DINNERS	BUNS
St. Edward's Boys	45	
Do. Girls and Infants	199	95
St. Luke's Boys	109	
Mill St. Church Mixed and Infants	163	25
St. Luke's Girls and Infants	139	70
Ball Haye Green Mixed and Infants	156	29
Compton Church Mixed and Infants	180	85
West St Wesleyan Mixed & Infants	196	103
Ball Haye St. Wesleyan Do	124	125
Mill St. Infants	32	45
Union St. Girls and Infants	83	63
British Boys and Infants	30	24
Catholic Mixed and Infants	76	46
TOTALS	1532	710

Accurate record keeping again distinguished a report by Robert Farrow. In 1893 the committee decided to appeal for worn clothing, and Farrow was again charged with its distribution. Meat and potato pies were introduced into the menu, and the dinners continued into the Edwardian years, by which time they were being held in the Butter Market Hall.

Robert Farrow clearly led a very busy life, for he also served on the management committee of the Memorial Cottage Hospital, he was a trustee of the Leek Burial Society and sidesman at St. Edward's Parish Church. He was also a keen supporter of the Oddfellows Friendly Society movement, becoming Provincial Grand Master in 1868. He was a great advocate of old age pensions of at least five shillings a week for all members of friendly societies. In all his activities, therefore, both professional and voluntary, the welfare of the individual was paramount, and his contribution to the shaping of Victorian Leek was immeasurable.

If Challinor's working relationship with Robert Farrow was productive and beneficial for the town, there were times when even Challinor had his critics. Anyone who places himself in the public eye by seeking election to his local council must be prepared to face criticism from his opponents - and occasionally be 'put on the spot'. In April 1860, just prior to the election, a particularly vitriolic, anonymous leaflet attack was launched against William Challinor and his colleagues:

On Saturday, April 21st, 1860 a printed leaflet, signed 'A RATEPAYER' and addressed to his 'FELLOW RATEPAYERS OF LEEK' was distributed.

The leaflet was critical of the present Improvement Commissioners for postponing the work of installing new sewers at the north end of the town. The reason, it appears, was the high cost of the land through which the sewer would pass, which would have meant a special rate of about fourpence in the pound. 'Ratepayer' pointed out that the saving of this cost was 'of more consequence to some of these Gentlemen than the lives, and health, and comfort of their fellow-men.'

Two days later a much bolder, more explicit notice was circulated, signed ANOTHER RATEPAYER. This boldly asked the question: *'How long are the affairs of the town to be decided by one man and his party?'* The leaflet posed three questions for the ratepayers of Leek to consider:

Are the Rates likely to decrease, if you appoint for Commissioners Land-owners who charge EXORBITANT prices for permission to make Public Works, and whose object seems to be SELF? Is it necessary or desirable that you should continue under the direction of ONE MAN and his party of LAWYERS and AGENTS?

Have we not Tradesmen and Manufacturers who would give their time and attention to the proper and ECONOMICAL management of Town affairs; Men who would study the interests of the RATEPAYERS and not their OWN?

The writer then urged the voters to *'Elect no Land-owners or Lawyers, and Agents for the future, and you will be right.'* Further printed leaflets followed on election day itself. One, to THE RATEPAYERS OF LEEK, was bold enough to cite a specific case:

In answer to the Circular as to why the Rates are so high, and where they have gone to, - surely the parties who are coming forward for re-election, and who have had the principal management hitherto, ought best to be able to answer that question.

The heaviest Law Costs incurred for some years, were for the Indictment against Mr Condlyffe, to compel him to put back his cottage a foot or two. Who was the chairman of the Meeting called to stop these costs? A Lawyer! and that undeterred either by Commissioners or Land-owners.

The Leek Town Act provides that no one who is a Commissioner can receive any remuneration or costs out of the Rates. The Law Clerks, therefore, who received the costs in Condlyffe's case have had and will have the benefit of the law costs in future to be incurred. Who appointed the Law Clerks? Why, among others, those who ask you for re-election!

The Establishment was challenged very vigorously by an increasingly militant liberal element. Elections in Victorian Leek were exciting times! Local printers were kept busy producing these last-minute campaign missives - the names of the printers Hallowes, Rider and Nall often appeared on these leaflets, which must have been produced immediately, and considering that type-setting would be by hand, overtime would probably be incurred by the compositors. (Rush jobs were not always welcomed by printers, often being greeted with muttered imprecations under the breath. Nevertheless, traditionally they pulled out all the stops and usually managed to meet the deadline.)

No attempt to counter this leaflet campaign was made by those attacked, and all the items were anonymous. Were they the work of individual ratepayers who held strong views? Or was there a concerted group who felt that some campaign of opposition was called for? And did the writers of the leaflets actually stand in opposition to the sitting Commissioners at the election? Whatever the answer to these questions may be, the campaign appears to have had little effect, for the retiring Commissioners, including William Challinor, were usually re-elected. Those who were privileged to have the vote at that time were clearly able to make up their own minds, and much of this elaborate campaign material would be lost on the many who did not have the franchise to vote.

Eight
THE SHAPING OF THE TOWN

IN LOCAL GOVERNMENT there has always been a significant relationship between the voluntary elected Councillors (or Commissioners as they were then) and salaried Council Officers. Sometimes these relationships ran smoothly and productively, at other times they were rather more abrasive. The town upon which William Challinor and Robert Farrow were to make their mark under the administration of the Leek Improvement Commissioners was greatly improved structurally by the Town Surveyors who worked in Leek from the 1850s to the 1880s - a period which saw extensive developments in Leek's roads and streets.

The post of surveyor carried a great deal of responsibility, for the work and achievements of the surveyor left a permanent mark on the shape of the town, and the roads and streets constructed under their management still largely exist today. The Commissioners clearly made great efforts to appoint suitably qualified and experienced surveyors, for none of these men were local. Nothing is known of their families or personalities; they were men who came to Leek to do a job of work, and the streets laid down under their tenure are still the streets we walk today.

Thomas Dale was the first Town Surveyor under the provisions of the Leek Improvement Act, taking up his appointment on 15th October, 1855. However, his term of office lasted only two years and Charles Slagg was appointed on 17th November 1857, followed by Thomas Le Burn on 12th August 1862, and Thomas Frost on 5th September 1865. Frost served the longest period, until 1882. These years marked a time of great improvement for Leek, as the 1855 Act began to take effect in the enhancement of the town, and the development of new housing areas, where new streets and roads were laid out.

These early town surveyors were responsible for laying out the streets of Leek upon which Sugden and Son, Thomas Brealey and other architects were to erect their buildings. They did little to disturb the existing original street pattern of the town centre, and their work was mainly on the periphery of the old town. Thus, Leek began to spread outwards, as the demand for housing grew in parallel with the burgeoning silk industry. In addition, many of the old streets were in need of improvement, and a number of street widening schemes were initiated for the principal thoroughfares. So the town surveyor had a significant role to play in the administration of the Improvement Commissioners, and he was able to make a permanent mark on the town.

Sugden and his contemporary architects would need to build up and foster an amicable working relationship with these men. We do not know how this was achieved and maintained, but we can imagine, human nature being what it is, the occasional difference of opinion. Mr Challinor's legal expertise may have been required when disputes became heated, but he was very skilled in this field. There was a continued record of progress, and Sugden and other buildings proliferated.

In his first report presented to the Commissioners on April 8th 1858, Charles Slagg commented on the extensive road repairs carried out during the year, using stone from local quarries. Mill Street, Abbey Green Road, Spooner's Lane, Ashbourne Road, Ball Haye Green, Ball Haye Street, Fountain Street, Well Street and Buxton Road had all been repaired, and Derby Street and West Street had been paved. Street cleansing had been greatly improved by the purchase of a mud cart. The main sewers, which were giving some cause for concern, were also receiving attention. The Chairman of the Paving and Sewerage Committee at that time was Josiah Brunt. He was succeeded by Charles Carr, and later by Thomas Brealey, who served for a number of years. These contemporaries of William Challinor were all business or professional men, for the working classes, not owning estate or property, had no part in the local government of the day.

Having made a start on road improvements in Leek, Charles Slagg quickly got to grips with his duties as Town Surveyor. It was by no means an office-bound job, and he would often need to get his boots dirty. His lengthy and detailed reports to the Improvement Commissioners suggest that he was a meticulous and painstaking man, who would supervise work on site as much as possible. During the year ended April 8th 1861 some ten miles in length of roads and streets were repaired, using stone from various local quarries, in the following quantities: 51 tons 7 cwt. from Froghall; 112 tons from Hollin Lane; 350 cubic yards from Gun; 98 cubic yards from Thorncliffe. Paving stone used during the same year comprised 75 tons 16 cwt. from Thorncliffe, at 8s. 3d. per ton, and 95 tons 14 cwt. 2 qrs. at 8s 6d. from Waterhouses. The area of paving done was 2006 square yards, 1346 square yards of which was of old stone re-used. A new limestone paving stone from Waterhouses was tried, and proved to be satisfactory. We should remember that there would be no mechanical aids for the labourers at that time.

The quarry at Thorncliffe was leased by the Commissioners from Messrs. Oliver and Lomas at a rental of £10 per annum. In 1860 the tenancy expired, and the owners reclaimed possession before about 50 tons of quarried stone had been removed. The owners refused to allow the Commissioners to take this away, and negotiations to resolve the dispute commenced. The outcome was that the Commissioners were granted a new lease at £10 per annum, plus an additional payment of two shillings per ton for all stone exceeding 100 tons which they may quarry and cart away in any one year, as well as any rubble or broken stone they may require. It was reported that this was the best deal they could get, and indicates that there must have been some hard bargaining.

Ambitious schemes for improving the town's sewers were under way in 1860. The town was divided into two drainage districts, South, Number 1 and North, Number 2, and much of the work was contracted to the Leek builders, Thomas Grace. By

1862 the town had about 6000 yards of sewers of all sizes, and every house in the district was within a distance of 100 feet of a sewer belonging to the Commissioners. The sewerage was carried under the River Churnet in two lines of 18 inch cast iron pipes, and deposited on land at Abbot's Meadows (echoes of Dieulacres Abbey). Charles Slagg's report of 1862 stated:

This fortunate circumstance of having plenty of grass land near the outfall, both of the North and South Districts, has relieved the Commissioners of the necessity of dealing with the sewage chemically, there being no deodoriser so good as the earth itself, where a sufficient breadth of it can be had over which to spread the sewage.

At the same time, the Commissioners were looking at the possibility of offering a contract for the removal of ashes and nightsoil, being of the opinion that an industrious contractor would do the work much cheaper, and be able to sell the material collected for fertilizer purposes!

During his period of service as Town Surveyor, Charles Slagg produced a document which tells us a great deal about the extent and size of Leek in the 1860s. His *Plan of the Town and Environs of Leek*, 1862 bears comparison with the earlier map of 1838, where the early street pattern is still seen, with certain additions, notably the railway and a number of new streets mainly on the fringe of the old town. It was a great contribution to the recorded history of the town.

Slagg's map of 1862 shows a large, open area of land largely owned by Mrs Shoobridge and Mr James Nixon lying between London Street and Ashbourne Road. Here the new streets which would eventually be constructed were Southbank Street, Fynney Street, Shoobridge Street, Leonard Street, Cromwell Terrace, Livingstone Street, Talbot Street, Moorhouse Street, Wood Street and Grosvenor Street. This extensive infill housing was an ambitious scheme, giving the developers the opportunity to build terraced houses of style and quality, for all classes of the growing population.

To the north of Derby Street, the Ford Street and Bath Street area was awaiting development when Slagg drew up his original map, but this would soon take place. Rosebank Street was constructed over land owned by Mr H L Johnson, silk manufacturer, formerly of King Street, but later resident at Rose Bank Villa, Rose Bank Street, an early Sugden house (1857) which is clearly shown on the map, but not named.

On the western side of the town, land off Canal Street, owned by Hugh Sleigh, was designated for Hartington Street, leading to Hugo Street and crossed by Dampier Street. Off Britannia Street, Chorley Street and Gladstone Street would be constructed on the late T. Atkinson's land. And on the extreme western edge of the town, Grove Street and Westwood Grove would stretch out over open fields on the Earl of Macclesfield's land. Other interesting features shown on Slagg's map include:

A brewery at Bridge End.

Sugden's 'Big Mill' (1860) on Mill Street

Kiln Lane is shown through to Westwood Lodge crossing the railway.

West Street is shown to Westwood Lodge.

Houses known as 'Petty France' are marked and named.

Strangman's Walk from Spout Street emerges near the railway station.

Leek Gas Works are marked.

An enclosed area known as Vicar's Close is shown near Newcastle Rd.

The site of Woodcroft Hall is shown, but not named.

Dickey's Gutter is shown from Stockwell Street to Ball Haye Lodge.

Ball Haye Green continues to Hare Gate Lodge.

Reservoir on Ball Haye Brook near the tannery on Ball Haye Road.

Other reservoirs marked 'Fish Ponds' are shown on John Cruso's land.

Reservoirs are shown at the top of Fountain Street and on the Mount.

Five brickyards are shown near the Workhouse, Ashbourne Road.

The Cattle Market is shown at the junction of Ashbourne Road with Derby Street. This is the area formerly known as Sparrow Park, upon which the Nicholson War Memorial was built in the 1920s.

Under the Leek Improvement Act of 1855 the original Act of 1825 was repealed. The 1825 Act limited the town to an area within a circle with a radius of 1,200 yards from the old Town Hall at the bottom of the Market Place. The limits of the town were extended under the 1855 Act to a circle, the radius of which was 1,500 yards measured from the lamp post in the centre of the Market Place. Charles Slagg based his map on this circle, which clearly defined the extent of the town at that time. Boundary posts, bearing the initials LIA (Leek Improvement Act), were erected at the points where the main roads crossed this circle, and a number of these still exist.

Slagg's splendid map was his final contribution to Leek, by which, together with his work on road improvements, re-paving schemes, sewerage and drainage works, he left a permanent impression on the town. One of his last projects was the improvement of Canal Street and the road leading to to the railway station, which, by that time, had become very busy. By 1863 Thomas le Burn had taken up his appointment as Town Surveyor.

With a new surveyor and a fresh approach, it soon became apparent that things were far from perfect. In his very first annual report to the Commissioners, Thomas le Burn was somewhat critical. He stated, *'On examining those roads when I entered upon my duties as your Surveyor in September last, I found them very much worn out, and with the exception of Cheadle Road and a portion of Buxton Road (which are still in pretty good repair), they required re-forming, being for the most part far too flat, thereby requiring a greater amount of material to bring them into proper form, than if the repairs had been attended to before the roads were so much worn.'* As is often the case, a new broom appeared determined to sweep clean! Nevertheless, Thomas le Burn would only hold the post of Town Surveyor for three years.

During that time, he supervised a major scheme in Stockwell Street. This entailed the widening and raising of the street, plus work on the adjoining sewers. The work was carried out by Thomas Grace, a local builder and contractor. The Town Lands Trustees contributed £100 towards the cost, and the Leek and Moorlands Building Society gave up about 40 square yards of land, with two cottages and a stable, on the south side, thus enabling the road to be widened to a uniform width of about 35 feet throughout.

It is interesting to note that, at this time the responsibility for street sweepings was given to a Mr George Caley, who was paid £6 10s per annum, out of which he had to provide a man and a horse to remove the sweepings daily!

The new Town Surveyor was Thomas Frost, and in his first report to the Commissioners, dated April 2nd 1866, he followed the pattern of his predecessors in stating that, following his appointment, he found the roads *'generally in a moderate state of repair'*. Canal Street always came in for much attention at this time, no doubt due to the fact that it carried much traffic related to the busy railway station. One of Frost's first tasks was to supervise the paving of one side of the street from the station to King Street.

In 1870 a scheme was in progress for constructing a wide street from the Cattle Market into Brook Street. This was to become Haywood Street, and the scheme was to be continued by the widening of Brook Street, thus making a good main road from the railway station direct up to the Cattle Market. For various reasons, it would appear that this scheme took some time to complete.

From 1870 to 1873 the Chairman of the Paving, Sewering and Building Committee was William Dawson Ainger. His initial reports as chairman were very positive and constructive, but for some reason, his last report, published in the Improvement Commissioners' reports of 1873, was very downbeat and censorious. What caused this sudden change of attitude is not known, and no clue can be found in Thomas Frost's accompanying report, which as usual was succinct and statistical, with no comment, opinions or judgements. This may have been a case of 'sour grapes' but clearly something had angered Ainger. Few escaped his wrath. The workmen were criticised for demanding more money, and if possible, less work. They had shown a marked disinclination to comply with orders, rules and laws, and poor weather for working did not help matters. The Committee had done its best to give priority to areas of work where traffic was heavy, or where deterioration was worst.

There had been several disputes with landowners over rights, and Ainger felt that more streets should be adopted by the Commissioners, but their unfinished state did not help this. There appears to have been some hold-up with the road from the railway station to the Cattle Market: *'The Committee have long expected an early opening of the new great thoroughfare into the Cattle Market from the Station, but their hopes like the apples of Sodom have fallen 'to ashes in the hand'.'*

Ainger's bitter report made the point that, if more paving work was to be done, a higher rate would have to be levied, and a larger staff of good workmen employed. He pointed out that the committee had worked strictly within its budget, and felt that unless the system was improved, *'a larger rate may easily be dribbled away, with very few comparative improvements, and a paving committee may go through all their troublesome and unpleasant labours, without satisfaction to themselves, or pardon from the ratepayers'.*

In spite of Ainger's misgivings, the Haywood Street scheme was completed during the following year. The new chairman of the Paving, Sewering and Building Committee was John Brealey and his first report was optimistic. However, the extra expenditure on flagging and kerbing led to the budget being exceeded by £120.

The contract for the removal of ashes and night soil was up for renewal and it was again granted to Ephraim Ridgway, for one year only, at a cost of £280, an increase from the £215 of his previous contract, which he had held for three years. With the increase of housing in the town, such an increase was inevitable, and Brealey appealed to the inhabitants to assist the authority in making the weekly clearance system work efficiently, for the better health of the town.

Thomas Frost's reports continued to give statistical details of the work carried out on Leek's roads and streets. In a typical year, an average of 2250 yards of paving would be done, and about 750 tons of MacAdamised stone laid on the roads. New streets were being added each year. The new Stone Yard in Cruso Street was established, with sheds for the stonemasons, and ample storage for materials, paving stones, flagging and kerbing.

Bad weather was frequently a problem. The harsh winter of 1875 caused the breaking up of the surface of many roads, and the necessary repair work led to another increase of expenditure beyond the estimated budget. Problems with the labour force would always be a cause for concern, and it would appear that the issues which confront local government and industry today are nothing new. Nevertheless, the works continued, and the committee was always seeking ways to improve the existing highways, and schemes to develop new streets were frequently being considered.

In this way, the shape of the town as we know it today, was gradually developed during these Victorian years. Alongside this development the silk and textile industry continued to flourish.

Leek Fire Brigade, Robert Farrow on the right with beard.

Brough, Nicholson & Hall, Cross Street offices and warehouse.

Nine
A FLOWERING OF SILK

A TWISTER

When a twister, a-twisting, will twist him a twist,
For twisting his twist, he three twines should in twist;
But if one of the twines of the twist does untwist;
The twine that untwisteth untwisteth the twist.
Untwisting the twine that untwisteth between;
He twists with his twister the two in a twain;
Then twice having twisted the twists of the twine,
He twisteth the twine he had twisted in twain.
The twain that in twining before in the twine,
As twines were intwisted, he now doth untwine;
'Twixt the twain intertwisting a twine more between,
He, twirling the twister, makes twist of the twine.

IT IS OFTEN MISTAKENLY STATED that the local silk industry owes its origins to the arrival of the Huguenots in 1685. An inventory of a certain John Wood of Leek, dated 1672, thirteen years earlier, states that he had silk and looms. Another inventory in the name of Matthew Stubbs, dated 1692, also mentions silk, mohair and buttons. The Huguenots were French Calvinists who were forced to flee Europe following certain periods of religious persecution. A few settled in Canterbury and London after escaping the massacre of St. Bartholomew in 1572, but a much greater number, about 50,000, sought sanctuary following the revocation of the Edict of Nantes in 1685. They undoubtedly exerted a great influence on the English silk industry, if not directly upon Leek.

The Huguenots were particularly skilful in silk weaving and were able to produce bright patterns in pure silk. From their settlement in Spitalfields, London, came many brilliantly flowering designs, much favoured by the fashionable society of London at that time. Demand increased during the 18th century, when patterned silk dresses and waistcoats were symbols of the height of fashion. The influence of the Huguenots began to spread and quality English silks were always sought after by the gentry of the day and their ladies. The society of the drawing room and the ballroom, romanticised in fiction, was clearly a strong feature of 18th century England.

The skill of the Huguenots was manifested in their technique of silk throwing by hand. Raw silk threads reeled from the cocoon were extremely fine, and the throwing process enabled these threads to be twisted together to produce a stronger yarn. Twisting and doubling then increased the thickness of the thread, and gave it greater tensile strength and elasticity. These basic techniques were, of course, slow by hand, and the expansion of production was restricted to the comparatively few who possessed the necessary skills, which would be handed down from generation to generation within the closed community.

It would take a significant advance in technology to bring about a major expansion of the silk industry, and this came in 1721, largely as a result of a piece of early industrial espionage. The chief motivator was a man named Thomas Lombe whose brother, John Lombe had clandestinely brought back from Italy the fundamental technology of the water powered throwing machine. Thomas Lombe took out a patent on this machine in 1718, and built his water powered silk throwing mill in Derby, on the River Derwent. This enterprise prospered and developed into a large, five storey mill, powered by an 18 feet waterwheel, and in this way the factory system was established.

However, presumably because of the rather underhand way in which it had been acquired, Lombe's patent was not renewed in 1732. Other manufacturers and prospective manufacturers had entered petitions of objection and Lombe was paid £14,000 compensation. But the technology was now widely available, enabling throwing mills to be established in locations where adequate water power and other favourable conditions prevailed, and Macclesfield (1743) and Congleton (1755) got their first silk mills, followed by other centres, including Leek. By the early 19th century several towns, particularly in the North West, had become silk towns.

William Pitt, in his General View of the Agriculture of the County of Stafford (1796), included a brief description of the early Leek silk industry:

Leek has a considerable manufacture in the silk and mohair way; the manufactured goods from which are, sewing silks, twist, buttons, ribbons, silk-ferrets, shawls, and silk-handkerchiefs. In these manufactures, as by information from Messrs. Sleigh and Alsop, and Phillips and Ford, manufacturers, and others, are employed about two thousand inhabitants of the town, and one thousand of the adjacent country. In this trade some good fortunes have been made, and it has been very flourishing; but the check on paper credit, which in a great measure hurt the confidence of all connexions, diminished the trade here; and the war must in some degree have dampened the demand for it abroad: yet the trade is now in a flourishing state, and considerably better than it was some months ago.

Economic forces and world affairs clearly exerted an influence on the Leek silk industry in the 18th century, just as the Imperial expansion of Queen Victoria's Empire would do in the 19th century.

Bailey's British Directory of 1784 lists the following eleven tradesmen, as being engaged in some aspect of the silk industry in Leek:

Joseph Badnall (Dyer)
John and Michael Daintry
   (Manufacturers of buttons, twist and sewing silk)
Knight and Fynney (Ribbon manufacturers)
Mellor and Bagnall
   (Manufacturers of buttons, twist and sewing silk)
Phillips and Ford

(Manufacturers of buttons, silk twist and ribbons)
Thomas Salt (Manufacturers of buttons, silk twist and ribbons)
Hugh Sleigh (Manufacturer of ribbons)
John Smith (Twist and button manufacturers)
Henry Smith (Dyer)
Joshua Strangeman (Manufacturer of buttons and twist)
John and Benjamin Sutton (Manufacturer of ribbons)

(It is interesting to note that this same 1784 directory lists a bookseller, Joseph Needham, trading in Leek. This is an indication of the relative prosperity of the town, for not many homes could afford to possess books. Books were a sure sign of affluence. A number of inventories of deceased persons from this period mention books and other symbols of affluence, such as mirrors, clocks and fine china. Also, the presence of four attornies at law, including a William Challinor, is a further indication of this prosperity, for lawyers would be called upon to administer the affairs of the wealthy.)

These early directories make many references to the manufacture of silk buttons, and this was a major factor in the early days of the local industry. There was still a demand amongst fashionable society for fancy silk-covered buttons and trimmings on coats, waistcoats and dresses, perhaps a throwback to the previous century. The production of these small-scale items was ideally suited to the local situation in Leek and the Moorlands, and an extensive cottage industry became established. The basis of the button was a small wooden mould which was covered with coloured strands of silk wound tightly over it. The work was highly suited to female labour, working at home, and cottages in both the town and countryside became centres of this growing industry. The silk was produced in the local factories or 'shades', and this would be delivered by hand around the district, to the cottages where the work would be completed. Payment was on a piece rate, and the weekly visit of the firm's representative would be very welcome, bringing more work, collecting last week's finished work, and any payment due.

In 1897, the Rev Thomas Brigden published *The Old Leek Sunday School: a Centenary Record*, in which he records the early life of James Wardle, a prominent Methodist:

One of the first Sunday School teachers, James Wardle, who became a man of mark both in his town and church, used to tell how at a very early age he was employed to carry buttons from the moorland cottage in which he was born, near Flash, to Leek, nine miles distant. The child walked both ways, and received 8d for the journey from the button makers, who clubbed together to meet this expense!

James Wardle was a life-long Methodist. He was one of the pioneer teachers in the Sunday School, and became a leader of West Street Sunday School for many years. The silk industry made him a comparatively wealthy man. He commenced business in the silk and button trade in partnership with his brother-in-law, Josiah Gaunt, trading as Gaunt, Wardle and Company. He was a generous benefactor to the Methodist Church. His gifts included the gallery and organ at the Ball Haye Street School, so that the building could serve as both Sunday School and chapel. He also gave a house for the resident minister in Regent Street, and provided £4381 to build Brunswick Chapel in Market Street. He died on 8 July, 1862.

The silk button industry was also very firmly established in the nearby Cheshire towns of Macclesfield and Congleton. James Wardle recalled his visits to Flash, and in the moorlands of the Staffordshire/Cheshire borderland there were many isolated homesteads involved in this cottage industry. This wild moorland area is interlaced with old packhorse roads, the trade highways of a bygone age. These old roads provided the means of access to this otherwise inaccessible region, as well as being the routes for the wider distribution of silk goods. Travelling pedlars, or 'chapmen' acted as distribution agents for the silkmen, and these intrepid entrepreneurs journeyed far and wide in the neighbouring counties.

The early years of the silk industry in Leek were largely centred around the 'shades' for the production of silk, and the simple dye houses, usually near the River Churnet, for the dyeing of the material. *Bailey's Directory* of 1784 lists just two silk dyers, Joseph Badnall and Henry Smith, both with dye houses in Mill Street, near the river. In 1844 silk mills began to develop their own dyeworks, and in 1851 *White's Directory* lists 33 silk manufacturers, many of whom would be doing their own dyeing. Three specialist dyers were listed - Charles Ball, William Hammersley & Co and Samuel Tatton, all with dyeworks in the Mill Street area.

A shade was a long, straight work room in which the looms were set up, and could either be a single storey shed (hence 'shade') at ground level, or a long attic room above a row of terraced houses. A common attic would extend over two or three houses, usually defined by a wide window, much larger than those in the houses below, which would be the living quarters for the families who worked the looms. These windows provided the optimum amount of natural light during the working day, thereby ensuring the maximum production. Access to some attic shades was by a separate, outside stairway. Surviving examples of attic shades can be found in the King Street, Albion Street and London Street areas.

Other silk towns, such as Macclesfield, worked a similar system in the attics of their houses, but here they were known as loom shops, or just simply, weavers' garretts. The weavers who worked the looms were known as journeymen weavers, and the looms were owned by the master weavers, or 'undertakers'. In 1818 a Parliamentary Committee was set up to enquire into the wages and conditions of silk workers, and Leek was included in this enquiry. The custom was that the wages in a particular place were set by the local magistrates, but this gave rise to a certain amount of disparity. The system was flawed, and in 1818 it became apparent that many weavers were being paid much less than others doing the same work. Furthermore, the onset of power loom weaving was causing more disparities between the workers.

Evidence taken by the 1818 enquiry revealed that engine

loom workers could earn 16s a week, whereas hand loom weavers' pay was only 12s a week, and attempts were made to get this reduced even further, to 10s a week. The matter was further complicated by the fact that there were differentials for the various types of goods produced, the best rates being for black silk handkerchiefs.

Steam power was introduced into the Leek silk mills during the 1830s, and in 1833 regular working hours were established under a new Factory Act. In 1839 Joseph Fletcher published his 'Report on the Hand Loom Weavers of Leek'. Assuming that Fletcher was accurate in his recording, this report provides a detailed account of the state of the local silk industry in 1839, soon after steam power had been introduced. Fletcher discussed the advantages of engine looms over hand looms, and gave details of the various products, rates of pay, and the organisation of the labour force.

A much more searching report was produced in 1841 by Samuel Scriven, in his report to the Commissioners on the employment of children in Leek. It was Scriven's job to conduct an enquiry into the working conditions in local silk factories, under the provisions of the Factories Regulation Act. His report was based on personal interviews with workers, many juveniles. Five factories were examined and Scriven was satisfied that working conditions were generally satisfactory, being *'well-regulated, spacious, lofty, and well-ventilated establishments'*. Conditions in the shades, however, were somewhat less than satisfactory, although the workers appeared to be happy in their tasks. He singled out one particular shade in London Street, which, he said, was situated *'in a yard at the back of a row of small tenements, each having a privy emptying into it, and nothing more provided to carry off the filth than a wide, open, shallow gutter leading to a cesspool equally exposed, and of itself enough to poison the whole neighbourhood. The passages, staircase, and rooms of the 'shade' are extremely dirty. I was told by the proprietor that it had not been cleansed for a period of seven years.'*

It is natural that, in this climate of industrial ferment, the ever-growing body of workers should feel the need to band together in some way to protect their interests. Such stirrings towards trade unionism were spasmodic, lacking in leadership and restricted by the lack of ability to read and write by many of the workers. The more literate and articulate silk workers were sometimes able to express themselves by writing letters, but these lacked co-ordination. Furthermore, such efforts were met with either indifference or antagonism on the part of the manufacturers.

In 1845 the Ribbon Weavers' Friendly Society was formed for the benefit of workers in such towns as Derby, Congleton and Leek but it appears to have had little effect on Leek, possibly because it was too broadly based. Locally, it was not until 1866 that the Amalgamated Society of Silk Workers was formed, and this had a Leek leader, William Stubbs, who was born in Leek. He was not a silk worker, being by trade a shoemaker, but he may rightly be regarded as the first trade unionist in Leek, and led the society for about forty years, becoming an important figure in the conduct of industrial relations in Victorian Leek. He stands alongside the more powerful and affluent silk masters as an influential figure in the town's history.

It seems likely that Stubbs continued to trade as a shoemaker whilst continuing his trade union duties on a part time basis. His period of service was not without its disputes, and it soon became clear that one union alone was not sufficient to look after the whole of the industry, with its complex job definitions. In 1871 a separate Trimming Weavers' Society was founded, with Charles Swain as secretary. Stubbs and Swain worked closely together, and later Stubbs took the dyers under his wing.

Most disputes were short-lived, and often over minor matters. The *Leek Times* of 8 April 1871 reported that Joshua Nicholson had lectured his female workers on the matter of cheap jewellery and dress. They objected to his views and about 100 walked out during the morning, paraded round the town (were they wearing cheap jewellery and dress, one wonders?) and returned to work after dinner.

However, during the early months of 1872, Leek experienced its first major dispute in the silk industry. The dispute was sparked off by a decision of J and J Brough, Nicholson and Co. to reduce the hours of working for their employees. This, of course, was welcomed by the workforce, but not by the other Leek manufacturers, whose employees started to agitate for the same terms. The new system was then adopted by all manufacturers, but the silk twisters, realising that the reduction in hours would lead to a drop in wages, began to agitate for an increase.

Industrial relations worsened, and strikes, lock-outs and street demonstrations followed. The dispute became very bitter, and deadlock was reached in March. Offers of arbitration were rejected and the local press carried much correspondence. William Stubbs and Charles Swain were deeply involved, but were unable to achieve a breakthrough. Robert Farrow, Leek's Sanitary Inspector, intervened to point out the adverse social effect the strikes were having on the children of striking workers.

The dispute stuttered on until a compromise formula was reached in April, both sides giving ground. The silk masters then re-opened the mills and the workers gradually returned to work. One effect of the strike was a strengthening of the trade unions and a consolidation of their efforts. From the manufacturers' side, the employers grouped themselves into an equally powerful trade association. Masters and men now found new strength in their separate industrial organisations. It is possible that Robert Farrow's remarks about the possible effects of the strike on workers' families played no small part in the workers' decision to return to work, for it was natural that the family came first.

The steady development of quality terraced houses for the growing force of silk workers during the latter half of the 19th century did much to improve living conditions. Men like Robert Farrow made a great contribution to raising living standards.

Illnesses of childhood were naturally very prevalent. A report on West Street Day School in the Wesleyan Methodist Circuit Year Book of 1889 reveals that, out of a total of 479 children on the books, the average attendance was 356. This average improved by the end of the century, by which time the total number on the roll was 491. The population of Leek was steadily increasing during the latter half of the 19th Century, as more and more people came to work in the local factories. In the 1851 census the total population was 9096, in 1861 it was 10174, and by 1871 it had risen to 11331, all of whom required somewhere to live, to see their children educated and to spend whatever leisure time they were fortunate enough to have. William Sugden's initial decision to settle in Leek because of the potentially large measure of future work was clearly justified.

This steady increase in Leek's population was largely due to the expansion of the silk industry, which required more and more workers. The occupations stated on the census returns were liberally sprinkled with operatives, and silk weavers, spoolers, piecers, ballers, dyers and so on proliferated, each process having its own designated worker. Their bosses were the new elite of Leek society. Names like Worthington, Ward, Sleigh, Brough, Wardle, Tatton, Davenport, Whittles, Bermingham, White were prominent on the Leek scene, and these became household names in the town, as the industry moved into the 20th Century.

You worked at 'Brough's' or 'White's' or 'Tatton's', and this was sufficient to identify your place of employment. The mill became very much a social unit. It was the place where local gossip, often scandalous, formed much of the conversation, and local and national affairs, political and otherwise, were vigorously debated. Lifelong friendships were formed, and marriages were made. As in all closely-knit groups, there would be quarrels and disputes from time to time. Following the principle of thrift, mutual benefit groups were developed, and 'easy savings' schemes established, often on an ad hoc basis.

Sports clubs were set up, and men played together in the various works' cricket and football teams. They marched off to war together, and all too often died together. The mill served as confessional, match-maker, advice centre, debating forum, social club and the hub around which the activities of the workforce revolved. For good or ill, the mill was a dominant force in the lives of Leek folk.

Families like that of George Fisher of Mill Street spent their entire working lives in the silk mills of Leek, from their teens to their seventies. They knew no other employment, and had little or no opportunity to break away from the mould. The met their wives and husbands at the mill, and marriage and family meant only a temporary break from work. It was not uncommon for workers to spend over sixty years with the same firm, doing the same job, year in and year out

A group of Leek cyclists, 1898.

Part of Slagg's map of Leek 1861.

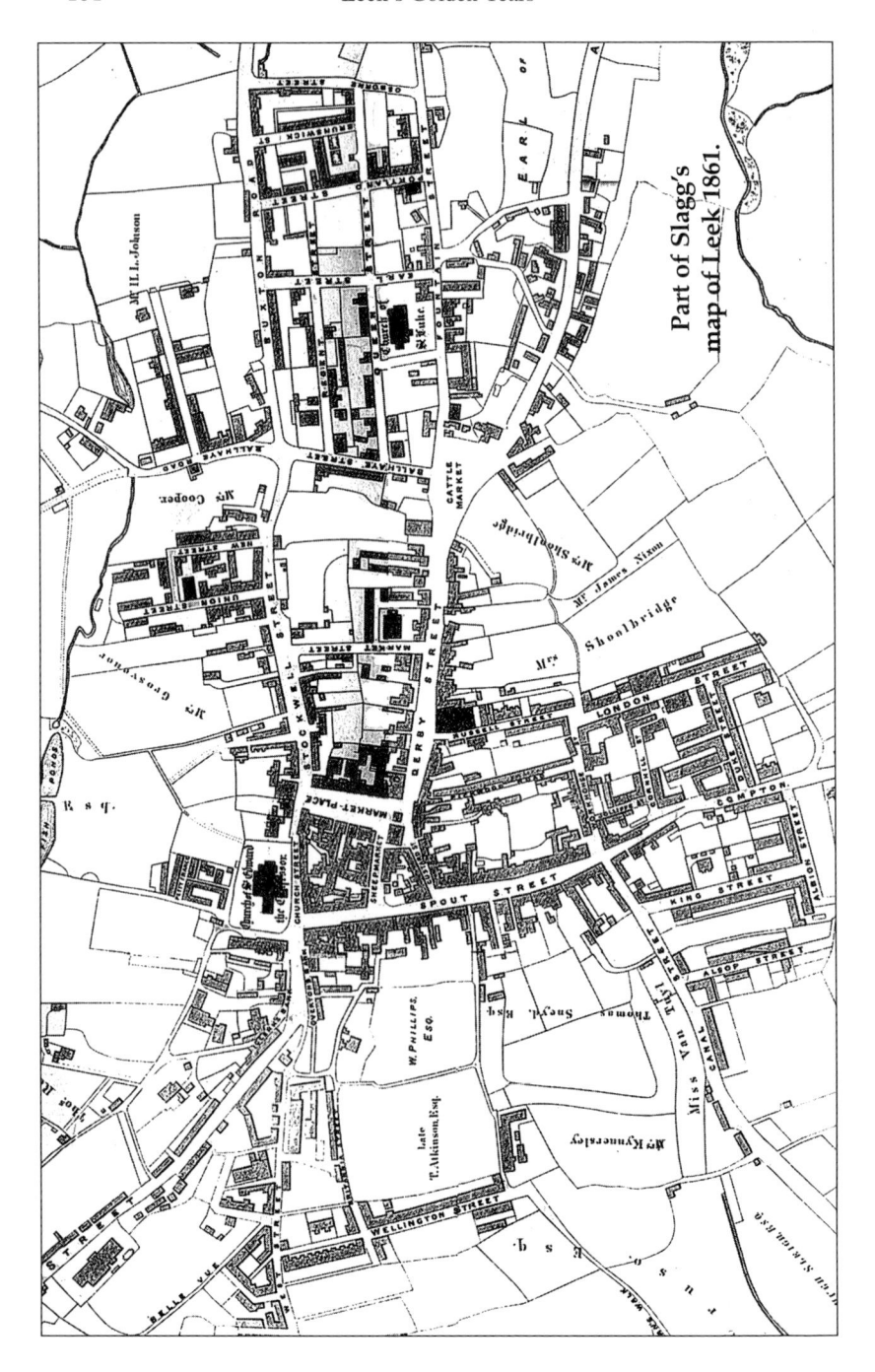

Ten

YORKSHIRE BUSINESS ACUMEN IN LEEK

TO WORK AT 'BROUGH'S' was to work for one of the largest companies in the area. In terms of the size and extent of its factory buildings and the number of workers on the payroll, Brough, Nicholson and Hall Ltd was a major factor in the economy of the Leek area. The complex of factory buildings - offices, warehouse and production sheds - covered the area bounded by Fountain Street, Cross Street and Ashbourne Road.

But until the arrival from Yorkshire of Joshua Nicholson, it had remained a small business. John Brough's original little silk factory, or 'shade', was founded in 1815 in Stafford Street, off Stockwell Street. Here, in 1818, he took a Mr Baddeley into partnership, and was then trading as Baddeley and Brough. By the time *Pigot's Directory* had been published in 1835 the firm had moved to a larger factory in Union Street and was trading as J and J Brough & Co. Still very much a family firm, John Brough's three sons, Joshua, James and John were gradually introduced into the business.

The precise location of the factory was known locally as Brick Bank, a steep, cobbled extension to Union Street, dropping steeply to the valley of the Ball Haye Brook, which marked the boundary of the Ball Haye Hall estate. The area is now a car park, at the edge of the appropriately named Brough Park. The factory stood on the left hand side of the street, and opposite, across the cobbles, was a row of tiered, terraced cottages, the homes of the silk workers - no excuse for lateness!

The year 1837 not only marked the accession to the throne of the young Queen Victoria, but it also saw the arrival in Leek of a young man, Joshua Nicholson. He had taken up the post of representative to the silk manufacturing firm of J and J Brough &

Co. He would be filled with enthusiasm - a new challenge, a new young queen on the throne, and a whole new world of opportunity opening up before him. Perhaps even the open moorland surrounding Leek would be to him a refreshing change from the dark mills of Bradford.

Joshua was born on 26 October 1812, the year of Napoleon's retreat from Moscow, at the little village of Luddendon Foot, between Hebden Bridge and Halifax, in Yorkshire. His father was a local builder and being the youngest son, he was apprenticed to a firm of wool merchants in Bradford. Nearly 100 years later the distinguished Yorkshire writer, JB Priestley, would find himself in a similar position, and was able to describe very graphically in his writings the somewhat stifling conditions of the stockrooms, warehouses and offices of the Bradford wool and textile industry. Writing in *Bright Day* (1946) Priestley's description would hardly have changed from Joshua Nicholson's earlier experience:

'Great bales of wool were being hoisted from carts or were swinging out from the upper floors of the warehouses, and shouts of warning echoed down the blackening canyons of those streets... The boy opened a door and showed me into a longish narrow room that had a counter on one side, near the windows, and on the other side reaching the high ceiling, a wall of bins or racks filled with wool samples in blue paper.'

It was a good training ground for an ambitious young man, in the cut and thrust of a hard-headed business environment. Joshua would be anxious to escape from these rather stultifying conditions, for the greater freedom promised by his new job with the firm of Brough in the Moorland Leek. He was 25 years of age when he arrived in Leek to take up his position. His salary was £250 a year, with a bonus and daily expenses of £1 when travelling. He had a few years experience behind him from Bradford, and the enthusiasm of youth to carry him forward.

He would need to be fit, for these were the days before the

railway and travel was by horse-drawn carriage. Leek was strategically placed on the turnpike road system and the town was served by regular coach services. Travelling in all sorts of weather, with a good deal of foot-slogging when he reached his destination, needed a good constitution, and meeting customers would not be easy, for the silk industry was very competitive in the 1840s. Nevertheless, he made a success of it, for Brough's business grew as he returned again and again with a book full of orders.

Some 42 years after starting his business, in 1857 John Brough senior was rather advanced in years. When one of his sons James died in 1857, it left a vacancy that was filled by Joshua Nicholson. The award of a partnership after 20 years service was a fitting reward. He was still only 45 years old and at the height of his powers, with much still to give to the firm and to the town of Leek.

Joshua Nicholson's wife shared his religious beliefs as a fervent and devout Congregationalist, and she was a generous supporter of public work. Her obituary in the *Leek Times* of October 14th 1893 refers to her *'gifts and subscriptions* [which] *were of a varied character, whilst her private charities were known only by the recipients'*.

In the early years the Nicholsons made their home in Regent Street. Their family comprised three sons, the youngest of whom, Harry Edwin, died in 1866 aged 22 after a long illness following a railway accident on 29 October 1863. The two surviving sons, Joshua Oldfield and Arthur, both went on to achieve great things in the silk industry, but in different directions. With the business doing well, Joshua and his wife moved to a larger house in Buxton Road. They later settled at Stockwell House, a solid, ivy-clad house just above Greystones in Stockwell Street, and within a stone's throw of Brough's earlier factories, just across the road.

Joshua's eldest son Joshua Oldfield Nicholson was born in Leek in 1839. Joshua senior clearly still cherished his Yorkshire roots, and sent his eldest son to Huddersfield College, to complete his education begun at the Leek Grammar School on

Clerk Bank. His college education concluded, he joined his father at Brough, Nicholson and Co., where he received a good introduction to the silk industry. He was like his father a man of ambition, and in 1855 he left the firm to take up an apprenticeship with Taylor and Birchenough, silk manufacturers in Macclesfield.

From his boyhood he was a gifted artist, and whist he was still at school he won a medal for art awarded by the South Kensington Museum. His enthusiasm for art led him to study at the Macclesfield School of Art. After working for Taylor and Birchenough for 13 years he left in 1869 to set up in business on his own account at Prestbury Road Mills. Like Sir Thomas Wardle in Leek, he became a local contact of William Morris, with whom he co-operated in the production of damask silks, for which Morris visited Macclesfield.

Joshua Oldfield was married in 1870 to Ellen Pidduck, a member of a well-known family of Hanley jewellers. The couple made their home at Ashfield, Upton, Macclesfield. He later moved his business to Hope Mill in Elizabeth Street. Although no longer resident in Leek, he never lost his links with the town. He stood as the Liberal candidate for Leek in the 1892 General Election, when he was defeated by the Conservative, Charles Bill of Farley.

Joshua Nicholson senior now found the time to become involved in the public life of Leek. In politics he was a Liberal, and his religious beliefs had led him into the Congregational Church where he was a regular worshipper. He was a keen educationalist, and this led him to support the extension of the work of the Leek Literary and Mechanics' Institute. William France, together with other silkmen, including John and Joshua Brough, led this enterprise in early adult education - a further example of the ways in which Victorian Leek was ahead of the times.

The Mechanics' Institute took over a small, low building near the top of Russell Street. In 1862 William Sugden was commissioned to build a new Institute on the site, which he did with great flair and style. The new building was three storeys high and incorporated many of the decorative features so typical of Sugden's architecture. The new Institute stood opposite to the site of the new Congregational Church which Sugden was to build the following year, 1863, in his Victorian Gothic style. Joshua Nicholson would have taken great interest in the developments in this little corner of Leek.

The aims of the Mechanics' Institute were directed towards working-class young men who wished to improve their education. For this reason, fees were kept low, but no doubt many would be prevented from attending because they were unable to pay. Nevertheless, the Institute prospered, and members were able to avail themselves of the newspapers and books in the reading room, which was open during the evenings. Lectures were arranged on a variety of subjects, and classes in basic subjects were available. These classes were later extended to include science, literature, music and art. A debating society and a chess club were formed, as the Institute began to fulfil a social as well as an educational role. The Institute was firmly non-conformist and there was some resistance to the move to open on Sundays.

In spite of his involvement with the Mechanics' Institute, Joshua Nicholson had an even greater trick up his sleeve. During the 1870s his mind began to turn over the concept of a very ambitious project for the town of Leek. As a Liberal, he had a high regard for the philosophies and beliefs of Richard Cobden, the British Liberal politician and economist who opposed class divisions and religious privileges, and believed in free trade and the emancipation of the working man. A simple 'Cobden Club' was founded in which these ideals could be discussed round the table by a group of like-minded individuals, and from this the seeds of Nicholson's 'grand design' were sewn.

The announcement of Nicholson's intention to build an Institute was made by Sir Philip Cunliffe-Owen, of the South Kensington Museum, at the distribution of the art class prizes in

November 1881, and the idea was received with great enthusiasm.

The concept of a great public building to house a library, an art gallery, a museum, a reading room, a school of art and rooms where study, lectures, debates and recitals could take place was revolutionary indeed, certainly for the small town of Leek. Nevertheless, Joshua Nicholson had the depth of vision and strength of intent (plus, of course, the financial resources) to see his project through, and the result was the Nicholson Institute.

The Leek architects, William and Larner Sugden, were commissioned to draw up the designs and oversee the building work, which commenced in 1882. For Larner Sugden, recently entered into partnership with his father, this was his great opportunity to give full expression to his talents and his enthusiasm for the revival of the Queen Anne style of architecture, which was making a great impact on dull and sombre Victorianism.

The foundation stone was laid by Mrs Nicholson, and the building was completed in 1884. The professional journal *The Builder* of October 18th 1884 carried a large, detailed article, following the official opening ceremony:

This Institution... occupies a very central site in Stockwell Street facing south to Market Street, whence an imposing and effective view of the grand entrance, with its lofty tower is obtained. This view is diversified by one of the ancient houses of Leek, stone-built and ivy-clad 'with many blinking windows, row on row', which, by the removal of a neighbouring building it has fortunately been found practicable to preserve. With its quaint garden of sunflowers and hollyhocks it imparts a charming old-world flavour to the whole scene and contributes very largely to the tout ensemble.

The building referred to is, of course, the 17th century 'Greystones', owned by Joshua Nicholson, with spacious gardens and grounds at the rear, on which the Institute was built. It stood in the way of allowing the Institute to be built with its entrance direct from Stockwell Street, and was considered to be of sufficient importance to have any thoughts of demolition annulled. The Society for the Protection of Ancient Buildings intervened, but with its strong local support, the fight to save Greystones would hardly be a difficult one. Amongst the local supporters of the S.P.A.B. were several silk manufacturers, including the Broughs and Thomas Wardle, another luminary in Leek's silk industry. It was Wardle who had introduced William Morris to Leek, when, in his quest for perfection in the colours for his fabric designs, he had during the 1870s availed himself of the facilities at Wardle's Hencroft Dyeworks, and the skills and expertise of Wardle the dyer. Morris was a leading figure in the S.P.A.B. and so was Larner Sugden! Indeed, Wardle, Morris and Sugden all served on the Society's committee. This accounts for the great sympathy which Greystones received, and enabled the Sugdens to plan the new Institute with such great love and care that the two buildings complement each other, rather than clash. There is not a jarring note, and the 17th and 19th centuries coexist quite happily in this little corner of Leek.

During the building of the Institute, Joshua Nicholson was living at the nearby Stockwell House, but a few yards up the street. He would therefore be able to keep a close eye on the work, which was literally taking place in his own back garden. Greystones continued to be occupied by executives in the firm of Brough, Nicholson, the first being Henry Salt after Arthur Nicholson, Joshua's son, had left to purchase Highfield Hall in 1885. Arthur left his mark on the building in the form of his initials in ornate ironwork on the tie bar above the top right-hand window.

There can be little doubt that the Nicholson Institute was Joshua's greatest legacy to the town of Leek. It was his generosity which provided the town with a building that was not only superb architecturally, but splendid in its concepts and ideals. *The Builder* October 18th 1884 provides a detailed description:

The style of the new buildings is a somewhat severe form of Classic Renaissance, and the materials used are thin, hard-fired local bricks with black joints, dressings of red Roche and mottled Alton stone, and Broseley tiled roofs. All the windows are glazed with faintly-tinted antique glass in lead quarries. The leading feature of the front is the tower, which rises to a height of about 100 ft. from the street. This has the spacious principal entrance doorcase at its base, supporting in the same composition the great staircase window with pedimented crown with carved urns; and large elliptical lights in each face of the upper stage. The domed roof and lantern are covered with sheet copper, which in a few years will, no doubt, assume the green paten which strikes one so often sees on such features in the old Dutch and other Continental towns.

The facade between the gable and the tower has a stone balustrading with urns, and contains a large window lighting the hall. The fanlights contain the effigies of four eminent men, representing the four last centuries, carved in high relief in stone from models by Mr. Stephen Webb, which are hung in the building. Tennyson stands for Literature and the nineteenth century; Sir Joshua Reynolds for Art, and the eighteenth; Sir Isaac Newton for science, and the seventeenth; whilst Shakespeare for the16th century may be said to reflect Humanity in toto. Above these 'animated busts' a carved scroll supported by griffins carries these words of John Milton's 'Areopagitica': 'A good booke is the precious life-blood of a master spirit, embalm'd and treasur'd up on purpose to a life beyond life'.

The internal structure of the building is unusual, in that there is no actual ground floor as such. The building consists of three floors, the central one being some nine feet above street level, approached by a flight of stone steps. On this floor the library and reading rooms were located, and the floor beneath it housed the School of Art, approached down a slope on the right hand side of the building. The upper floor, which appears to be the second floor from the street, but is in effect the third, contained the art gallery, museum and meeting room.

This original structure and use is largely applied in the present day, which makes the Nicholson Institute unique, being one of only three such institutions in the whole country which still conforms precisely to the same founding principles in 2001 that applied in 1884.

The Nicholson Institute was opened with great ceremonial on Thursday, 16th October 1884 by Lord Wrottesley, Lord Lieutenant of Staffordshire, and it must have been a proud moment for Joshua Nicholson to see the successful culmination of his plans, and speculate on its fruitful future. The town was en fete for the occasion, and there were many decorations and illuminations in the streets. Decorated arches, usually reserved for royal occasions, were established in some locations. These carried moralistic slogans, such as 'If a good man thrives all thrive with him', or 'To the valiant heart nothing is impossible', and 'Honour to whom honour is due'. Others ventured into the more classical, with 'Ars longa vita brevis' and 'Arte favente nil desperandum'. Flags and bunting hung from shops and houses, and the Market Place was ablaze with gas-lit illuminations.

The weather for the great day was rather drizzly, which would be typical for October, but this did not deter the crowds from turning out. The grand procession included several bands and representatives of numerous local societies and the churches. The Leek Improvement Commissioners, visiting mayors, magistrates and town officials were escorted by the Queen's Own Royal Staffordshire Yeomanry, under the command of Captain Heath.

Later in the evening a display of fireworks took place in the Cattle Market, attracting a large crowd as darkness fell. The *Leek Times* reported that 'it was almost midnight before the streets became deserted and the illuminations ceased'.

The inaugural exhibition of oil paintings and water colours staged in the Art Gallery included works by major artists such as Raphael, Canaletto, Landseer and Wright of Derby. Victorian artists were well represented by D.G. Rosetti's *Water Lily* and *Joli Coeur*, G.F. Watts' *Una and the Red Knight* and *The Angel of Death* and five paintings by W.P. Firth under the title of *The Road to Ruin*. A collection of art treasures and bronzes was supplied on loan from the South Kensington Museum. The Gallery was open daily from 10 am to 10 pm, and there were admission charges, with season tickets available.

Sadly, though, having seen his great ideal established, Joshua Nicholson did not survive for another year. He died in August 1885. His wife survived him for a further nine years, continuing to live at Stockwell House. His elder son, Joshua Oldfield Nicholson, in Macclesfield, took a hand in his father's affairs. He was instrumental in setting up the initial selection of some 12,000 volumes for the Nicholson Institute Library, which occupied him for several months. His knowledge as an artist was also of great value in those early days.

At the memorial service for Joshua Nicholson at the Congregational Church - the church he had seen erected and generously supported - the Rev J Hankinson referred to his diligence in work and business:

To him the world was a stage, on which he was called to act his part. As a citizen of the world he felt that he had both rights and responsibilities, and he would not that either should be ignored. To him life was worth living; it had in it much blessing, of which he was forward to avail himself. In his early years he had a hard training - he passed through sore and severe discipline. Truly he had to bear the yoke of his youth, which we are told is 'good for a man', and he bore it bravely. It was soon found that here was an eager spirit - one full of energy, pluck and determination. Never was he afraid of work; even as a boy he loved it. Never was he abashed by difficulties - they served the more to arouse his vigorous nature. Ere he attained to manhood he was all awake to the events and activities of life. Already he had begun to take a keen interest in affairs - public, political and religious. He was quick to form positive opinions, was never slow to express them. Especially did he show an aptitude for business, and in this particular sphere he seemed to revel. His intellect, his ardour, his enterprise were devoted to it in an intense degree, and indicated his resolve if possible to command success. He was, perhaps, a little impatient if others did not quite share his enthusiasm. What he had to do he did with all his might. He could do nothing by halves. In a word, there was an intensity in his character which calmer, quieter, more passive temperaments could hardly understand, and but little appreciate.

The Rev Hankinson naturally went on to refer at length to Nicholson's support of the Congregational Church and his generosity towards many worthy causes, saying that he was *'dearly cherished as a kindly benefactor'.* The words of the minister seem to suggest that Nicholson had been in failing health for some time prior to his death; *'When health permitted how regular was his attendance at the services of the sanctuary, and not seldom was he present at some risk to himself.'* This quintessential Victorian funeral oration, warm in its appreciation of the man and his achievements, was delivered before a large congregation.

Every community in Victorian England seemed to have its father figures - men of integrity who had made their fortunes and were prepared to plough some of their wealth back into the community. It was inherent in the building of the Empire - 'I am your father and your mother' was a philosophy often projected by the civil and military settlers in lands like India. In a community like Leek, in order that men like Joshua Nicholson might be able to endow the town with benefits, it is obvious that their wealth must have been generated within that community, and by the citizens of that community. This makes their generosity no less laudable. They were held in awe and respect by the townsfolk, many of whom would be numbered amongst their workforce, and would never deign to refer them as less than 'Mr.' and address them as 'Sir'. You touched your cap to them, if you met them outside the workplace. Men like Joshua Nicholson were respected figures in the community, and Victorian England could not have achieved what it did without them. Often their power and influence remained within their families, and in this case the mantle in Leek fell upon Joshua's younger son, Arthur Nicholson.

FOOTNOTE We cannot leave the firm of Brough, Nicholson & Hall without some reference to the third director, John Hall. He was born 7 January 1840, the son of an Ipstones farmer. He was educated at Cheadle and Ipstones, and in 1854 he joined the firm of J. & J. Brough - 17 years after the arrival of Joshua Nicholson. By that time the firm was well established and about to embark on a period of great expansion. John Hall's energy and skills were a great asset to the firm and much of the planning and development were attributed to him. He became a partner in 1868 and a director in 1876. He saw the firm grow from employing less than 100 people in the old Union Street days to about 3000 in the Leek and Cheadle factories at the time of his death in 1930, at the age of 90.

He was a Wesleyan Methodist, holding many offices in the church. He became a J.P. and served as Chairman of the School of Art and the Technical School. In 1874 he established West Street School as the first mixed school in Leek. He lived at Ball Haye Hall - although he did not own it - and was a great supporter of the scouting movement.

The old Leek Grammar School where Arthur and Joshua Oldfield Nicholson received their early education,.

Eleven
THE DYNASTY CONTINUES

WITH HIS BROTHER JOSHUA OLDFIELD NICHOLSON firmly established in his own business in Macclesfield, it fell to Joshua Nicholson's youngest son, Arthur, to continue in his father's business in Leek. By the time of Joshua's death, 24th August 1885, the firm of Brough, Nicholson & Co. was well established, with a strong reputation for quality products, full order books and customers throughout the land. Joshua's business acumen and hard-headed Yorkshire judgement had enabled him to establish a staff of very able and committed men, who ran the business on sound principles. The extensive factory buildings covered an area of several acres, bounded by Ashbourne Road, Well Street, Cross Street and Fountain Street, where over 1000 workers were employed. The publication *Leek and District Illustrated* (1896) gives a good account of the business at that time:

Their processes commence with the treatment of the raw material, some of which the firm themselves import directly from Yokohama, China and other silk producing districts, but the bulk of which comes through the ordinary channel of the London open markets. The raw material passes through many processes before it emerges in that state of perfection which the public are used to, and in these mills the latest improvements in methods and machinery, some of which are their own patents, are adopted in order to attain the highest possible results. Their leading articles include the manufacture of every description of silk thread, such as sewing silks, embroidery and art crewel silks, machine and tailors' twists, braids, ladies' trimmings, beltings, bindings, laces etc., all of the highest class, and largely in demand among the principal traders in the country.

Joshua Oldfield Nicholson was three years old when Arthur was born on July 15th 1842. The two boys spent their early childhood together in a good solid Victorian family home, first on Buxton Road, then at Stockwell House. It was a somewhat sheltered existence, their devoted parents saw to that, having lost a son as a result of an accident. They both went to the Leek Grammar School and then completed their education at the Huddersfield College.

The old Leek Grammar School, standing in a prominent position on Clerk Bank, its venerable old grey stones reflecting the solid standards and principles of education, was established by Thomas Parker, Earl of Macclesfield, in 1723. At that time it stood on a level plateau above a steep slope through which Mill Street was eventually cut when the road was turnpiked in the late 18th century. A severe, no-nonsense kind of building, with a strong air of discipline about it, the school might have been a daunting prospect to a young boy, but it established a good reputation for sound education in Leek.

The first master, appointed by the church, was a man named Thomas Bourne. Subsequent masters were appointed by the Earl of Macclesfield for the time being, but the church was involved, for much of his income came from the George Rhoades Charity. The Rev. Rhoades was the son of a former vicar of Leek and under the terms of his legacy provision was made for the education of a small number of local children whose parents did not have the means to pay for their education. The number of poor children was usually six and this social mix meant that the school was ahead of its time.

The church always had a strong involvement, the master or his assistant doubling as the curate or holding some other appointment at St. Edward's Church, or as chaplain to the workhouse. This arrangement usually worked well, but there were occasional tensions. For example, in the mid-19th century a curate named Ribbans was the subject of an acrimonious correspondence between the church authorities and left under a cloud.

The school catered for a few boarders, usually 3 or 4, and there would be about 24 pupils on the roll. It is not known how well the school was supported by the gentry of Leek. Many would no doubt wish to send their sons to more notable establishments, but it was in the refined atmosphere of the Leek Grammar School that the two young Nicholson brothers received their early education, in the mid-19th century.

True sons of their father, the silk industry was clearly in their blood. It was good, sound Victorian business practice that sons entering the family business should not automatically start at the top, but gain an overall experience by starting on the lower rungs of the ladder. This was certainly the case with Arthur who joined the firm of Brough, Nicholson & Co. in 1856 as an apprentice, learning the trade in the various departments.

His early years were dominated by a desire to succeed in his chosen career, and he did not marry until September 20th 1882, when he was 40 years old. His bride was Miss Marianne Falkner, of Manchester, and they had a family of three sons and a daughter. Their eldest son was Arthur Falkner, followed by Malcolm and Basil Lee, and Christine.

Like many of his contemporaries, Arthur Nicholson seemed to possess a boundless energy. Deeply involved in the business, and a devoted family man, Arthur Nicholson still found time to become involved in public work across a wide spectrum. He was made a Justice of the Peace in 1883, and was Chairman of the Leek Bench for many years. In politics he followed his father in being an active Liberal supporter. He was Chairman of the Joshua Nicholson Lodge of the Liberal League, which was supported by many local people including Larner Sugden. Indeed, Nicholson's eldest son, Malcolm, and another member of the Sugden family, M A Sugden, were joint honorary secretaries, so there was strong family involvement. The office was at the Liberal Club in Market Street.

Arthur Nicholson was elected unopposed to the Staffordshire County Council in 1889 and, with the exception of a short break of 3 or 4 years, continued to serve until the time of his death in 1929. He became an Alderman, served on the Education

Committee and was Chairman of the Staffordshire, Wolverhampton and Dudley Joint Tuberculosis Committee. When Westwood Hall was opened as a grammar school for girls in the 1920s he became Chairman of the Governors.

Arthur Nicholson was knighted for his services to industry and public life in the King's Birthday Honours List of December 1909, under the Liberal Prime Minister, Herbert Asquith. A further honour came his way, when in 1916 he was called upon to fill the ancient office of High Sheriff of the County of Stafford.

The burgeoning building society movement also attracted his interest. He became Chairman of the Leek and Moorlands Building Society in 1890. His knowledge of properties in Stockwell Street enabled him in 1894 to negotiate for the purchase of the site of 15 Stockwell Street which became its new offices. The building, which still stands today, was the work of John Brealey, a local architect and brother of Thomas Brealey who designed the Buttermarket and the old Fire Station.

He clearly had great skill in handling and understanding financial matters. His obituary in the *Leek Post* February 16th 1929 said *'his handling of the figures at the annual meetings made even that gathering quite an occasion to be anticipated, for few financiers could make figures tell such a pleasing story as the former Chairman has often done.'*

Arthur Nicholson was one of the seven trustees of the Cottage Hospital appointed by Mrs Allsop. He was also trustee and adviser to the Leek Benevolent Burial Society until pressure of business caused him to retire. He contributed generously to the North Staffordshire Royal Infirmary and the Biddulph Hospital. Following the family tradition he was a generous supporter of the Congregational Church. He held the post of chairman of the Congregational Church Finance Committee for some 20 years and was treasurer, and later chairman, of the Staffordshire Congregational Union.

Progressive and wealthy Victorian families usually made their mark on the community in which they lived and the

Nicholsons were no exception to this rule. These father-figures commanded a great deal of respect; you touched your cap to them and addressed them as 'Sir'. In the workplace you never referred to them as anything more familiar than 'Mr.' for you knew your place. Like his father Joshua before him, Arthur Nicholson would set a high standard in the attainments of himself and his family, his business and the town.

Highfield Hall was a substantial mansion built of red brick with stone facings and leaded light windows, approached from the road from Leek to Macclesfield. It stood in extensive grounds of over five acres, with rhododendrons, shrubs and trees lining the carriage drive from the main road, which terminated in a wide, gravelled forecourt. The imposing portico was supported on two circular stone pillars on either side of the panelled oak door. A feature of the house was a large conservatory and sun loggia on its south-west aspect. The house had extensive stabling, which would have appealed to Arthur Nicholson when he purchased the property from Edwin Cliffe Glover in 1885. Highfield Hall became the home of the Nicholsons for many years.

The move to Highfield released Greystones in Stockwell Street for occupation by a fellow director, Henry Salt, for about 40 years. On leaving school, Henry Salt was apprenticed to J. and J. Brough & Co. but his abilities came to the notice of Joshua Nicholson who sent him back for another year's schooling and personally trained him in book-keeping and commercial methods. He progressed through the counting house to the position of cashier and eventually company secretary, and later, a director. It was said that such was his extraordinary memory he could remember the exact state of the account of every customer on the firm's books at the end of each month. He was a Wesleyan Methodist and served as Circuit Steward to the Leek Methodist Circuit. He worked hard for the cause of the Cottage Hospital, being Chairman of the Hospital Committee when the appeal was launched to build an extension in 1908. From 1870 he was a subscriber to the Leek and Moorlands Building Society and was a director for 52 years. From 1912 to 1929 he was Chairman of the Board and he succeeded Sir Arthur Nicholson as President in 1929. He died at Greystones on 3rd February 1923 at the age of 82, his loyalty to the Nicholson company remaining solid to the end. He would no doubt regard Arthur Nicholson and fellow director Benjamin Nixon not only as colleagues but as friends.

When Arthur Nicholson took over Highfield in 1885 he continued to allow the free use of part of the grounds by Leek Cricket Club. The extensive and well-trimmed lawns in front of the house ended in a low stone wall. Between this and the main road, the broad oval of level ground, ringed with trees and shrubs, provided a fine arena for the game and continued to be the home of Leek Cricket Club, founded in 1844. Nicholson's relationship with the club was usually a very amicable one. His son's, Malcolm and Basil, were both competent cricketers, and he provided the club with a pavilion. However, there was one incident which soured this relationship for a time, and demonstrated Nicholson's firm Liberal principles and sense of justice, as well as reflecting the social mores of the time.

It occurred in 1894, when Arthur Nicholson was President of the Cricket Club. At the Annual Meeting in September 1894 the Treasurer reported a deficit of £40, mainly due to the falling off in donations to the Professional Fund. This prompted Mr Marcus Prince to ask if Leek was big enough to afford a professional. The employment of a professional would give a club some standing, particularly if the player was famous. At the time, the Leek professional was J.W. Kirkby of Maidstone, Kent. The members wished for the club to maintain its status, and it was decided to arrange a concert to raise money. In addition, it was agreed that playing members should pay their own match expenses, and that working men who could not afford to pay should raise a fund amongst themselves for that purpose.

This decision clearly annoyed Arthur Nicholson, who was moved to take drastic action. He wrote to the secretary of the

Cricket Club in uncompromising terms:

October 2nd 1894
To Mr. Percy Miller,
Hon. Sec., Leek Cricket Club,

Dear Sir, - I have read with regret the report in the Leek Times of the annual meeting of the Leek Cricket Club. It is a pity to see the club so heavily in debt, but the course decided upon in order to retrieve this position does not seem to me a wise one. The only possible outcome of the resolution respecting 'travelling expenses' will be the entire exclusion of working men from the club, for a large majority of the playing members especially in the second eleven - are quite unable to spare money for this purpose. Hence such a resolution is to them practically a notice to quit, and the result would be that the ground would be almost exclusively reserved for well-to-do players quite capable of paying for a ground if they required one.

As I strongly disapprove of the working men being thus shut out, I cannot grant the use of the Highfield ground for so restricted and, in my opinion, selfish a section. Therefore, I shall be glad if you will at once make known to your committee this determination, so that should the course decided upon be irrevocable, they may have ample time during the seven or eight months which intervene before the new season commences in which to provide themselves with some other ground. In that case I will relieve the committee of the cottage at any time they may wish, but if the ground is not utilised by the Leek Cricket Club I shall still hope to see cricket played there.

I am, dear sir, yours truly,
A. NICHOLSON

Most of the working men players would be employed in the silk industry, and as a manufacturer, it might be said that Nicholson would not want any extra drain on the mens' pockets that might prompt demands for increased pay. Nevertheless, his letter expressed a genuine concern and highlighted the differences between the social classes in sport at that time. The 'old school' syndrome was still very prevalent. Gentlemen versus Players was an annual fixture on the cricket calendar, and score cards printed the names of the 'gentlemen' with full initials plus rank or qualification whilst the 'others' were granted surname only. This system obviously reached down into the ranks of Leek Cricket Club.

Nicholson's letter prompted the calling of an extraordinary general meeting of the club, which was held at the Swan Hotel and was well attended. Arthur Nicholson was not present. The club's 'heavy' debt, which was the main element in shaping the decision regarding working men, was £40. The meeting was reluctant to rescind the original decision, although it was felt that a working men's fund could be set up. Chief spokesmen for the working men were Mr T Armitt and Mr T Tipper. It appears there was an element in the club which did not believe in men playing cricket when they had a wife and large family, and a remark had been passed to the effect that any man with a wife and seven children and 15s a week ought to stay at home.

Mr M Prince thought that Mr Nicholson's letter was uncalled for and that he had been wrongly informed of the facts. The letter was also unfortunate because it began to set class against class, which had never been the intention. He, personally, had no wish to be involved with any cricket or football club where the question of class came in, and should always oppose any feeling which helped to set working men against what Mr Nicholson called the 'selfish section'.

Several members questioned Nicholson's true motives in sending his letter, feeling that he might be wishing to have the ground for his own employees. There was a doubt that they could work together amicably in these conditions, with what amounted to a 'notice to quit' hanging over them. Eventually Mr Armitt proposed that the resolution of the annual meeting be rescinded. Mr Tipper seconded, but this was defeated, 13 voting for and 17 against.

As a result of this decision a split occurred in the membership of the cricket club. One group, consisting mainly of the silk manufacturers, traders and professional men, left

Highfield, keeping the name of Leek Cricket Club. They played their matches on the Beggars Lane ground. The remainder of the membership stayed at Highfield, having fulfiled Arthur Nicholson's conditions, forming a new club that played under the name of Leek Highfield Cricket Club.

My grandfather, Arthur Poole, served for some time as a 'collector' for the Highfield Club, and always spoke proudly of his work. Such was the determination of the Leek working class to ensure that the great national game remained accessible to all and not just the privileged few.

The two clubs became great rivals in local league cricket and some keenly fought local 'derbys' were played. The rift was not healed until after the First World War, when the two clubs settled their differences, reunited as one club, and returned to Highfield. A strong club was the result, which enjoyed much success in the 1920s, when the resources of so many clubs had been decimated by the casualties of the war. The reformed Leek Cricket Club continued to enjoy the generous - and genuine - support of Sir Arthur Nicholson.

On May 20th 1911, Leek Highfield entertained their rivals, Leek Cricket Club, for the annual 'Derby' match. The occasion was marked by the opening of a new pavilion which Sir Arthur Nicholson had generously provided for the club. Present at the event were Lady Nicholson, Sir Philip Brocklehurst, Arthur Falkner Nicholson and H R Brunt, the Leek captain. Sir Arthur performed the opening ceremony, and hoped that the pavilion would be a great convenience to the players and the club, and to the many visitors who came to play cricket at Highfield.

Sir Arthur Nicholson clearly loved Highfield. Its rural location enabled him to work a schedule of conservation for the extensive wooded grounds. He engaged the Sugdens to carry out work on the house, moving into the lodge whilst the work was done. But his greatest passion was perhaps the breeding of shire horses. The Highfield Stud attained a high reputation in competitions for shire horses at many of the principal agricultural shows throughout the country. At the London Show in 1917 his champion stallion won the main prize, and his mare, Rayscroft Forest Queen was the supreme female champion. He also owned a herd of pedigree dairy shorthorns and a flock of Suffolk sheep. For a time he was president of the Staffordshire Agricultural Society and a member of the Dairy Shorthorn Association.

It was a passion he shared with George V, and when the King and Queen Mary spent some time at Highfield during their visit to Leek on 23 April 1913 Sir Arthur's shire horses were a centre of attraction when they were paraded before His Majesty.

The tragedy that engulfed Europe in 1914 made its mark on the Nicholson family. All three sons became serving officers in the First World War, and one was to perish in the conflict. Arthur Falkner Nicholson, the eldest son, had followed his father into the business. He was elected to Leek Urban District Council in 1911, a position he returned to after the war, when he became Chairman of the Finance Committee. He served for one year as High Sheriff of Staffordshire, and later as Deputy Lieutenant for the county. He had a distinguished military career. He was for a long time in command of the Leek Battery, and served with it at the front, where he was wounded in the shoulder by shrapnel. After the war he was placed in command of the 61st Brigade, and was appointed Lieutenant-Colonel in 1924.

Malcolm Nicholson, the second son, had followed a legal career, and was called to the bar in 1913. At the start of the First World War he was attached to the 2nd North Midland Brigade, and later transferred to the Flying Corps. He, too, was promoted to Lieutenant-Colonel, and received the O.B.E. for war service. He married the daughter of Mr and Mrs Chambers, a prominent Birmingham family.

Basil Lee Nicholson, the youngest son, was educated at the Priory School, Malvern, before passing to Rugby, and thence to Burschied, near Cologne, and Vevey, Switzerland, where he completed his education. He then joined the firm and was in charge of the dyeing department at Bridge End, where he was showing much promise when the First World War broke out.

At the start of the First World War, 'C' (3rd Leek, Staffs) Battery ('The Old Leek Battery') was part of the 231st Brigade RFA, of the 46th North Midland Division TF. The Battery's headquarters in Leek was the barracks in Alma Street, and the officers were Major Challinor, Lieut. Arthur Falkner Nicholson and Lieut. Basil Lee Nicholson. By 1915 the Battery was serving in the Ypres Salient, involved in the battles at Hill 60 and Hooge. It was here that Falkner Nicholson was injured by shrapnel from a German shell. He was taken to a dressing station. Lieut. Basil Nicholson had just returned from leave when he heard of his brother's injury. He was determined to take reprisals from the attacking Germans and led a party to the front line trenches. From the forward Observation Post he was viewing the results of his attack when he was shot in the head by a German sniper, killing him instantly.

Basil Nicholson was buried in the churchyard at Dranoutre. His brother Falkner and his colleagues in the Leek Battery were present. His military grave is just inside the entrance to the churchyard, where he was laid to rest with full military honours.

The news was devastating to his parents, Sir Arthur and Lady Nicholson, and of course to all the people of Leek. Writing home, a fellow officer in the Leek Battery, Major W. F. Challinor, recalled the high regard in which Basil Nicholson was held:

Isn't it sad that our first casualty should have been Basil. I hardly like to think of him, and of the intimate talks and episodes we have had together. However, this is war, and it may be the same with any one of us, at any moment, otherwise we are very fit except Falkner, who is in a rest home some miles from here. I cannot write any more, as our Battery now requires much attention, in the circumstances, though we have other officers sent temporarily to help.

Sir Arthur and Lady Nicholson received a telegram from the King and Queen:

The King and Queen are grieved to hear of the death of your son, and offer their heartfelt sympathy in your loss. Their Majesties remember with so much pleasure their visit to Highfield.

Over the next four years Col W F Challinor's observation that *'this is war, and it may be same with any one of us, at any moment'* became a reality for many more Leek families. At the end of the war, when local communities throughout the land were establishing war memorials, it was the Nicholsons who took the initiative to provide Leek with a suitable monument to the fallen.

Described by the Leek Post as the 'Great White Tower of Remembrance', the clock-tower war memorial was built of Portland stone, to the design of Thomas Warrington and Sons, of Manchester. The builders were Messrs E and A Frith, of Macclesfield and Leek, and constructional problems extended the projected building time by about nine months. The chief source of trouble was discovered as the foundations were being dug. The subsoil was very waterlogged due to an underground water course which followed the line of Fountain Street, Haywood Street and Brook Street. This meant that considerable excavation was necessary, and much deep cement was laid to secure a firm foundation, to consolidate the base and keep out the water. The building work was supervised by W E Beacham, the Leek Urban District Council surveyor.

The memorial stands 90 feet high and is 22 feet square at the base. It rises from a 43 feet square platform, raised by steps a few feet above street level. The iron gates were made by Harts of Salford, and the bronze tablets bearing the names of the fallen were the work of the Birmingham Guild of Handicraft. The paving around the tower was done by local builder, Thomas Grace.

The names of First World War battles in which local men were involved appear on all four sides, above the clock - on the north side, Hooge, Loos and Ypres; on the south side, Somme and Bellengise; on the east side, Ramicourt and Bohain; on the west side, Lens and Gommecourt.

The clock, which is electrically driven, was made by Gent

and Co. of Leicester, and a stand-by accumulator battery provides an emergency supply in the event of a short-term power failure. The movement for operating the hands of the clock is capable of varying its power to counteract the battering of storms and gales. The clock faces are seven feet in diameter, and can be illuminated at night.

The memorial, which cost £16,000, was the gift to the town of Sir Arthur and Lady Nicholson, in memory of their son, Lieut. Basil Lee Nicholson and all the other local men who died in the conflict. The many names on the tablets were collected by Mrs Horace Wardle. Every care had been taken to ensure that no name was omitted, and a list had been placed on public display for several weeks, as well as several advertisements in the local press, to enable the townsfolk to ascertain that all names were included. The tablets are on the east and west sides of the tower. The one on the east side has 208 names, and the one on the west has 211 names - a total of 419 names, arranged in alphabetical order. The dedicatory tablet in memory of Basil Lee Nicholson is at the front of the monument.

The unveiling and dedication ceremony took place on Thursday, 20th August, 1925. It was half-day closing for the shops, and most of the silk mills closed down for the occasion, enabling a very large crowd to assemble at the bottom of Derby Street, and many laid their own floral tributes around the monument when the official ceremony was over. Traffic came to a standstill.

Lieutenant Colonel Arthur Falkner Nicholson, Sir Arthur's eldest son, presided at the ceremony, and Sir Arthur handed over the title deeds to the town. In his speech, Sir Arthur stated that all legal steps had been taken to ensure that the monument became the property of the town and its citizens. The site was in the joint ownership of the Trustees of the Leek Town Lands and the Leek Urban District Council, and the necessary consents of the Charity Commissioners had been obtained. *'I now leave it in your care and keeping, and in that of the public of Leek, with the earnest hope and faith that it will be cherished and prized for all time'.*

Lieutenant General Sir Charles Harrington, GBE, KCB, DSO (GOC Northern Command) unveiled the main tablet. The side tablets containing the names of over 400 local men were unveiled by Cyril Plant and Frank Prime, Boy Scouts whose fathers died in the war. The memorial was dedicated by the Lord Bishop of Stafford. The platform party also included Sir Arthur's other surviving son, Lieutenant Colonel Malcolm Nicholson, together with General H M Clayton, Rev J D Jones, Rev J Ogmore Morgans, Captain C Kendall, Mr G H Wilson (Chairman of Leek Urban District Council), Mr A H Shaw, of Challinors and Shaw, and representatives of the architects.

The Monument, fondly known to Leek people as 'Sir Arthur's Wristwatch', was his last major contribution to the life of the town. He died at Bournemouth, where he was spending some of the winter in a milder climate, on February 9th 1929, at the age of 86. His life had spanned the Victorian and Edwardian years.

The funeral of Sir Arthur Nicholson, February 1929, heading for the service at Leek Congregational Church.

The Royal visit at Highfield, 23 April 1913.

Highfield Hall, home of Sir Arthur and Lady Nicholson.

Visit of King George V and Queen Mary to Highfield Hall, 23 April 1913.

'Sparrow Park', site of the Nicholson War Memorial.

The Nicholson War Memorial, dedication ceremony, 20th August 1925.

194 Leek's Golden Years

The unveiling of the Nicholson War Memorial 20th August 1925.

Twelve
WORDS WERE HIS BUSINESS

THE NEWSPAPER has played an important role in the development of society, the reflection of political opinion and the recording of events for nearly 400 years. The invention of printing as a means of reproducing text or illustration on paper led to the introduction of news-sheets as early as 1609 in Germany. The first English newspaper was probably the *Weekly News*, edited by Nicholas Bourne and Thomas Archer, which made its first appearance in 1622.

During the English Civil War printed broadsheets were widely used as a means of conveying often biased, and frequently scurrilous, political opinions to a wider public. These were often crudely printed and covertly distributed but they played an important role in the shaping of public opinion, for very forthright views were expressed in uncompromising terms - these broadsheets were early examples of what is often euphemistically referred to today as 'the power of the press'.

By the time of Bonnie Prince Charlie's Jacobite Rebellion in 1745 newspapers like the *Caledonian Mercury* were able to publish detailed reports of the progress of the march of the Highlanders and the counter-measures of the Duke of Cumberland to defeat them. There are therefore good printed reports, assuming they are accurate, of the progress of the rebellion through Leek and the moorlands.

Improved printing techniques and the wider availability of cheap newsprint paper led to the growth of newspapers. Steam printing began in 1814 and the rotary press was introduced to the Britain in 1857. Newsprint paper made from wood pulp became widely used during the 1880s. The repeal of certain so-called 'taxes on learning' in the mid-19th century also contributed to the spread of newspapers. Advertisement tax was abolished in 1853, newspaper stamp duty in 1855, and the duty on paper in

1861. Another factor during the Victorian years was the higher literacy rate. All these elements combined to shape the spread of the press towards the mass distribution of newspapers which prevails today.

The first local newspaper of any substance was the *Staffordshire Advertiser,* which made its appearance in January 1795. (The earlier *Wolverhampton Chronicle and Staffordshire Advertiser* appeared in 1789 but failed after only four years.) The new paper was the first to attempt press coverage on an entire county-wide scale, including news from as wide an area as Leek and Cheadle in the north to Wolverhampton and Walsall in the south, and embracing the Potteries, Newcastle-under-Lyme, Stafford, Stone, Eccleshall, Brewood, Lichfield, Tamworth, Burton, Rugeley, and Uttoxeter. Its full title was the *Staffordshire Advertiser and Political, Philanthropic and Commercial Gazette,* thus reflecting many of the aims of the press at the time. Its editor and publisher was Joshua Drewry, who like many printers in those days had served his apprenticeship in Derby.

The paper was a large broadsheet, about 20 inches by 14 inches, consisting of four pages of closely-set typescript. It was common practice at the time to blatantly 'lift' whole items of national and international news and blend in items of local news and court cases. There were no banner headlines, indeed the small type size would not be easy to read in the dim light of oil lamps or early gas lighting. The *Advertiser* set new standards as a quality provincial newspaper, and survived competition from a number of contemporary local papers established in the larger towns of Staffordshire. Its major competitor, certainly in North Staffordshire, was the *Staffordshire Sentinel,* first published in Hanley in January 1854. At first this was a weekly publication, but an evening edition commenced publication on 15th April, 1873. This was the first daily newspaper in the county.

The *Staffordshire Advertiser* continued as a weekly newspaper, published on Saturday and covering the entire county, until the mid-20th century. In its heyday it had the reputation as perhaps the most widely read local newspaper in the Midlands. It was at its height in the mid-19th century when Matthew Henry Miller worked for the *Advertiser*, as a local correspondent.

Matthew Henry Miller was born in Birmingham on 7th February 1843, the second son of James and Eliza Miller. His father was a silversmith and was manager to Messrs Bent and Parker of Newhall Street, Birmingham. M H Miller was educated at Severn Street School and his family were strong non-conformists, attending the Ebenezer Chapel in Steelhouse Lane. He remained a Congregationalist all his life.

Printing was in his blood, and on leaving school he became apprenticed to Josiah Allen, of Livery Street, Birmingham. In his early teens he won the *Boy's Own* Paper prize, open to all England, for an essay entitled 'A Young Printer's Autobiography'. He came to Leek in 1864 to join the printing business of Robert Nall, in Stanley Street, as manager. This would be a considerable achievement for a young man of twenty-one years.

George Nall, father of Robert, came to Leek from Bakewell in 1828, and set up in business as a printer in Spout Street (now St. Edward Street). He came with a solid grounding in printing gained at the famous Derby firm of Bemrose, where he was a partner. The firm of Bemrose and Sons Ltd. is still in business today as a leading name in the printing industry.

George Nall moved his business to Sheepmarket in 1835 and demonstrated his expertise by introducing copper-plate printing to the town. This high quality printing, with its clean, sharp lines and fine detail, enhanced the appearance of the business stationery and letterheadings of his customers, many of whom would be the silk manufacturers. Nall also undertook general jobbing work and produced a number of books and booklets. His son Robert was apprenticed to his father, and eventually became a partner in the firm. Following his father's death Robert continued to run the firm in his own name from new premises in Custard Street (now Stanley Street). Robert Nall was not a young man in 1864 when Matthew Henry Miller joined the firm, and he would no doubt welcome the services of a younger, more dynamic man who came with a wide experience in the printing industry.

Miller's first connection with the press was as correspondent for the *Birmingham Daily Post*, a position he held for many years. He was also on the outside staff of the *Staffordshire Sentinel*, in addition to his work for the *Staffordshire Advertiser*.

On 30th July, 1870 he commenced the publication of the *Leek Times*, and shortly afterwards, on 26th September, he married Annie Lovatt, the daughter of John Lovatt a silk manufacturer in Leek and partner in the firm of Lovatt and Gould. Miller was a family man, and in 1881 he was living at 11 Westwood Terrace in Leek with his wife and six children - Percy, Nellie, Harry, Lizzie, Frank and Sidney. Most of the children, boys and girls, were given the second Christian name of Box, but the significance of this is not known. The family later moved to a larger house in the newly-developed Southbank Street, where stylish Victorian town houses had become available to middle class families. A further move to Wood Street, came later, when the family had grown up, and it was here that Miller died in 1909.

The *Leek Times* started as a four page newspaper, using a partly printed London sheet and printing two pages of Leek news. Miller's initial problem was to persuade local traders to take up advertising space in his new paper, yet to make its mark, instead of existing papers and the local almanacs and directories. However, the *Leek Times* was a success, and its size and price were adjusted to meet the changing circumstances. It was published each Friday from a workshop in Bath Street, later moving to larger premises in Market Street.

Miller's fearless criticism of local, county and national affairs soon resulted in the paper gaining a considerable circulation as the years rolled on. Politically, Miller was a keen

Liberal and his newspaper did not hide this fact. Nevertheless, its columns were open to both the Liberal and Conservative parties, for he was always scrupulously fair in his reporting. On the other hand, the *Leek Post* openly supported the Conservative cause, and the two papers, from their two different viewpoints, managed to co-exist. It may be said that, for a small town, Leek was fortunate to have the choice of two newspapers supporting opposing political viewpoints.

The democratic sympathies of the *Leek Times* were however well known, and in local trade disputes the workers were always sure of warm-hearted support. Charitable causes too, found the paper of inestimable value, and Miller gave enthusiastic support to the successful Cruso Nursing Fund. Funded by an endowment from the late Mrs Cruso of Foxlowe, this fund provided financial support for working class families in times of sickness and need. Nonconformity also found the paper to be a true friend, and many were the tributes paid to it by the leaders of the Free Churches in Leek.

The *Leek Comet* was another of Miller's ventures, published weekly on each Wednesday and designed to attract farmers and others attending the Leek Market. It was a brave venture, but its limited appeal was difficult to sustain and owing to lack of support it was discontinued after a few months.

In Matthew Henry Miller, Leek had a journalist of high esteem and experience. Although outspoken in tone, he was scrupulously clean in aim and sentiment, and the *Leek Times* was followed with keen interest. Miller was a founder of the Birmingham Press Club, one of the first of its kind in the country, and was a member of the Council of the Institute of Journalists.

An example of the fearless nature of Miller's editorial comments, and at the same time, his sense of justice, can be seen in his reporting of a proposed Royal Visit to Leek. In the bitterly-cold winter of 1895 there was a good deal of poverty and distress in the town and the local Charity Organisation Society had launched a fund to provide free hot dinners for the children of

Leek. M H Miller was serving on the Poor Children's Dinner Fund committee at the time, and the fund was generously supported by leading citizens and traders.

At the same time another committee was planning the celebrations for the forthcoming visit of HRH the Duchess of Teck on 1st March 1895. Opinions were divided on the amount that should be spent on decorations and celebrations for the visit of the Duchess, and several members, including Mr Larner Sugden and Mr A Ward, had withdrawn their support. Thomas Wardle was able to see both sides of the problem. Writing to the committee, he said, *'I think the Duchess ought to be received in Leek as becomes her rank; but more especially as her mission is one of attempting to help to some solution of the decaying state of the English silk industry caused solely by foreign competition from the labour sweated markets of the Continent. I have been told in Leek that H.R.H. would herself desire that money promised for decorations should be given to the poor. Probably she would if it were put to her, but my opinion is that we can both feed the poor and receive H.R.H. in a manner worthy of Leek and herself. I can speak for myself and am doing what I can for the poor and for the reception.'*

Into the arena stepped Matthew Henry Miller, with some bold editorial comments in the *Leek Times* 9th February 1895:

ROYALTY v. DISTRESS.
This may be said to have formed the text of the discussion at the meeting of the Royal Visit Committee on Thursday evening, and the result may be regarded as a happy compromise between two subscription lists. Without leaving ourselves open to an accusation of snobbery, we may say that expense must necessarily be incurred in receiving a Royal friend of the silk industry in a befitting manner, and Mr. Wardle is of the opinion that this can be creditably done and the poor looked after as well. We hope this is so; but the dual object can only be carried out by the opening of the purse strings of the wealthy. Tradesmen and the better paid artizans will inevitably be more attracted by a fund to relieve the bitter distress, of which they see so much more than the rich, than one to entertain even the most distinguished visitor. However, the

committee, in the face of all this have been most moderate in their estimate of what they deem to be really necessary, and as the surplus funds are to be devoted to the relief of distress, we can only trust that the Royal visit subscription list will show a handsome balance on the right side without materially interfering with gifts to the fund which has for its sole object the alleviation of the poverty that unfortunately so largely prevails in our midst.

In the following issue of the *Leek Times* Miller again returned to the theme:

March 1st will not only find the Duchess of Teck at Leek, but the Dukes of Teck and Schleswig-Holstein, and as the object of the visit is the betterment of the silk trade we trust their reception will be worthy of their rank and mission. In face of the distress, visible to all but the wilfully blind, it has been wisely decided to limit the reception expenses and give the residue to the poor. Fifteen pounds only will be devoted to decoration, and the cost of the address, luncheon, band and other contingent expenses will bring the bill up to about eighty pounds. It is, however, hoped that sufficient funds will be subscribed to enable the committee to turn over a handsome sum for the relief of the poor, in order that the visit may not only permanently improve the staple trade of the town but immediately benefit those who are in dire distress and want.

Miller clearly had a deep social conscience. He gave much space in the Leek Times to the support of the Poor Children's Dinner Fund, and to the committee set up to provide dinners for old people. In an amusing editorial in the issue of December 23rd, 1893 he gave publicity to a charity football match between Commercials and Tradesmen, describing it as a match in which 'anything goes', no previous knowledge of the rules being necessary:

'There will be only one ball and it will be good form to kick it very hard and very often. Each player must kick something, and should any one miss the ball and kick his own chest, he may adjourn for the necessary repairs and refreshment; but if he should kick somebody else's chest, the kicker and the kicked may retire for the same purpose, and they

shall be sole judges of when they are able to resume kicking. Every player is to have free use of hands and feet, and the interference of referee or linesman will be deemed out of place and a violation of the freedom that is so dear to every Englishman.'

Miller's sense of humour and barbed wit was apparent in much of his writings for the paper. In the following issue of December 30th 1893 he gave a glowing report of the subsequent dinner, when 250 old people were fed at the Town Hall, and a further 100 meals delivered to the homes of those unable to attend - a report which would have given him considerable satisfaction to write.

Another of Matthew Henry Miller's interests was cricket. Although he was only 21 when he arrived in Leek, there are no records that he played the game in Leek. However, when a Yorkshire County XI visited Leek in August 1875 to play a three-day match against a team of 22 Leek players, Miller acted as umpire. He was a personal friend of Arthur Shrewsbury, a famous Nottinghamshire and England player, who played for Leek on a number of occasions, no doubt due in no small measure to Miller's influence. Miller's talents and contacts as an entertainer also came into play at the annual dinners and fundraising events for Leek Cricket Club. By 1889 he was a member of the committee of the Club, a position he held for several years, occasionally taking the chair. In 1894, when the division occurred in the club over the dispute about working men's expenses, Miller's Liberal leanings led him to remain with the new Leek Highfield club, as a vice-president. He made no attempt to disguise his feelings in a subsequent editorial in the Leek Times, at the start of the next cricket season, May 18th, 1895:

CURIOSITIES IN CRICKET.
For the first time in the 51 years during which the Leek Cricket Club has existed an appeal, in the shape of a bazaar, has been made to the public for pecuniary relief, and this has been done under circumstances not a little curious. Consequent upon the adoption of the principle that

those who could not afford to pay their own expenses ought not to play cricket, a rupture took place at the last annual meeting, and the working men players thinking, and thinking rightly too, that their exclusion was the point aimed at, were not slow to show their full appreciation of the situation. The owner of Highfield, who for many years had freely given the use of the ground, took sides with those who were unable to help themselves, and joined issue with the reformers. True the club is in debt, but the deficit is traceable to the fact that the well-to-do members of the team had received for years their expenses in common with the working-men players, instead of paying them out of their own pockets. Cut off from a free ground, the apostles of independence, so strongly of the opinion that those only who could afford to pay should play cricket, have found themselves in need of £500 before a ball was bowled, and an appeal to the public, all and sundry, is made for that sum.

Appropriately enough, a field at Beggar's Lane has been taken, and here the 'independent beggars' are for the present located. It remains to be seen how far they will uphold the credit of Leek in the local cricket world. Upto the present they have shown no sign of fulfilling the responsibilities of their position, and a great change will have to take place before it will be clear that they are able to sustain even the damaged prestige of the last few years.

One wonders how these rather barbed remarks were received by the supporters of Leek Cricket Club! Miller often signed his column under the pseudonym of 'Kweer Kuss' - a not inapt pen-name! (He also used this nom-de-plume with a series of humorous items and anecdotes which he published in the paper from time to time.)

Miller kept his connection with the Highfield club until his death in 1909, when tributes were paid to him as *'a valued chronicler of Leek cricket'*. He did not live long enough to see the healing of the breach, but remained a Highfield man until his dying day. Many local people whose politics tended towards the Liberal or the Left felt the same. My own grandfather worked as a collector for the Highfield club for a while, and would have no truck with 'the Beggars Lane lot.' There was definitely a strong political element in the split!

Matthew Henry Miller's Liberal politics were often in evidence in his column in the *Leek Times*. On one occasion he pointed out that the local Conservative MP, Charles Bill, had attempted to introduce a bill in the House of Commons *'to prohibit the sale of intoxicating liquors to persons of drunken habits'*. The bill was treated with some ridicule, when it was pointed out that its provisions would undoubtedly include some of Mr Bill's own supporters. *'As a temperance reformer, therefore, Mr. Bill has not been a brilliant success'*, commented Miller. Nevertheless, two years later, in 1895, Charles Bill, MP attempted to reintroduce his bill, and again it failed. Miller was quick to point out *'Mr Bill's fame as a legislator has remained stationary since May 1893'*, and *'it seems improbable that the innocent, impracticable proposal will mar the Government or make Mr Bill's reputation as a statesman.'*

Miller's comments on the result of a subsequent General Election were equally forthright. In the Leek Times of Saturday, July 27th, 1895 he wrote:

THE RESULT.
Just on the eve of going to press the result of the poll was declared as follows: Mr C Bill, 4705; Mr R Pearce, 4091; majority for Mr Bill, 614. We candidly confess that we are disappointed. We thought that the straightforward, honest, clean fashion with which the Liberal candidate had fought would have commended itself to a majority of the electors, but the tactics of the last contest have again prevailed. Mr Pearce, however, has come to stay, and whenever the opportunity serves he will again fight the battle of Liberalism.

Miller's prediction came true, for Pearce returned to fight the General Election in 1900, when he was again defeated by Bill. Success, however, came in 1906, when Pearce polled 5749 votes, to defeat Bill's total of 4275. Sadly, however, Miller did not live to see the excitement of 1910, when the Liberal Robert Pearce, in the second General Election of 1910, defeated the Conservative Col. Bromley Davenport by 590 votes, having narrowly lost by a mere ten votes in the earlier election.

Although he clearly wore his political heart on his sleeve, Miller was always prepared to give space in the *Leek Times* to major events involving the local Conservatives. For example, in April 1887 he gave a glowing report of the opening of the new Conservative Club at the site of the old Crown Hotel in Church Street. *'The ceremony was of such a character as will long be remembered in the annals of Conservatism in Leek, and the complimentary dinner to Mr Davenport at the Town Hall in the evening was one of the most successful gatherings which have been held in the town of Leek for many years past.'*

Harry Tichborne Davenport was MP for the Leek Division at the time, and it is interesting to note that he was also known as H T Hinckes. Following his death in March 1895, Miller paid a warm tribute to him, in glowing terms: *'During the three heavy campaigns in which he took part, viz. 1880, 1885 and 1886, he fought fairly and kept his reputation clean, and his memory will remain a pleasant one to friends and foe alike. In the language of the Moorlands, he was 'a tidy little mon', and there is a good deal of deserved admiration hidden away in the rough but affectionate phrase.'* Any newspaper should be scrupulously fair, and Miller was exemplary in this respect.

In local politics and matters concerning the government of the town, Miller was a shrewd observer and fearless critic. When the members of the new Leek Urban District Council - successors to the Improvement Commissioners - met for the first time in 1895 Miller made no attempt to hide his disapproval of the decision to exclude all reporters from the meeting, on the grounds that the business under discussion was of a private nature. He could not understand why this historic first meeting of the new council should go unreported and wrote that *'the reporters retired, not to wait in a draughty passage on a frosty night, but to more congenial quarters.'* Miller was at a loss to understand this action, since the main item of business appeared to be the election of a Chairman and Vice-chairman. With tongue in cheek he named the Chairman, John Brealey, and the Vice-chairman, R S Milner - *'exactly as we forecasted last week'*, he added.

On the issue of the proposed new Buttermarket and Fire Station Miller sided with the ratepayers who opposed the scheme: *'No one dreams of such a white elephant being thrust upon the town'*, he wrote, in his editorial of Saturday, August 15th 1896. He seized upon the point that the Local Government Board had decreed that the council had a right to build shops in conjunction with a covered market but it would go beyond its powers to erect shops in conjunction with a fire station.

The matter became a live issue in November 1895 when the Leek Urban District Council was barely a year old. Miller accused the Markets and Estates Committee of perpetrating *'a cleverer piece of special pleading* (that) *has never before marked the municipal history of any town.'* The Council, it appears, was making the point that the provision of a covered market could be easy and inexpensive, but Miller made the point that no councillor would dare face the electorate with such a proposal, but the intention was there, just the same. He referred, somewhat disparagingly, to the councillors as *'the Wise Men of the Moorlands'*, guilty of formulating *'nonsensical legislation'*.

By the autumn of 1896 the Red Lion Hotel had become something of a political football in the matter. In his aforementioned editorial of August 15th 1896 Miller made the point that that the Urban District Council had bought the Red Lion for the purposes of a general market, and if it were not to be used in what he saw as a flawed and doomed scheme it should be sold. Miller was very outspoken on the manner of the sale, pointing out that the property should have been put to public auction. On October 24th 1896 he made the point that the Council had not employed the reasonable and usual means to ascertain the real market price of the property. He went on to say:

When we hear of nearly two thousand pounds being given for an obscure beerhouse on the eastern side of Leek, and of three thousand pounds for a modest beerhouse on the western, surely it was not extravagant to suppose that a fully-licensed family and commercial hotel, with extensive stabling and outbuildings, situate in a commanding position in the Market Place (adjoining the site of the new public butter-market about to be erected by the Leek Urban District Council), and doing a large commercial as well as local and market business, would realise an amount large enough to dwarf the figures we have given. In any event, a transaction would have been fair, square, and above board, and in every possible way would have absolved the Council from the blame of not adopting the ordinary method of selling a property for which there was every reason to believe there would be a stiff fight. As it is, it will never be known whether three thousand pounds was a high, moderate, or ridiculously low price.

By that time Miller had clearly accepted the inevitability of the Buttermarket, but he was not finished with his criticism. A few weeks later, on October 24th 1896, he published a letter in the *Leek Times*, written in local dialect and supposedly from a reader. However, one wonders if this was Miller himself, using this method to express his strong feelings on the issue.

TH' RED LION JOB
(To th' Heditur o' th' LEEK TOIMES)
MESTER HEDITUR - That piece yo put in th' Leek Toimes abite th' sale o'th Red Lion, is a heye oppenur: it reminds me of an ould sayin' that sum folk stale a hoss out o'th feelt, wheer others darner look o'er th' edge. An' its pratty plain that there's bin some gillory abite th' bisness autogether. If th' Britannia pub's worth 3500 pound, ony body's sense ull tell 'em that th' Red Lion's woth 500 pound moer at least. Whoose faut is it that its bin soud, nay, gen away so chep? They are a rum lot, are our district councillors. When they want to buy ony land, they gin about twice as mich for it as its woth: but when they want fur sell they almost gin it away. If a workin' mon has to carry halfe a donkey load o' brick up a two story ladder, an' he happens to stond still t' three minutes to rest hissen a bit, he's caud a hidle beggar. An' if some chaps hav' getten th' street up to mak a drain, an' happen to put their pick or shovel down to streiten their backs a bit, they's caud lazy scamps and ar toud

they desarve th' sack. Bur Mester, awm shure aw'th time wasted by aw'th kommisshuners men put together for restin' their backs an' leetin' their pipes, for monny an' monny a yeer, wudner cost th' ratepayers hauf so mich as our ekonomikal councillurs hav' thrown away o'er this Red Lion biseness.
A WORKIN' MON
Leek, Nov. 10, 1896

There was another scheme to construct a new access road from Market Street, that would, it was said, afford a better view of the north front of the Town Hall. Miller's comments were very scathing: *'Now who, in the name of common sense desires to see the north wall of a monument of unsuccessful speculation'*. He went on to say, *'The present scheme includes the building of some new shops. Let this be opposed tooth and nail... There are already too many shops and too many shopkeepers, and is it reasonable that public money should be spent to provide further opposition and competition?'*

This is, of course, a common plea whenever new schemes are suggested, and indeed the same kind of comments were being made about new schemes in the mid-20th century! Nevertheless, Miller stuck to his guns, and used his column in the *Leek Times* to urge everyone to attend the forthcoming Public Meeting on the issue, even though their views would probably be disregarded. His column concluded with the comment: *'It is the duty of everyone who objects to the town being saddled with the white elephant of a covered market to attend the meeting and stoutly oppose any proposition tending in that direction.'*

The covered market was, of course, ultimately built in 1897. Matthew Henry Miller, it appears, was sometimes the champion of lost causes!

Whatever we may feel about Miller's opinions and ideas expressed in his editorial comments, he was certainly an able and erudite chronicler of the changing scene. History can be very grateful to him for providing very full reports of the meetings of the Commissioners, and later the Leek Urban District Council and other local bodies. These were almost verbatim and provide the historian with a unique and detailed record of the way in which the affairs of the town were conducted, and an insight into the personalities and motives of those involved. A hundred years on, we can judge these men by their decisions and the effect, for good or ill, on the town. Miller was always scrupulously fair in giving unbiased coverage to all shades of opinion in the debates and reserved his own feelings for his editorials. Thus, from the columns of the *Leek Times*, we can form a clear and balanced impression of the working of local government in developing town of Leek.

Miller was a master of the use of hyperbole. The *Leek Times* of Saturday, October 18th 1884 carried a very full account of the opening of the Nicholson Institute, but Miller's best rhetorical style was reserved for his editorial column:

The Ides of March have come and gone, but they have brought no disaster as they did to Caesar, but have rather witnessed the inauguration of an event of happiest omen. The beautiful building, with its still more beautiful contents, is opened, and the Nicholson Institute henceforth takes its place amongst those other beneficent gifts of worthy men who go honour to their country and their countrymen. It stands in our midst, a proud monument of an unselfish desire to benefit and bless. Kind hearts are more than coronets. Kings and potentates may confer titles, but they cannot create noble men - noble deeds alone can do that, and without them the pride of blood is a fiction and a farce. Envy is compelled to slink about and hide its hateful and contemptible form in the presence of an event like that on Thursday, and all good men and noble natures rally round him who generously seeks the happiness of others by the sacrifice of self. Gathered about Mr Nicholson were men of all shades of political opinion and belief, and the rich and the poor were there, and all these discordant elements were united into a harmonious whole by the magical wand of a good deed. And the deed is wise as well as good; for generations after Mr Nicholson has put off his harness from the battlefield of life he has fought so well, men shall rise up to call him blessed... But, as Emerson affirms, it is what are called the 'masses' that are our misery and our danger, as well as our disgrace. We do not want a mass of festering ignorance in our midst, but a multitude of bright-eyed, rosy-cheeked happy individuals, and if we must have these we must have education, and culture, and wisdom, and what can act more powerfully in this direction than such noble benefactions as the Nicholson Institute. We want to level, as far as possible, the terrible gulfs that separate class from class, not by dragging down the lofty, but by lifting up the lowly... It was a wise and graceful thing for Mrs Cruso, whose kindness of heart and wide-spread sympathies are known and respected of all, to take out the first book, and have her name inscribed as the first borrower. We cannot better conclude than by quoting the words of the lamented Prince Leopold: 'Those men who with great wealth at their disposal elect to spend it in mere sumptuousness and luxury, are repaid indeed by admiration from certain persons, of a certain kind. But far richer is the reward of those who, after spending what is needed to maintain with dignity their place in society, devote the remainder towards furthering the happiness of their fellow-men. Far off generations shall rise up and call such men blessed, and the names they leave behind them shall be ranked with such names as those of Peabody in London, of Owens or of Mason at Manchester, or Firth at Sheffield.' We may now add, and of Nicholson at Leek.

Matthew Henry Miller's sense of humour was often apparent in his writings. He often used the plural pronoun 'we', so often used for 'I' by monarchs, but also used by editors. The demise of a rival newspaper in January 1896 produced this somewhat droll editorial comment, which was headed THE DEAR DEPARTED:

It is our sorrowful duty this week to report a death in the family of newspapers, at the early age of three years and nine months. We refer to the Staffordshire Post. For some time past the deceased had been in delicate health, and in spite of constant care and costly attention, it passed away, on Tuesday night, arm-in-arm with the old year, to that bourne from which newspapers rarely return. By those who knew it best, its memory will be held dear; but those who had not the privilege of its close acquaintance will rejoice greatly that its end was peace. De mortuis nil nisi bonum.

Perhaps Miller did not fully endorse the principles that the *Staffordshire Post* stood for - or maybe he saw it as the removal of a rival to his own newspaper, a competitor for sales, and hence his livelihood!

But perhaps Miller's sense of humour was best demonstrated in his occasional column of brief items which he collected under the heading 'Week by Week'. Even in the issue of *Leek Times* dated Saturday, January 26th 1901 - printed as a black-bordered edition commemorating the death of Queen Victoria - he could not resist a humorous anecdote on the subject of the late Queen:

It is difficult to believe that even in the remotest corner of Morridge that there was either man, woman or child who had not heard of the late Queen. And yet it seems to be so. On Wednesday, a country woman remarked to her family that the Queen was dead. 'Who's that, mother', said a girl of six or seven winters, 'somebody yer wesh for?'

Another example, typical of the usual content, appeared in a later edition: A famous pianist, almost as celebrated for the length of his hair as for his music, purchased a penny paper from a newsboy whose face was dirty beyond the ordinary dirtiness. The pianist paid for it with a threepenny-bit and the boy had no change. Said the musician, *'Go and spend it on getting your face washed.'* The boy plunged his hand in his pocket, pulled out the threepenny-bit, and shoved it into his customer's hand. *'Ere, guvnor'*, he said, *'you keep the fruppence, and git yer 'air cut'.*

Miller usually signed his column by using his pseudonym 'Kweer Kuss'. In other columns, headed 'Epitome of News', and 'Miscellaneous Intelligence', Miller collected brief items of news from far and wide, some whimsical, some humorous, some obscure, and under the heading 'Bits of Fun' he published rather more jokey items, although it has to be said that the standard of humour in these was not usually very high. This type of journalism is still used today in the more popular tabloids.

However Miller's propensity for gathering together a variety of unrelated items from many sources would stand him in good stead when he turned his hand to publishing the books on Leek's history for which his name will always be remembered.

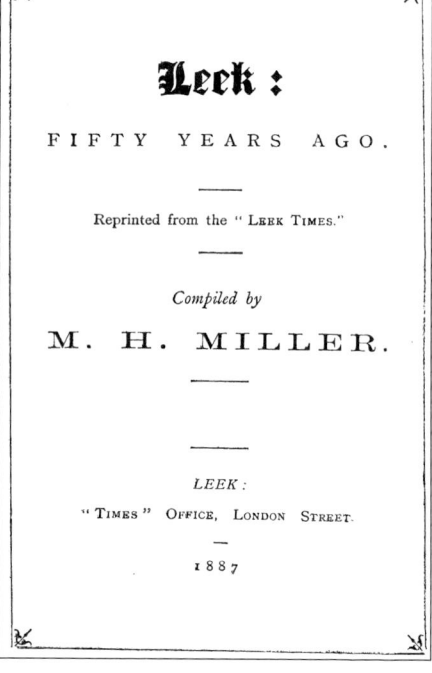

"THE ABSTRACTS AND BRIEF CHRONICLES OF THE TIMES."
—*Shakespeare.*

Olde Leeke:

Historical,

Biographical, Anecdotal, and Archæological.

Edited by

MATTHEW HENRY MILLER, M.I.J.

Reprinted from the "Leek Times."

LEEK:
PRINTED AND PUBLISHED AT THE "TIMES" OFFICE.
1891.

Leek :

FIFTY YEARS AGO.

Reprinted from the "LEEK TIMES."

Compiled by

M. H. MILLER.

LEEK :
"TIMES" OFFICE, LONDON STREET.
1887

Thirteen
'OLDE LEEKE' AND ALL THAT

AS EDITOR OF A LOCAL NEWSPAPER Matthew Henry Miller was in a unique position to collect and preserve printed records and memorabilia from bygone years. His contribution to the recorded history of his adopted town is immeasurable, but he was not an academic historian. He did not attempt to interpret history, he simply recorded items of historical interest, some trite, some commonplace, some hearsay, some mere gossip, some whimsical, some fanciful, some downright unreal and conceptual. It is left to historians who have followed after him to sift through his vast supply of printed material, but there are rich pickings for the diligent searcher - some nuggets among the dross, some gold in the clay. It is on this basis that Miller's contribution to local history will be judged to be invaluable.

Most towns of any size seem to have had their Victorian historian, usually someone from the business or professional classes who had the time and energy to apply themselves to the task of recording the history of the place. These were the days when records were not as well archived as they are today, and there were no electronic aids to the recording of local history. The researcher had to rely on much oral evidence, and such limited records as might be available. Many of these would be family papers, still in private hands or solicitors' offices. Consequently, the well-connected local person stood the best chance of gaining access to original documentary material. Victorian Leek was fortunate to have two such men: John Sleigh and Matthew Henry Miller.

John Sleigh, Barrister at Law, was the pioneer, his first *History of Leek* being published in 1862. This was an octavo (about A5) edition of some 312 pages, printed by Robert Nall of Leek. It contained few illustrations, but took a broad look at Leek's history across the years. A substantial chapter on geology by Thomas Wardle, occupying about one third of the book, completed the volume. In 1884 he published the second edition of his history - a much larger, lavishly-illustrated volume, which included the coats-of-arms of notable local families in full colour and detailed genealogical charts. Fine, engraved plates of local scenery, buildings and personalities were printed on high quality paper, and for the text a heavyweight, deckle-edged paper was used. This handsome volume was published in three limited editions, each in a different binding and individually numbered. A total of 851 copies were produced, of which 15 were printed on hand made paper and bound in calf leather. A further 234 copies were printed on hand made paper and bound in a light brown leatherette grained bookcloth, and the remaining 602 copies were bound in a grey, smooth bookcloth. Each subscriber received his own personal copy.

Matthew Henry Miller gave a generous full page in the *Leek Times* of Saturday, May 3rd 1884 to a verbatim report of a lecture by William Challinor on the subject of John Sleigh's new *History of Leek*, given under the auspices of the St. Luke's Young Men's Society at the Temperance Hall, on Friday, April 25th. The meeting, presided over by Rev. W. Beresford, attracted a large audience.

Challinor, in his opening remarks, stated that, over the past twenty years, his friend Mr Sleigh *'had been accumulating a great mass of information from the British Museum and from many public and private sources... the result was a beautiful volume, a copy of which was on the table, and which he thought they would agree with him did Mr. Sleigh infinite credit, and was a great credit to the publishers, Messrs. Bemrose of Derby, and was in point of fact a monument of research and able investigation, and was perhaps the best local history in England'.*

Challinor's lecture was spiced with his own humorous anecdotes, which provoked laughter from his audience from time to time. His closing remarks, as an impression of some interesting aspects of Leek's history, are worth recording, and we can be grateful to Matthew Henry Miller for allowing space in his newspaper for them to be recorded in full:

I would observe that some often speak of the good old times, but I think on the whole, the new times are better, considering all things. I remember in my early days seeing bull baits and bear baits in the town, when the poor bull, fastened by a long chain to a long stake driven in the Market Place, was torn at by ferocious bull dogs, and surrounded by a crowd hardly less ferocious, and among them a few gentlemen, who, as a bystander once remarked to me, seemed stronger in the arm than in the head. (Laughter)

I remember the stocks, through which the legs of drunken men and other offenders were fastened, and which were by the side of Mill street, opposite Clerk's Bank. I remember dreadful fights between men in the streets on market days, and an old sexton a number of years ago told me how women from Scalding Bank and Quarrel Hole near Mill street used to be taken to be ducked in a ducking stool in the Churnet, because they were supposed to be rather vicious and noisy, but, as you are aware, we have no vixens now-a-days - (laughter) - at any rate no such mode of punishment - but instead of these we have Bands of Hope, one of the hopeful signs of the day, reading rooms, and amateur theatricals, illustrating that 'All the World's a Stage', and most young lawyers in it turning players. (Laughter)

We have with the aid of our friend Mr Ritchie (whom I hear beneath me), Mr Farrow, and others, a great improvement in our sanitary arrangements, and in certain departments of health, and the beautiful springs from under the Roches have been brought in healthful abundance through the town.

Locomotion by railways is cheaper and swifter than the old coaches were; and in reference to this subject, I am glad to say that I attended and took part at a meeting in London some months since, at which the North Stafford Company determined to make a loop line a little beyond Macclesfield, which will give a better route for the Potteries and Leek to Buxton and that part of the country. As regards the buildings in the town they are no longer 'poor and mostly thatched' as Blome says they were about 200 years ago, and although we have lost the Black's Head and several timbered buildings of that description, we have instead Mr.

Sleigh's fine medieval-like houses in St. Edward street, recently built; and within the last few months we have seen rising among us like some new creation, Mr. Nicholson's dome-topp'd tower and institute, erected by one who, rising from the body of the people, has been able by the right hand of his industry and strength of will, to erect a worthy memorial for the benefit and improvement of the people (cheers), where newspapers and books and works of art are to be enjoyed in future by the townspeople, without money and without price, and among the best books there, certainly one of those that will be most prized by Moorlanders, I am sure you are agreed with me, will be my friend Mr. John Sleigh's recent edition of his 'History of the Ancient Parish of Leek' to which I have referred this evening. (Cheers)

I will now conclude with a few lines apropos to the subject matter of this evening:

> What varied scenes surround,
> Our Moorland town's approaches,
> Hill, valley, fertile ground,
> The heather and the Roches.
>
> Wide Cheshire's level plains,
> And honeysuckled hedges,
> Fair Rudyard's lake, that hides
> The wild duck in its sedges.
>
> And you bleak Morridge hill,
> From whence the distant Wrekin,
> Looks a small dome-like cloud,
> From the horizon peeping.
>
> In the dense forest shade,
> That once the town surrounded,
> The grisly boar has strayed
> And wolf and fox abounded.
>
> The spotted stag has stood,
> And seen his antlers quiver,
> In the pellucid flood,
> Of our now dye-stained river.
>
> Streets that now feel the blast

Of many a rude north-wester,
Have seen King Edward pass,
And mail-clad Earls of Chester.

The Abbot's white monked train,
Prince Charlie's Highland pladdie,
And following in his wake,
The kilted soldier laddie.

And some were greeted fair,
And some the people jeered at,
The last though pelted sair,
The Moorland lassies peered at.

The Abbey ruins lie,
Shorn of their ancient glory,
But the old Church towers high,
Majestic, grey and hoary.

Each house with varied style,
By contrast though arouses,
Bank, Roe Buck, and just built,
Sleigh's medieval houses.

Proud doth th' Art Temple stand,
Of Nicholson our neighbour,
By industry's right hand,
Reared for the sons of labour.

And last not least, our guide,
Through many an ancient mystery,
Sleigh's last historic work,
England's best local history.

The meeting ended, as did many of Challinor's lectures, with the singing of 'Auld Lang Syne' and there was a choral item during the interval. Miller's complete record of the lecture gives us an insight into Challinor's technique as a lecturer, for he was certainly able to hold the attention of an audience, and his grasp of local history was impressive - although, of course, the railway developments he referred to did not materialise in the way envisaged at the meeting of the railway company he had attended.

It is likely that it was Leek's eminent Victorian historian, John Sleigh, who first stimulated Miller's lively interest in local history. Sleigh sent fragments of local and county history to Miller, and thus he was caused to take an interest in the past life of his adopted town. He published substantial selections of these paragraphs in a column in the *Leek Times*, and as a consequence, a modest little book of 168 pages was issued under the title of *Leek Fifty Years Ago*. This was priced at one shilling, and as it appeared in 1887 its contents reflected a wide variety of images of life in Leek at the start of Queen Victoria's reign. Miller chose not to include any introduction to the material, nor did he attempt to interpret the items. They are not classified in any way, and this hotch-potch selection stands or falls on its own merits. Nevertheless, it is an invaluable contribution to the annals of local history, for much of the material is not available in any other form.

With such wide-ranging contents, it is difficult to be selective, but three examples will serve to illustrate the range and scope of items in this remarkable little book - one historical, one anecdotal and one humorous.

A small personal memory of working as a child in the local silk industry in the 1830s is recorded under the heading JUVENILE LABOUR:

A lady correspondent says: 'Fifty years ago, when our gracious Majesty ascended the throne, I was six years of age, and worked a piecer for Mr Anthony Ward. My hours were from six o'clock in the morning until half-past seven in the evening (Saturdays included), and I was paid 1/3 per week if I was a good girl and minded my work. In the afternoon I was wrapped up in a shawl by the tenter and put to bed in a bobbin-box and allowed to sleep for an hour. How happy and contented the children of today ought to be, with their school, short hours, and better wages! I often think how swiftly the years have rolled away in favour of the working classes.

There is no reason to doubt the authenticity of this item,

which dates from a time before the hours worked by children were controlled.

Miller had developed an ear for local stories, and Leek has always produced an abundance of such. Like many oral traditions, a story never loses anything in the telling, and the following could well be an example:

OLD TOMMY GRIFFIN
Fighting used to be a very common occurrence in the Market Place on market days, and the belligerents were often marched off to the 'Hole' under the old Town Hall. Tommy Griffin arrested one man for the offence, and took him to the Hole, but after fumbling a good deal found he had left the keys at home. Turning to his prisoner, he said, 'Stay here awhile till I fetch the keys,' the silly remark eliciting loud laughter from the numerous bystanders. Upon consideration he found it best to wait for Billy Alcock, his deputy.

Tommy Griffin and Billy Alcock were obviously employed as constables who would have the responsibility of policing the town. The story confirms the presence of cells, or lock-ups, beneath the old Town Hall at the bottom of the Market Place.

An example of Miller's sense of humour, and his ear for a good story, is illustrated by an item headed *NEDDY EARLS AND THE CHURNET*:

It is a very long time ago since Neddy Earls ventured into the River Churnet, and Neddy himself never forgot it. Boasting one day of his ability to swim and otherwise amuse himself whilst in water, he was induced at last to demonstrate his aquatic abilities. Loth enough but unable to escape, Neddy took off his clothes, and very gently put in one foot. Gasping slightly he inserted the other and then got knee-deep. 'Up to me knees and non frightened,' said Neddy. Advancing slowly the water soon reached his breast, but Neddy, puffing and blowing, repeated 'Up to me arms and non frightened.' Then the stream reached his chin, and still he answered with a sigh, 'Up to me yead and non frightened.'

The moment, however, the water reached his mouth, he screamed, 'O'eryead, o'eryead; frightened; pu' me out, pu' me out!'

A nice story, neatly told! Matthew Henry Miller had the talent to become a humorous writer of distinction! And he continued to include such items in the *Leek Times* long after his little book was published. The following little item appeared in the issue of 14th November, 1896:

In a commercial room not five hundred miles from the Old Church, a young bagman tried to be funny at the expense of an old gentleman with a bald head. For some time the latter ignored the insolence of his assailant, who had imbibed well if not wisely. At last, however, he turned round and said, 'Yes, I am bald, and no man knows the fact better than I do, but I would rather have it so than be in possession of such a head of hair that you have.' 'Why,' was the reply, 'there are not many better roofed in than I am.' 'That is quite true,' was the calm response, 'but it reminds me of a daisy.' 'What, reminds you of a daisy! What do you mean?' The old gentleman for some time refused to gratify the curiosity of his questioner, but the other persons present having become interested, he gave his explanation. 'Well, if you insist, I will tell you. The reason, young man, why your head of hair is like a daisy, is because it grows upon a soft green sod!' During the roar of laughter that followed the rude fellow left the room in search of his bed - and more respect for bald heads.

Another sharp little item, from the Leek Times of 24th October, 1896, would find a place in any anthology of humour:

Monday was a gala day in the lives of a happy couple who toed the mark at All Saints' Church. The gay bridegroom, who carried without a blush the sixty-six winters that have passed over his head, gallantly led his blushing bride, his junior by sixteen years, to the altar, where the knot was well and truly tied, the consent of his mother having been previously obtained. Amidst the hearty good wishes of not a few, and a generous supply of confetti, rice, and old slippers, the happy pair drove away, en route for Shoobridge Street, where the honeymoon will be spent.

'The best way, it seems, a deep sorrow to smother
For the loss of a wife - is to marry another.'

Whatever else he may have achieved during his time in

Leek, Matthew Henry Miller will always be remembered for his *Olde Leeke*. The original volume, sub-titled *'Historical, Biographical, Anecdotal and Archaeological'*, was printed at the Leek Times office in Leek, and published in 1891. (The book also has the imprint of Thomas Mark, printer, Leek.) Miller dedicated the volume to the Earl of Macclesfield, Lord of the Manor of Leek and Lowe, and it was sold to subscribers. The names on the list of subscribers, printed at the end of the book, numbered 269, and included many of Leek's prominent citizens as well as names from further afield, who would no doubt have had some contact with the town. There were two names from abroad: A J Barrat, of Balaclava, Russia, and John Keats, of Bagnall Hall and Paris. The Earl of Macclesfield is listed, with his address: Shirbourne Castle, Tetsworth, Oxfordshire.

In his preface, Miller acknowledged the help he had received from John Sleigh, W S Brough and the Rev. W Beresford, who had supplied much of the material, and W R Kean and A Mosley of the Leek School of Art, for illustrations. The success of *Leek Fifty Years Ago* had given Miller the spur to produce *Olde Leeke* in a much more lavish and expanded form. Like its predecessor, *Olde Leeke* contained a wide range of articles, arranged in no particular order or logical sequence.

Such was the success of the book that, nine years later, in 1900, Miller was encouraged to produce a second volume, as more material had become available, mainly through his lively column in the *Leek Times,* and with help from John Sleigh, Rev W Beresford, Sir Thomas Wardle, W S Brough, P L Brocklehurst, Rev Gustavus Sneyd and Thomas Cooper. Artwork was provided by Lucy Nixon, G R Rigby, D E Larner and the late W R Kean, of Leek School of Art. This volume was dedicated to Philip Lancaster Brocklehurst of Swythamley. The number of subscribers had increased to 379, mainly from the Leek area, but from as far afield as London, Sheffield, Kent, Manchester, Nottingham, Bedford, Bristol, Exmouth, Southport and Dublin. The volume included the 1838 map of Leek, copied in 1899 by R

Ewan. This was a facsimile of the original, the only variations being that Ewan omitted the hachuring which indicated the hills, and he used his own style of lettering.

Given their shortcomings, Miller's books have provided a rich source of information to local historians for many years, for much of the information contained therein is not available in any other form. The social history of Leek in Victorian times comes alive in the writings of Matthew Henry Miller. Like a magpie gathering his treasures, if he thought an item was worth including, Miller would include it. We should perhaps be grateful that he did not always attempt to interpret his material.

In a modest way, Miller also produced a number of booklets and pamphlets, mainly reprinted from the pages of *Leek Times*. These included an obituary booklet of 14 pages on the silk manufacturer, Stephen Goodwin (1888), a 22-page publication on the silk industry by L B Bernhart (1893) and an advertising pamphlet for the Oddfellows Association (1893). His sense of humour was illustrated by the publication in 1889 of a booklet entitled *Shakespeare and other on the Leek Commissioners* in which he wittily attached well-known quotations from literature to individual Improvement Commissioners, some of which were rather pointed! And, perhaps something of an oddity, in 1882 he produced a 64-page booklet, reprinted from the *Leek Times*, entitled *Cetewayo, his experiences in England*. The authorship of the article was attributed to 'Sir Kalm Obsahvah, KGC' - perhaps another of Miller's sideways swipes at history, the Zulu leader being the foil, in this instance!

Matthew Henry Miller's contribution to the society of Victorian Leek was very far-reaching. In shaping and reflecting public opinion he used his newspaper and his press experience to good effect. His interest in and promotion of the history of his adopted town found a permanent record in his books and publications. And his talents as a public entertainer, humourist and elocutionist gave pleasure to a great many people. Along with other local personalities he was a regular performer in the old Penny Readings which were held at the Temperance Hall in Union Street on Saturday evenings. These usually consisted of readings of straight poems, many drawn from classical sources and English literature, and monologues, some tragic, some serious and others humorous.

Miller also performed on the amateur stage with the old Leek Volunteer Theatricals, one of several dramatic societies which existed at the time. The company performed plays from the classical repertoire and in an article in the *Leek News* of December 1935, the writer William Warrington (under his pen-name of 'The Small Boy in the Market Place', and himself involved in amateur theatricals) commented: *'Mr M H Miller, editor of the Leek Times appeared as an amateur actor, and, if he was as entertaining as he was in private life, I should think he was very good.'*

Such was the reputation of the Birmingham exile who came to Leek and made the town his home. Matthew Henry Miller died on 25th October, 1909.

THE ITINERANT TAX INSPECTOR

TAKING OVER, AS IT WERE, the baton in the Edwardian era, when it came, the new chronicler was, like Matthew Henry Miller, an 'import' to the town. William Henry Nithsdale was a Scotsman, employed by the Inland Revenue as a local tax inspector. The nature of his work was such that he was sent to a local town where he spent only a few years before being moved

An iconic picture of Nithsdale from his book *In the Highlands of Staffordshire.*

on to a different location. He was not allowed time to put down roots, and such men were always 'on the move'.

Nithsdale was the agent for the Inland Revenue in Leek during the Edwardian years. He arrived about 1904 and was gone by 1910, but during this short time he developed a deep love for the district, and he was able to harness his twin talents of writing and photography to leave a lasting testimony of that love.

His work was encapsulated in a little book entitled *In the Highlands of Staffordshire* published in 1906, and you can almost hear his lilting Scottish brogue coming through in his delightful little travelogue. When the book was first published Leek was a prosperous little township, still basking in the glory of its Victorian 'golden years', and he has given us a vivid, lively and racy account of his impressions gained during excursions awheel and afoot throughout the area, usually by pony and trap or by bicycle. The book is enlivened by a selection of his own photographs, for he was a talented cameraman, always with an eye for the unusual. Many of his photographs were made into picture postcards and produced commercially for sale to visitors to the area.

Nithsdale's book gives us a witty and keenly observed account of life in Leek and the Moorlands in a bygone age. There are fine descriptions of Leek's market day, the working of a silk mill and the Leek and Manifold Valley Light Railway, as well as impressions of Rudyard and the local countryside, spiced with stories of local 'characters', for he had a keen ear for a good story and a sharp eye for a good photograph.

For his record of the passing scene during the Edwardian years, at a time when few others took up their pens, we can be very grateful to William Henry Nithsdale - our itinerant tax inspector.

Fourteen
A MAN OF MANY PARTS

FEW HUMAN DWELLING-PLACES are so remote and lonely as Highhurst, and no one out of love with solitude would care to live there long. But the inmates at Highhurst come of a race which loves solitude, and Highhurst has never harboured other than its own race. The house itself and the farm buildings are excellent for their purpose and admirably suited to the situation in which they are placed. Once you have ascended from Bleak and gained the edge of the moor, Highhurst may be seen some three of four miles distant on top of the next and higher spur - the last southern spur of the Pennine range. Between the moor and the ridge upon which Highhurst stands, in a deep and narrow valley, is the source of that strange river which after making its way through the gorge, at length reaches the limestone. There it sinks beneath the surface of the earthcrust, to emerge again, after pursuing its mysterious underground course, near to its confluence with the river Dove. Across the valley there are several footpaths, but only one road by which Highhurst may be reached. This road is of such a character that no bicycle nor motor car could make its way upon it, and no driver would risk his neck and his horse by driving either up or down it. It is a mountainous road, its surface a mass of loose stones, and it is impassable after a fall of snow or in heavy rain. Communication with the world therefore is but intermittent. In the direction of the old market town of Bleak, the nearest railway station is eight miles away: on the other side there is no station nearer than St. Anne's Well which is not less than twelve miles distant.

So begins a remarkable novel by a remarkable man - *Life's Desert Way* by Kineton Parkes. This descriptive opening passage paints a familiar picture in words to anyone who knows the moorland area between Leek (*Bleak*) and Buxton. The countryside of the area around the Roches, Morridge and Axe Edge, where the River Manifold (referred to as 'that strange river') rises is well described. It sets the scene for a story located in the Staffordshire Moorlands area, written by a man who was not a native of the district, but who had clearly developed a good understanding of the local countryside, and a literary style of the many erstwhile novelists of the day who turned their hands to writing, but who were never destined to achieve national recognition. Did he, however, see himself as another regional novelist, following in the footsteps of Arnold Bennett, to whom he dedicated one of his novels? The literary styles of the day were clearly much in evidence in his fictional writings.

William Kineton Parkes was born at Aston Manor, Warwickshire, on January 18th 1865, the son of William and Ann Parkes. The 1881 British Census reveals that he was then living with his parents at the family home, 10 North Brook Street, Birmingham. Kineton then had three younger brothers, Frederick, Ernest and Thomas, who were still at school, and two younger sisters, Bertha and Florence.

From this solid, middle-class background, young Kineton was educated at King Edward VI Grammar School and Mason's College, Birmingham. On completing his education, he took up a position as a merchant's clerk at an office in the city, where no doubt (to preview one of his future Gilbertian roles), he *'copied all the letters in a big round hand.'*

He had a lively and intelligent mind, and became keenly interested in music, the arts and literature, with a particular leaning towards the history of art. Working in the city, he would be aware of the world of the provincial theatre, where drama, opera and musical productions would be performed regularly. Science subjects also exercised his intellect, and he developed a good working knowledge of botany and physics.

The Nicholson Institute with its library and school of art, had quickly made its mark on the local community, fulfilling the growing interest in the arts by the people of Leek, seeking an escape from the humdrum daily round of factory work. The music and drama societies in the town were enjoying good support and there were enthusiastic audiences at the various drama productions staged at the Temperance Hall. In the cultural sense, Victorian Leek was a very lively town, with a wide range of events taking place on a regular basis. There was no shortage of cultural activities for those who wished to take part in them.

It may be said that Victorian Leek needed a personality of the calibre of Kineton Parkes. The town that had rubbed shoulders with the Pre-Raphaelite movement through its links with William Morris and his association with Thomas Wardle was fertile ground for someone like Parkes. The ambitious and imaginative Queen Anne and Victorian Gothic styles of architecture of the Sugdens had created an attractive townscape in which the silk industry was flourishing. In a sense, Leek was made for Parkes, and Parkes was made for Leek. Furthermore, he was an incurable romantic.

He married Margaret Anne Simpson, daughter of Daniel Simpson, a retired tobacco manufacturer at the New Court Congregational Chapel, Islington on 2 September 1889. He described his profession as 'journalist' at the time. They were to have two sons - Gabriel Kineton, born in Birmingham in 1891, and Maxwell Kineton, born in Leek in 1892.

Music and drama involved people from all social classes Leek. Choirs in particular broke through the class barriers, for those participating included factory workers, clerks, shop workers, managers, employers and the professions. Anyone possessing a good voice and sufficient enthusiasm could take their place in a choir and many came through the chapel and church choirs, which were numerous at the time. It was not so easy, however, for the working classes to break into the dramatic societies, where leading parts in plays or operettas were usually taken by the more well-to-do, who would have the means, the ability and the time for such things.

The Nicholson Institute became a great centre for cultural activities freely available to the people of Leek, and it was always run on sound business principles. The first to hold the post of Librarian and Curator at the Nicholson Institute was William Hall, from 1884 to 1889. He was appointed by a committee of local business and professional men, under the chairmanship of John Robinson, JP.

The Public Libraries Act was adopted on November 3rd 1887, and the local authority became more involved. The Leek Improvement Commissioners appointed William Challinor, Henry Davenport, Thomas Shaw, John Ward, Thomas Wardle and Robert Wright, with the addition of Joshua Oldfield Nicholson, Arthur Nicholson, Frederick Eastwood and John Robinson to form a Public Library Committee. This committee was responsible for the entire running of the Institute.

Following William Hall in 1889 this committee appointed Angus McCleod to the post of Librarian and Curator. He stayed for only two years. William Kineton Parkes was appointed in 1891 at which time the Institute was governed by John Robinson, JP as President and John Hall, JP as Chairman.

Kineton Parkes was just 26 when he came to Leek. How would this personable young man fit into the solid, middle class, society of Leek? And how would they react to him? He had something of the 'angry young man' about him, and even showed himself as a bit of a rebel at times. Nevertheless, he would remain in Leek for 21 years, until 1912, taking the Nicholson Institute into the 20th century.

His first impact was upon the running of the Nicholson Institute itself. The range of classes and subjects taught expanded rapidly under his initial guidance, and by 1896 the teaching staff, full and part-time was as follows:

A.P. Basher - Script shorthand and typewriting
L.B. Bernhart - French
Ralph Bott - Pitman's shorthand, algebra, etc.
William Craigmile - Head of School of Art
W.H. Eaton - Teacher, School of Art

P.H.V. Hammersley - Hon. lecturer on ambulance and sick nursing
S. Hunt - Instructor in woodwork
Lucy Nixon - Teacher, School of Art
Kineton Parkes - Botany, physiography, physics, etc.
Harry Phillips - Photography
Howard Ridding - Chemistry, dyeing, etc.
Margaret Sant - Cooking and laundry work
Emily Smith - Dressmaking
J.J. Sykes - Mathematics, Latin
George Tudor - English grammar, book-keeping etc.
(J J Sykes also served as the master of the Leek Grammar School.)

The wide-ranging syllabus of subjects also included classes in botany, building construction, geography, history, leather work, machine construction and drawing, metal work, modelling in clay and plaster casting, ornament and design, wood carving and work in brass and copper - a good blend of art and craft, business and practical subjects. By 1898 classes in gardening and pianoforte tuition had been added.

A number of the lecturers and tutors remained with Kineton Parkes throughout his stay in Leek. William Craigmile continued as head of the School of Art, and with Parkes made a formidable and influential partnership. There is much evidence to suggest that Parkes, whilst possessing a good sense of humour, had a strong personality and did not suffer fools gladly. He may sometimes have appeared curt and brusque, but he was a perfectionist with a keen desire to 'get things done'. If this meant getting his own way, that was how he worked.

Nor was he slow to chase up unpaid bills, and even overdue donations. It was the custom to present prizes for effort to students who had done well, and to cover the cost of these, usually books, an appeal was made to manufacturers and businesses, and if any promised payments were late he was not slow to drop a short reminder to the person concerned.

Like many of his Victorian contemporaries, Kineton Parkes

appears to have been a man of boundless energy. In addition to his duties at the Nicholson Institute, he found time to write many books and pamphlets, contribute articles to learned journals and periodicals, and edit other works. His broad range of interests is illustrated by the wide variety of this work. In 1887 he published a 31-page essay on Thomas Carlyle and a 16-page pamphlet on individualism in art. In 1888 he followed this with another booklet entitled Shelley's Faith, its development and relativity. This was privately printed, and only 25 copies were produced on hand-made paper. He was a Shelley devotee, for that same year he produced another booklet on Shelley's Revolt of Islam for the Birmingham Branch of the Shelley Society. This was printed on Whatman paper, and limited to 30 copies. These small, limited editions laid the emphasis on quality rather than quantity.

Parkes clearly had an interest in the Pre-Raphaelites, for in 1889 he produced a 52-page book on the movement, published in London by Reeves and Turner. *The Painter Poets*, in the Canterbury Poets series, was selected and edited, with an introduction and notes by Kineton Parkes. This was a 256-page book, published in 1890, in London. He was also joint editor of *Igdrasil*, a monthly magazine of literature, art and social philosophy, largely devoted to Ruskin's works.

The Leek Press was a venture in which Parkes was involved. This was set up to produce specialist papers, usually on art or literature, printed locally by Charles Kirkham. The first in the series was *The Relation of Art to Education and Social Life* by Walter Crane (1892), again, a quality limited edition on hand-made paper. Crane became a president of the Nicholson Institute, and created some designs for the interior decoration of the William Morris Labour Church on Overton Bank Leek (Quaker Meeting House). Parkes would find in Crane a kindred spirit, and the association was formed in his first year in Leek.

Another Leek Press pamphlet of 23 pages was an article by Parkes on *The Libraries of Paris*, reprinted from *The Athenaeum* magazine (1893). A much more ambitious project from the Leek

Press was *The Library Review and Record of Current Literature*, a massive two-volume work of over a thousand pages, edited by Kineton Parkes and published 1892/93. *The English Republic* by W.J. Linton, on the other hand, revealed an interest in social science. This was a book of 216 pages, edited by Kineton Parkes and published in 1891 in London.

Particularly close to his interests and beliefs was the journal *Comus*. He edited this slim monthly magazine, which covered art, literature, music and drama. The first six issues were published in Birmingham, and the last six in London.

Among the many other journals he contributed articles to were: *The Midland Naturalist, The Ruskin Guild Journal, The Sun, The Artist, Victorian Magazine, Atalanta, Studio, Poet Lore* and *The Athenaeum*.

Like Arnold Bennett in the neighbouring Potteries towns, Kineton Parkes' novels had a largely local setting. The books had a London distributor, and often received good reviews in the national press. Of *Life's Desert Way*, *The Times* said: *'There is a great deal of work, and indeed, thought put into the book.'* The Scotsman deemed it to be *'both a clever and a solid book'* and the *Daily Telegraph* said *'the writing is good'*. In *Love à la Mode* Parkes used epigrams and wit to create an amusing and thoughtful novel. All in all, as a relatively minor regional novelist, he enjoyed a reputation well beyond his local area.

Kineton Parkes had an eye for beautiful things - a great asset in his chosen career. It is perfectly natural that a librarian should have a feeling for fine books, and this was manifest in an appreciation of The Sutherland Binding in 1900. This fine and elaborate bookbinding was executed by G.T. Bagguley of Newcastle, and named, by request, in honour of the Duchess of Sutherland, of Trentham. White leather of the finest quality was frequently used, with delicately tooled designs in a variety of rich colours as ornament, sometimes with, sometimes without gold tooling or stamping. The opening paragraph of the pamphlet is an illustration of his aesthetic feelings:

The gentlest of all the arts is that of bookbinding, and the most refined of all avocations is that of book collecting. Some of the dearest of men and the most charming of women have been the happy owners of rare books beautifully bound. The man who has a room lined with books cannot be base; and the woman whose boudoir harbours beautiful things cannot be frivolous. There are books and books, however, and they have their corresponding range of bindings. While no book written or printed is wholly contemptible, there are many books which cannot deserve the dignity of binding. When upon the work of a great writer a great printer lavishes the resources of his craft, and the master binder encases it in leather without and vellum within, with decorations rich in gold and colours, perfect in balance and design, then surely greatness is reached: the apotheosis of the Book!

Another small publication attributed to Kineton Parkes was *A Guild of Cripples* (1903). This was an article reprinted from the *Manchester Evening Chronicle*, and it provides an insight into Parkes' charitable activities, and a further link with the Duchess of Sutherland. In July 1908 the Duchess held a bazaar and fete at Trentham, on behalf of the Cripples' Guild and Cripples' Home. Kineton Parkes contributed a well-researched article on the history of Trentham and the Sutherland Family to the lavishly-printed souvenir brochure for this event.

Millicent, Duchess of Sutherland was a great supporter of local charities in North Staffordshire, and was Patron of a number of organisations. She established the Potteries Cripples' Guild in 1900, and this later became the North Staffordshire Cripples' Aid Society. A lady with a deep social conscience, she pioneered the campaign to restrict the dangerous use of lead in the pottery industry. She served with the Red Cross in France during the First World War, where she was awarded the Croix de Guerre.

As might be expected for a man who clearly enjoyed the company of ladies, Kineton Parkes was effusive in his praise of the Duchess. In his article for the souvenir of the bazaar and fete, he writes as follows:

In the Duchess the Duke is fortunate in possessing a wife who is able to support so admirably the important public and philanthropic duties which fall to the lot of a great family. She is a leader in London, in Scotland, in Staffordshire and Shropshire, of every movement which promises well for the general welfare. The Duchess is a keen business woman, and can get at the heart of a proposition more quickly than others less gifted with the analytic power. United with these exceptional powers of organisation, the Duchess of Sutherland possesses also the poetic gift. This was evidenced in her play 'The Conqueror' which was produced in London by Mr. Forbes Robertson a year or two since; and it is evidenced more frequently in the speeches the Duchess makes from time to time on behalf of some philanthrophic or educational project. These speeches are essentially poetic in their feeling, as all who have come under their spell willingly confess. They are rhetorical without the hollowness of rhetoric, and they are emotional but devoid of emotionalism. The Duchess brings to the arts which she practices, a humanism which commends her efforts to all who are prepared to that which is evolved from the workings of a cold or academic brain.

He managed to persuade her to become patron of his other great enthusiasm - the Leek Amateur Opera Company.

During the late 19th century fashionable theatre audiences in Victorian London were enchanted by the Savoy Operas of Gilbert and Sullivan. This extraordinary partnership created an enduring theatrical tradition, producing 'hit' musical shows that have stood the test of time. Within ten years or so of their first performances by the original D'Oyly Carte Company at the Savoy Theatre in London these same operas were being performed in Leek to a high degree of perfection, and with a great display of talent and skill.

The Leek Amateur Opera Company was founded in Leek in 1893 with the express purpose of bringing the delights of Gilbert and Sullivan to local audiences. Kineton Parkes was a leading figure in the company. Not only was he deeply involved with the administration, he also played most of the leading character roles, following the tradition established by the D'Oyly Carte Company.

Writing in the 1935 edition of *Leek News* the Small Boy in the Market Place says:

The Lord-High-Everything-Else of the Society was Mr Kineton Parkes, a most delightful man and a born showman, and my recollection of this Society was that it was run on showman's lines. Mr Parkes seemed to be Business Manager, Secretary and Producer and took all of the principal parts. Not that he was not good - indeed he was excellent - but it is bad for a Society for one man to rule and take the principal parts. His sister, Florence, was perhaps the best soubrette Leek has given us, but the Society as a whole lacked talent.

The writer, William Warrington, later acted as producer of the same Gilbert and Sullivan operettas in the 1920s and 30s, so we might detect a touch of 'sour grapes' in his comments.

Kineton Parkes's physical appearance, personality and demeanour were perfect for the characters, and he carried off the roles to perfection. Indeed, it may fairly be said that he was born to play the parts of the Lord Chancellor in *Iolanthe*, Sir Joseph Porter in *H.M.S. Pinafore* or Jack Point in *The Yeomen of the Guard*, roles which demanded not only a good singing voice, but also an acting talent.

Performances were in the Town Hall in Market Street, and rehearsals were held on Wednesdays at the Maude Institute on Clerks Bank. The orchestra was usually composed of members of the Leek Orchestral Society. Records show that productions were well supported and the large audiences very appreciative. Many well-known local personalities became leading members of the company in the early days - Edward Challinor, Marcus Prince, J G Beckett, A E Southall, Ada Allday (of Birmingham), Constance Unwin and Lexy Munro, together with members of his family, Mrs Kineton Parkes and Miss Florence Parkes, the younger sister of Kineton.

The Leek Amateur Opera Company was an enterprise of great style, vision and ambition - perhaps even over-ambition.

Kineton Parkes was obviously very single-minded of purpose, pressing firmly to get exactly what he wanted. In spite of this he was clearly no business-man, and often had to admit that he had 'mislaid' certain bills and invoices. Although the company enjoyed great success and popularity in its stage productions, it always struggled financially in the early years. Productions were expensive to stage, given the level of perfection strived for. Indeed, in 1900 Parr's Bank wrote to the company about an overdraft of £31 which had been outstanding since 1896. It was usually necessary to pay D'Oyly Carte a fee of £10.10.0, and sometimes £2.2.0 for band parts. Costumes were hired from a professional company, B J Simmons & Co. of Covent Garden, London.

Each show during the early years appears to have been produced at a loss, but no expense was spared in providing 'comforts' for the performers. For instance, the refreshments account for the 1896 production of Pirates of Penzance included an amount for *'beer and stout for about 60 persons for 3 nights'* as well as sandwiches and food. Printing costs were always high, as were the charges for hire of rooms and the construction of scenery. Nevertheless, money was still found to support a project close to the heart of Kineton Parkes, the Nicholson Institute Picture Fund, and a sum of £28.3.6 out of the takings from the 1895 production HMS Pinafore was paid to R Jack for a large painting of an old dye house. This picture is still in the local collection, in the care of the district council.

The performance of Gilbert and Sullivan's HMS Pinafore in November 1895 was very much a family affair. Kineton Parkes, with his usual theatrical flair, played the leading role of the Right Hon Sir Joseph Porter, KCB (First Lord of the Admiralty), and also in the cast were his wife, playing the part of Little Buttercup, and his sister, Florence, whose dancing skills were used to good effect. Also imported to Leek was another actress from Birmingham, Ada Allday, playing the part of Josephine. The photograph of the cast in the Leek News of 1936 is one of the few known photographs of Kineton Parkes. The report on the production said that the part of Sir Joseph *'was efficiently filled by Mr Kineton Parkes, who successfully resisted the always-present temptation to exaggerate the distinct peculiarities of the naval official.'* Of Mrs Parkes, the report stated: *'Though lacking the physique usually identified with the popular part of Little Buttercup, Mrs Kineton Parkes acted and sang in a most admirable fashion, and over and over again won general applause.'*

In his domestic life, Kineton Parkes appears to have been a somewhat restless spirit. He lived in Leek for 21 years, between 1891 and 1912, and during that time he lived with his family in at least five different houses. His first home was Eastwood Cottage, Ball Haye Road, but by 1896 he had moved to 29a Queen Street, one of the Sugden houses. The 1901 Census reveals that he was living at 10 Hugo Street with his wife and their two sons, Gabriel Kineton Parkes, age 10, and Maxwell Kineton Parkes, age 8. One of his colleagues, William Craigmile, head of the School of Art, was lodging with the family. His next move was to 8 Shirburn Terrace, Ashbourne Road, and by 1907 he had moved to a house in Spencer Avenue. All these were good, solid Victorian town houses, which would appeal to Kineton's aesthetic instincts.

Kineton Parkes was an incurable romantic. His love for all things beautiful included attractive ladies, and in this sense it may be said that he had a roving eye. He was obviously much happier in the company of ladies, and does not appear to have been ungracious to them, or curt and off-hand, as he was with men, who often felt the shortness of his tongue. His love of the stage brought him into contact with attractive women who often had a more out-going personality than the average late-Victorian female, and less inhibitions. The feminine figure, usually unclothed, appeared in a number of his books on art, but never in a salacious way. To Kineton Parkes, a woman was a real person, an object of affection, to be admired, revered, respected and loved. He had several mistresses, and he and his wife parted by mutual consent when they left Leek. Mrs Parkes returned to Birmingham where she became involved with the women's suffrage movement.

They had two sons. Gabriel, known as 'Gib', married Helena West, daughter of John West of Leek, and after a distinguished military career, went into agriculture. He died at Great Dunmow in 1978. Maxwell left England for New Zealand in 1914, where he died in 1933.

Kineton continued his involvement in the art world, spending much of his time in London, where his influence and reputation led to him becoming a highly-respected figure. He continued his writing, contributing many articles to learned journals. In 1931 he published a major two volume work entitled *The Art of Carved Sculpture* in Chapman and Hall's Universal Art series.

He lived in Elvaston Place, South Kensington, near to the museum which held much of his areas of interest. He had a large private collection of works of art, including modern sculpture, watercolour paintings, oil paintings, drawings and prints. He was an acknowledged expert on the works of WJ Linton, the distinguished engraver and socialist with whom Walter Crane served as apprentice.

In *Who's Who in Art* Kineton Parkes, always the performer, stated his recreations as skating and pianoforte. He died in London on 17 April 1938 aged 73.

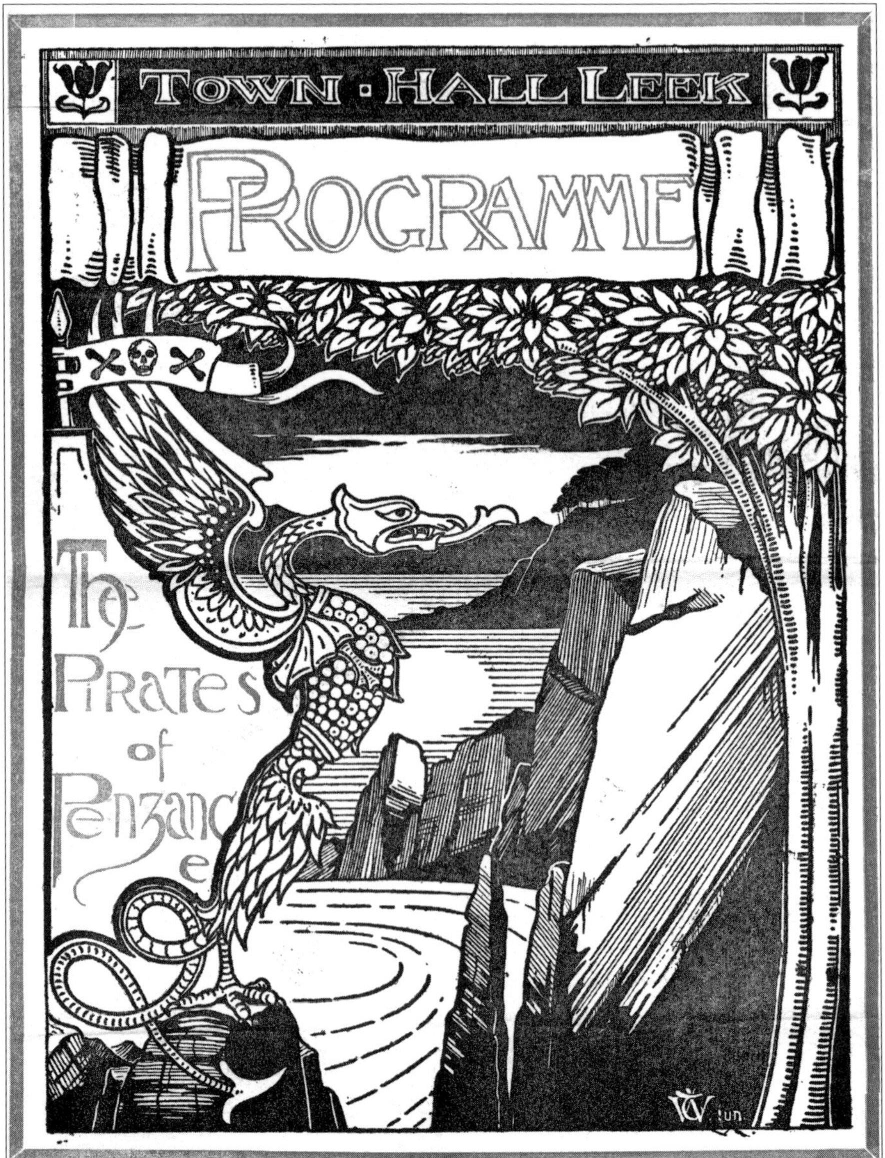
TOWN · HALL LEEK
PROGRAMME
The
Pirates
of
Penzance

Leek Amateur Operatic Company.
1895.
TRIAL BY JURY.   Mrs. SPANKARRAY'S FIVE-O'CLOCK.
H.M.S. PINAFORE.

PROGRAMME
of the production of Gilbert & Sullivan's Comic Opera in Two Acts,

THE PIRATES OF PENZANCE
Or, The Slave of Duty,
By the Leek Amateur Operatic Company; by special permission of R. D'Oyly Carte, Esq., of the Savoy Theatre, London.

Wed., Thurs., Fri., Nov. 25, 26, 27, 1896.

CHARACTERS:

Major-General Stanley	...Mr. KINETON PARKES
The Pirate King	Mr. MARCUS PRINCE
Samuel (the Pirate Lieutenant)	Mr. J. G. BECKETT
Sergeant of Police	Mr. W. E. BRINDLEY
Frederick (the Pirate Apprentice) ...	Mr. EDWARD CHALLINOR

Mabel		... ... Miss ADA ALLDAY
Edith.... ...	Major-General	Miss FLORRY PARKES
Kate	Stanley's Daughters	... ... Miss LEXY MUNRO
Isabel ...		Miss ANNIE GOLDSTRAW

AND

Ruth (a Pirate Maid of All Work)... ... Mrs KINETON PARKES

The cast of the Leek Operatic Society production of 'HMS Pinafore', November 1895.

THE MOORLANDS PRESS:
*
A New Series of Works of Fiction dealing with Actualities.

VOLUME I.

LIFE'S DESERT WAY
By KINETON PARKES
(Author of *Love à la Mode*)
PRICE 6/-   CROWN 8VO.   370 PAGES.   CLOTH BOUND.

KINETON PARKES.
From a photograph by Mrs. Esther Wood: the block kindly lent by the Proprietors of the *Manchester City News*.

A leaflet advertising one of Kineton Parkes' published books.

Letter written by Kineton Parkes to Edward Challinor.

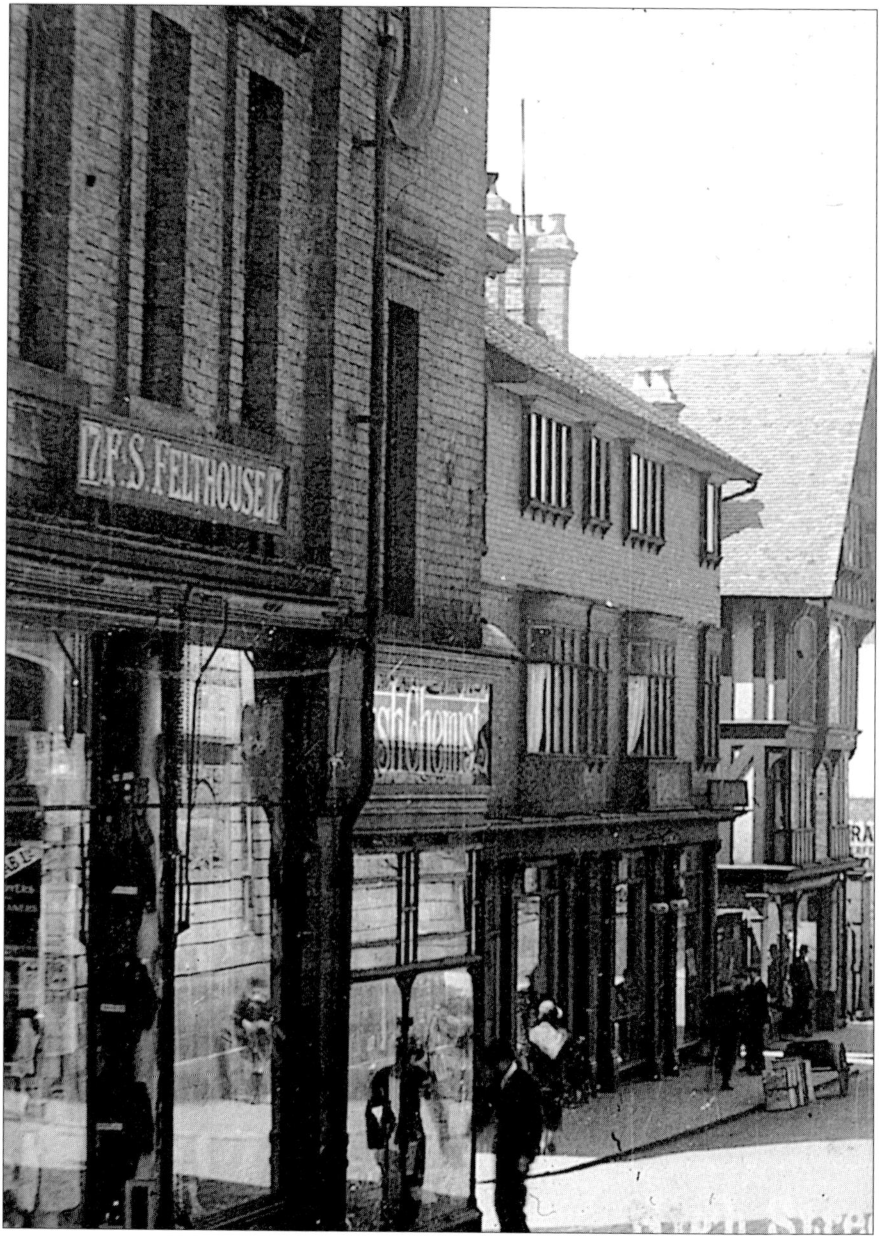
17 F. S. FELTHOUSE 17

High Street from Sheepmarket, the new Grand Theatre on the left.

SOME NITHSDALE PHOTOGRAPHS

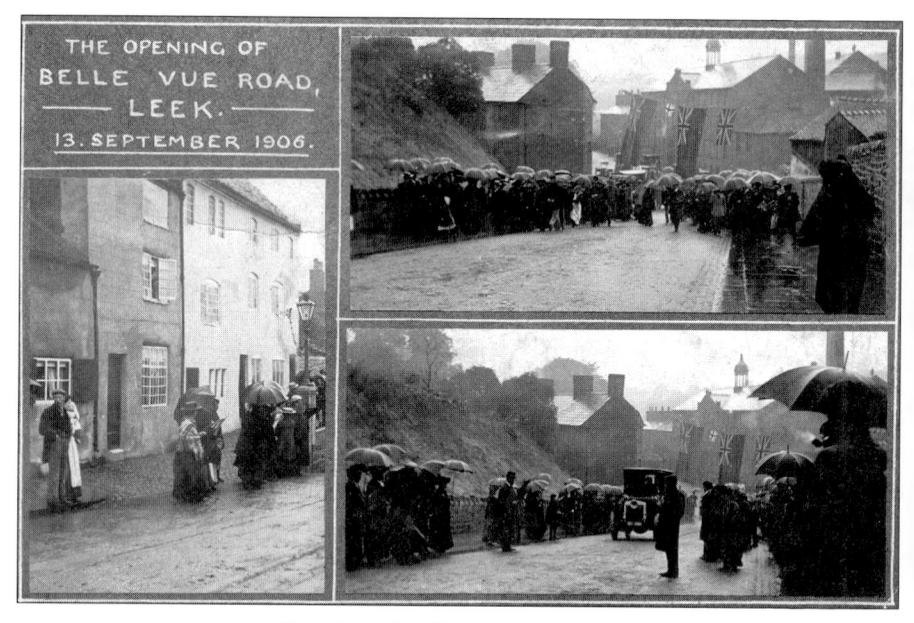

Opening of Belle Vue Road, 1906.

Mill Street about 1906.

A silk twister and his helper in Leek.

A typical silk 'shade' in Leek.

PIONEERS OF CYCLING IN LEEK

Members of the Leek & Moorlands Bicycle Club, taken soon after its foundation in 1876.

Leek Cyclist Club 1910
Back: W Howard, S Godwin, W Constantine, S Newall, H Smith, C Simpson, H Walters
4th row: TW Hawksworth, F Salt, WH Capper, C Pickford, JJ Carding, F Coates, H Rigby, GH Wilson
3rd: H Hill, J Trafford, H Cater, A Armitt, C Brassington, H Kirkham, WH Robinson, J Fowler, GH Pickford
AJ Hall, J Wilkinson, G Watson, G Bestwick, RA Crombie, T Bestwick, WH Hill, R Manuell, E Trafford, GW Cook
Front row: J Hudson, T Messham, A Barnett, W Kinsey, TS Myatt, C Heath, WT Cook,
JP Fellowes-Smith, A Billington, S Taylor

Fifteen
TIME OFF

OUR LEADING PLAYERS HAD a strong influence on the leisure, cultural and sporting activities of the town and its commercial, industrial and social life. Joshua Nicholson was involved with the Literary and Mechanics Institute and later the Nicholson Institute. Larner Sugden had the Labour Church. William Challinor had his poetry and lectures. Arthur Nicholson had his shire horses and his involvement with the Cricket Club. Matthew Henry Miller had his writing and entertaining, and Kineton Parkes had the Opera Society and the library, School of Art and art gallery. Together their activities established this town as a cultural centre, where the talents of all classes could find expression.

For a town with a hard-working population, where workers had limited leisure hours, there was a surprisingly large amount of things going on. Certainly if a person showed any kind of talent - sporting or musical - they were encouraged to take part. Indeed, it is often said that the possession of any such talent would go some way to ensuring a much better chance of being offered a job! So what did Victorian and Edwardian Leek have to offer?

To start with the real upper classes, even the nobility, there was the LEEK RACES. Between 1833 and 1867 horse racing was held regularly in Leek, usually in October each year. (The month of the old Leek Wakes.) In 1868 the Leek Races became the North Staffordshire Races, the annual autumn meeting being held in Leek. The races were always well-organised, and supported by the prominent citizens of the town and district, whose generous annual subscriptions made the venture financially viable. Much money was certainly involved.

The first record of races was in 1833 when they were held on Monday and Tuesday, 21/22 October, over the Birchall Dale Course. The stewards were Francis Cruso and John Heathcote; William Alcock was Clerk of the Course, and George Keates was the secretary and treasurer. The Subscription List for 1833 was headed by John Davenport MP and Edward Buller MP. The rules were strict, and stated, for example: *'No person will be allowed to erect a Booth, Shed or Stall until he has agreed with the Clerk and paid his subscription. Also dogs found on the Course will be destroyed and every person crossing the adjoining fences or in any way wilfully trespassing will be prosecuted.'*

In the early years entries were usually small, the maximum being six horses and often less. Nevertheless the races were clearly popular, enjoying regular support. Balance sheets during those years never showed a large profit, the income being largely paid out in prize money to the winners. Each year there was a payment *'to Mr Hockenhull, for the use of the course'* and to the Leek Band, in addition to the regular expenses of printing, postage advertising, beer for the band and casual labour to maintain the course.

An odd entry in the subscription list for 1844 is a gift of ten shillings from someone listed as *'An enemy to races'*! That year James Bloore was the Treasurer, and John Heathcote Hacker and Andrew Jukes Worthington were the Stewards.

At a meeting at the George Inn on 17 September 1849, a committee of five was appointed to organise and promote the Leek Races to take place in Wakes Week each year. The first five members were John Wain, Abraham Howes, John Whittles, E Smith Walters and James Robinson. The Racing Committee met at the King William IV Inn, Church Street, on 6 October 1851 *'to inspect the proposed new ground at Leek Edge as to its condition and suitability on which to hold the proposed Races'*. This move does not appear to have materialised as in 1863 the Leek Races were still being held on the Birchall Dale Old Course. Thomas Maskery was Clerk of the Course, a position he held for a number of years, and the Treasurer was William Allen. The accounts showed a healthy balance of £50 3s 0d.

In 1867 the Leek Races were held for the last time under that name, at the Highfield Park Course. The following year the event assumed the title of the North Staffordshire Races, Autumn Meeting, Leek. The prestigious list of Stewards was Lord Alexander Paget, Lord Berkeley Paget, Captain Hyde Smith and W F M Copeland Esq, with Thomas Maskery still holding the office of Clerk of the Course. The races were the Churnet Valley Stakes (a field of 9); the Hunter and Yeomanry Stakes (a field of 4); the Ladies' Purse (a field of 6); the North Staffordshire Handicap (a field of 11); the Highfield Stakes (a field of 10) and the Horton Stakes (a field of 5).

In 1870 the races were held at Highfield on 8/9 August. Mr T Maskery continued his service as Clerk of the Course and the distinguished list of Stewards was Lord Waterpark, Lord Henry Paget, Lord Alexander Paget, Lord Berkeley Paget, Captain Hyde Smith, P L Brocklehurst Esq, Robert Bentley Esq and W F M Copeland Esq.

Perhaps a little more accessible, provided you could afford to buy a bicycle, was the LEEK AND MOORLANDS BICYCLE CLUB, which was founded in 1876, and is probably the oldest cycling club in the country still operating today. It did enjoy good support from all classes. In those days before the motor car, the club provided not only healthy exercise, but the means of opening up the countryside to a broad cross-section of the townspeople.

The Club was founded on 3 August 1876, in the Old Plough vaults. The founders were W T Cook, C Clulow, J Deakin, W H Hambleton, G Watson and J Fisher. Cycling in those days was a strenuous adventure. The primitive machines and the rough roads made cycling an adventurous pastime that demanded considerable energy and also involved not a little risk.

The club runs of the early days, though short, contained

plenty of incident and excitement. The first run in the history of the club was to Congleton on 19 August 1876, when four members turned out. A week later three members ventured as far as Hanley, but the following week only two members turned out for the run to Kingsley, Froghall, Ipstones and Bottomhouse. The fourth run, to Cheadle, attracted seven members, but one turned back at Wetley Rocks and one stayed at Cheadle.

The club eventually changed its name to the Leek Cyclists' Club, and the first President was the ubiquitous William Challinor, who, in 1892, presented a silver cup to be competed for over a five mile grass course. W T Cook, the club's first captain, served the club in various capacities for over sixty years.

CRICKET in the summer and football in the winter were, of course, the main sporting activities. Both sports were played to a high standard locally, and their development ran parallel to the industrial growth of Leek. As trade and the silk industry expanded so there was a growth in the number of works teams which were established, and a number of league and cup competitions emerged.

William Challinor was the Chairman at the inaugural meeting of the Leek and Moorlands Cricket Club on 20 May 1844, and many of his colleagues in industry and the professions became involved. The movers and shakers of Victorian Leek provided the main body of support for these sporting activities. The first organised match was against Norton CC on Monday 30 June 1845, but there is no record of the result.

It is a comment on the class distinctions of the time that by 1855 the Cricket Club was able to afford to pay a professional. J Copson was paid one shilling per match, with a free dinner and £1 per year for carrying the club's baggage. In other words, although he was employed because of his cricketing skills, he was very much the paid servant of the club and had to carry out many other duties in addition to playing regular matches. This is something of a reversal of the status of a professional today.

Nevertheless, over the years, the Leek Cricket Club attracted a number of players with first-class experience in the game.

The class element was also evident in 1895 when the 'split' occurred over the matter of the workmens' expenses, resulting in the establishment of Leek Highfield as a separate club. As we have seen in the chapter on Sir Arthur Nicholson, this was not resolved until after the First World War when Sir Arthur continued to allow the free use of his Highfield ground to the club.

It would seem appropriate, at this point, to mention a man who was an outstanding cricketer for Leek and who only narrowly missed the distinction of being one of the leading characters in our story - Robert Schofield Milner. A silk manufacturer, he had mills in Union Street and Langford Street, established by his father, William Milner, yet another Yorkshireman to make his home in Leek.

In his public work over 40 years, Robert Milner was firstly one of the Leek Improvement Commissioners and later served on the Leek Urban District Council. He served many organisations, including the Memorial Hospital Trustees, the Board of Guardians and the Old Age Pensions Committee. His passion to support education led him to establish the Milner Bequest - an on-going fund which provided grants to enable the less well-off to have a better education, and a lasting memorial to a man who contributed much to the public life of the town.

Robert Milner was a staunch Liberal and a great admirer of WE Gladstone. He gave great support to Robert Pearce, the Liberal candidate who fought several elections and who finally became Leek's MP at the 1910 election. Milner was one of the most popular and effective of local liberal speakers.

He died in 1925, and his obituary in the *Leek Post* stated that *'he was never known to do another an unkindly act... he was a man in whom everyone had implicit confidence.'* He was a man who name is perpetuated in several aspects of the life of the town, but he deserves greater recognition, and his large-hearted nature and stature belies the rather minor role he plays in our story.

The first recorded FOOTBALL match took place on 15 October 1870. Organised by the Recreation Club, two Leek teams opposed each other and the game was played under the Rugby Rules. During the 1876-7 season Leek adopted the Association Rules, the first recorded match being played on 20 January 1877, against Uttoxeter. For a time, it was not clear under which set of rules a particular match was to be played, and much confusion ensued when players alleged that their opponents displayed a total lack of knowledge of the rules!

Many local football clubs were established, as the game was accessible to all classes, with works' teams playing in a number of local leagues. A high standard was attained and in 1884 the Leek club entered the English Cup. Their first venture into this higher competition was not successful, for they were beaten by Northwich Victoria by 4 goals to 3. Next season they fared much better and reached the third round of the English Cup. Their opponents were Queen's Park, Glasgow, and the historic match was played on Saturday 3 January 1885, on the Westwood Lane ground before a crowd of 3000. It was an exciting match, but Leek lost by the narrow margin of 3 goals to 2.

There was great proliferation of junior football teams and leagues in the later Victorian years, with many of the silk factories forming teams. Cup competitions were fiercely fought affairs. Support was very good. Families like that of George Fisher turned out in their numbers to roar their team on. The large crowd that lined the touchlines for the cup match between Leek YMCA and St Mary's on 30 March 1907 included many ladies.

RUGBY UNION Football continued to be played on a ground to the north of Highfield Hall, a number of players playing there in winter, and playing cricket in summer. Later, athletics, with the Leek Harriers, and angling were amongst the outdoor activities available to the people of Victorian and Edwardian Leek.

The 1880s were marked by a great upsurge of interest in MUSIC AND THE ARTS in Leek. One of the high points of the town's cultural activities was the visit in 1884 of no less a person than Oscar Wilde. He gave a lecture in the Temperance Hall on the subject of 'The Ethics of the Home' to a small but appreciative audience. How Leek folk reacted to his wit and style is not known, but no doubt the audience would be somewhat elite. The working man would be seeking his entertainment elsewhere.

The Temperance Hall in Union Street was formerly a Congregational Chapel. It was built by a breakaway group of Congregationalists who left the main Derby Street church during the pastorate of Rev James Morrow (1813-1836) to form a separate church. Following the building of Sugden's new Congregational Church in 1863, the two groups re-united at Derby Street, and the Union Street chapel was sold to the Temperance Society, becoming the Temperance Hall.

The hall was used for theatrical performances, both amateur and professional, and one of its most popular events, appealing to all classes because the admission charges were low, was the Saturday night Penny Readings, which played to packed audiences. Poetry, monologues, sketches, minstrel turns and musical items made up the programmes, and performers included William Challinor, Matthew Henry Miller, Ralph de Tunstall Sneyd, J G Beckett, J Lovatt, Dr Ritchie, W Doxey, Sam Godwin and Mrs Hobson. The Temperance Hall ended its days as the Majestic Cinema.

In his article in the 1935 edition of *Leek News* the 'Small Boy in the Market Place' has some memories of amateur theatricals in Leek. The pen-name masked the identity of William Warrington, who became involved himself in amateur theatricals. He writes of a production of *The Rivals* by the old Volunteer Theatricals in which Sergeant Bolstidge took part:

I recollect how his movements so reminded us of him as our Drill Instructor teaching us to 'Right turn', and 'Smartly come to attention' etc. And his dialogue was about as intelligible as his words of command 'As unt' (eyes front) and so on. I remember his entrance when he came to say farewell to Julia seemed like 'Left, right, left, alas Julia. Left, right, left, right - right turn - attention - feet at an angle of 45 degrees - I come to bid you a long farewell'.'

The Small Boy's article also mentions three very attractive young actresses - Alice Sherratt, Tillie Slater and Alice Birtles - as well a several actors, including Willie Young, Marcus Prince, Edward Challinor and Sergeant Govier.

The Leek Philothespian Club was formed in the 1880s *'for the performance of plays, recitations, and other methods of dramatic entertainment'*. The rules of the club made provision for the appointment of a Stage Manager and Acting Manager, and the club was run on very strict lines. Members only were allowed to attend meetings or rehearsals, and *'nothing done at the club shall be divulged outside'*. Members were required to attend punctually *'10 minutes before the time appointed to commence rehearsal unless satisfactory reasons be given for absence'*, and no member was allowed to perform with any other society without the permission of the club.

The first Acting Manager and Secretary was John Wardle and the Stage Manager was James Newall. The first performance took place at the Temperance Hall on Thursday and Friday, 17 and 18 January 1884. The evening began with a prologue, specially written by W Lea, and spoken by John Wardle, which concluded as follows:

> *Concluding, I may say none of our pains*
> *Are undertaken with the hope of gains.*
> *We're acting simply for the drama's sake,*
> *To clear the cost is all we want to make.*
> *With this short introduction then I'll go,*
> *And pull the curtain up and start the show.*

This was followed by a one-act comedy entitled *The Spitalfields Weaver* - an appropriate theme for a silk town. The central piece was a melodrama, *The Corsican Brothers*, complete with visions, duels and ghosts and with sufficient rhetorical exaggeration to give full reign to John Wardle's thespian talents, in the dual role of two twin brothers. After such heavy drama, the audience was sent home happily with the farce *Diamond cut Diamond* with John Wardle playing a comic role. Such was the pattern of the performances of the Philothespians - a blend of heavy drama and hilarious farce, which was very much the established pattern of Victorian theatricals.

It was not long before John Wardle grasped the nettle and tackled the role which made Henry Irving famous - that of Mathias in the most renowned of all the Victorian melodramas, *The Bells*. The ghastly tragedy was played to full measure, wringing every drop of pathos out of the audience. The report in the local press stated that the part *'affords opportunity for the employment of some of the most powerful and impressive strokes of the tragic actor's art, and Mr Wardle rose fully to the heights of the occasion'*. This heavy fare was lightened by the final play - a farcical comedy entitled *Raising the Wind*, which would send the audience happily to their *'carriages at 10-30'*.

A rival group, the Volunteers Theatricals, were also performing plays in Leek. A very attractive actress with the Philothespians, Miss Alice Birtles, sent a letter to the secretary saying that she had been offered a part in the Volunteers' production of *The Rivals*. This was contrary to the rules of the Philothespians and by this defection Miss Birtles had effectively resigned.

Other prominent players with the Philothespians included comic actor A E Quinn (who later became Stage Manager), C W Eaton, F Taylor, E Hunt, J G Parkinson, T H Birch, J Collins and F Mee. Female performers, following the defection of Miss Birtles, included Miss A Allen, Miss S Rider, Miss M Foster, Miss C Wilson, Miss M Allen, Miss M Bishop, Miss E Robinson, Miss M

Hassall and Miss E Vigrass. Music was always a part of the performances, and S H Mee later became the Musical Director.

The Philothespians tackled their first full-length Shakespeare production in 1888, when they performed *The Merchant of Venice*. John Wardle, who always played the leading roles, was Shylock, and Miss M Bishop played the part of Portia. The play was well-received by large audiences; indeed the local press always gave enthusiastic reviews of all performances.

This group of amateur actors was a hard-working enterprise, presenting plays at least twice a year, in the spring and autumn, and also gave charity performances. In September 1886 they put on a special performance in aid of the Leek Church Cricket Club, and a few weeks later, in November, they performed at the Theatre Royal, Longton, in aid of the Cottage hospital.

The 1880s were the main years of the Philothespian Club. By 1888 several members including A E Quinn and Miss Gater had resigned. An attempt to perform *The Taming of the Shrew* was abandoned and the company resorted to repeat performances of former successes. In July 1889 the Committee *'resolved to endeavour to obtain a cast for Heir at Law to be played early in September'*, but the end was in sight. The club had successfully brought a measure of culture to Leek, giving the townsfolk the opportunity to enjoy outstanding plays of the day. Members of the Philothespians continued to perform in the Saturday night 'Penny Readings' held in the Temperance Hall, but the stage was now set for the advent of Kineton Parkes.

In addition to local amateur performances Leek also received regular visits from travelling theatrical companies. One such group was the 'RAG AND STICK' THEATRES - an apt description of their stage - these companies travelled around with several flat-bodied waggons which were lined up side by side and then covered with large sheets of canvas after the manner of a circus tent. Within the temporary structure were performed plays, from Victorian tragedies to rip-roaring farces.

The most popular location was 'Sparrow Park' at the eastern end of Derby Street, where the Nicholson War Memorial now stands.

One such travelling company was the Victoria Theatre, proprietor Mrs MC Sinclair, and boasting as its patron Sir Henry Irving. During its week long visit in April 1899 it performed *The Three Musketeers* among other plays. Charges for admission ranged from the most expensive reserved seats at 1s 6d, to the gallery at 3d. Such prices - and an evening of theatrical entertainment - were in the reach of families like George Fisher's.

On a more sophisticated level, visiting companies also performed in the Old Theatre in the Swan yard. Restoration comedies and classical plays were in the repertoire of these professional players and the warm and comfortable indoor venue would attract the upper classes.

A local romantic story that would not be out of place in a Victorian play concerns one such family and an actress. The family - the wealthy Gaunt family - lived at Gaunt House in Derby Street, the large house set back from the street and now fronted by the shops known as Gaunt Buildings opposite the NatWest bank. It was sometimes known as 'Knit-Knot Hall' because the family made its wealth from the silk industry and banking. Richard Gaunt fell in love with an actress, Harriot Mellon, who then became very famous. He proposed to her but she turned him down to marry the banker Thomas Coutts. She later became the Duchess of St Albans. But before this illustrious elevation she was a frequent visitor to Leek.

The top social event of the year was always the LEEK INVITATION BALL. This was organised with great flair and style by Mrs Cruso of Foxlowe. Mrs Cruso was highly-respected by the townsfolk of Leek; indeed, it was said that they thought more of Mrs Cruso than they did of 'their own dear Queen'. Such was her status that Foxlowe, the fine Georgian house at the head of the Market Place, was known simply as 'Number 1 Leek'. It always played a prominent role in Royal visits and elections, for Mr and Mrs Cruso were prominent Conservatives. (It was a twist of fate that Foxlowe would one day become the headquarters of such a Left-wing organisation as the Textile Trade Union!) William Challinor was a regular visitor, his calls being a blend of social, business and political matters.

In his article in the 1937 *Leek News*, 'The Small Boy in the Market Place' (William Warrington) gives us this little insight into Mrs Cruso's character:

At one election when the Liberal candidate was returned and was being chaired past her house she bowed to him and waved her hand, and when some of her conservative friends remarked on this she replied, with her great gift of fairness and dignity, 'He is now my member.' The same gentleman who told this tale reflected on the anomaly of the Times when a woman of Mrs Cruso's intelligence, position and wealth had no parliamentary vote but her under gardener had.

Mrs Cruso, a rather large lady, 'held court' in her spacious drawing room, her household servants having prepared the room for visitors were on hand to supply dainty refreshments as required - a perfect picture of Victorian gentility. Her generous nature was embodied in her support for the Cruso Nursing Association and her endowment of the Cruso Aid in Sickness Fund, both of which provided for the welfare of the working classes of Leek when they met hard times.

Mrs Cruso was formerly Anne Searight, born 12 August 1812, whose father was a merchant trader in Liverpool. Her uncle was Hugh Ford, of Ford Green Hall and also owner of Ford House on the corner of Market Street and Stockwell Street. Visits to her uncle brought her to Leek, and in 1851 she married John Cruso of Foxlowe. She was his second wife, and he died in 1867. Mrs Cruso herself died in 1893.

The list of invitations to the 1887 Ball, headed by Mrs Cruso and party, reads like a roll-call of Leek's leading citizens. The Sleighs, the Challinors, the Wardles, the Sneyds, the Wards, the Watsons, the Worthingtons, the Broughs, the Nicholsons, the Milners and the Princes. Over 300 invitations were sent out to people far and wide. Industry, the professions, the gentry and the clergy, from Stoke-on-Trent, Newcastle, Macclesfield, Ashbourne, Uttoxeter and Manchester. Not all attended, of course

William Warrington, writing in the 1931 edition of *Leek News* recounts an incident concerning Mrs Cruso and the public ball, a story which, both in its subject and style, might have come from the pen of Arnold Bennett:

An anecdote showing what a great lady she was and what an example she set to Victorian snobbery occurred at a public ball where a cord across the room divided the elect from the herd. A young tradesman noted for his skill in dancing (which skill was evidently handed on to some of his descendents who in my youthful days were equally noted for the same accomplishment) made a bet that he would dance with Mrs Cruso. How he surmounted the dividing cord history does not relate, but it is on record that she danced with him with utmost grace - using the word in both its meaning of 'good-will' and 'elegance'. One of the above-mentioned descendants of the young man told me that after that Mrs Cruso always danced with him and his brother.

The Red Lion, kept for many years by Mr Henry Swift, was the location for many balls and dances. Mr Swift, another of Victorian Leek's Dickensian characters, was described by the 'Small Boy in the Market Place' as *'an old gentleman, rather like a pouter pigeon, because he had rather thin, bird-like legs and a fat stomach like a pouter's chest, and used to wear a heavy brilliant watchchain and rings, and a crimson velvet smoking cap on the top of a crimson face.'* The article, in the 1932 edition of *Leek News*, gives the writer's contrasting impressions of the society balls at the Red Lion and the more unsophisticated dances at the Cock Inn next door:

At this time balls used to take place in the Assembly Room there [Red Lion], *and the Market Place would be crowded to watch those attending alight from their carriages - for that would be all most people ever saw of dances, for there were no Saturday night public dances in those days as there was nowhere to hold them - but , yes, on second thoughts, there was one place where dancing took place on Saturday night, and that was in the top storey of the Cock Inn next door to the Red Lion, and I remember having a vague feeling, as the couples tore madly past the open windows (it was the days of gallops, polkas and other strenuous dances) that it was the place where we were told we should go to if we were not good.*

This vivid, first-hand impression suggests that these rather more raunchy, bacchanalian affairs, in the sweaty atmosphere of the attic of the Cock Inn, were where the working-classes found their entertainment when their wage packet, such as it was, would be fresh in their pocket on Saturday night.

The Market Place also staged open-air concerts by the Volunteer Band on Monday evenings. These were very popular, attracting large numbers of spectators, and gave the townsfolk an opportunity to socialise, as it cost nothing to attend. The 'Small Boy in the Market Place' recalled how the audience, young and old, ranged from the gentry and the middle classes to screaming children playing round the bandstand. He remembered the spot where *'the Misses Allen, of the Swan Hotel, held their court. They were very popular and renowned for their beautiful figures - no doubt the result of drilling by their father who was one of the Balaclava heroes of the Charge of the Light Brigade - there was generally a crowd of young men anxious to bask in their favours.'* (Sergeant-Major Allen, who kept the Swan, fought in the Battle of Balaclava. His tomb-stone, designed by William Sugden, stands in Leek Cemetery. He is, perhaps, one of Leek's neglected characters, and deserves greater recognition.)

A large amount of the leisure time of the townsfolk of Leek, however, was centred on the CHURCHES AND CHAPELS, and their influence was widespread. All the major denominations of the Christian were represented in the town, and most held Sunday Schools and other activities for young people. There was a Wesleyan Institute and a Church Lads' Brigade, and later scouting groups became established. Nearly all the churches had choirs and several had concert parties where impromptu entertainments were performed to appreciative audiences. The National School had a library, reading room and Young Men's Society.

Church-based activities flourished because there was always a ready-made meeting place. And of course, the high level of Victorian piety meant that all churches and chapels were well-attended, giving rise to large buildings with a huge number of seats - a factor that would create a problem for the churches years later when attendances began to decline rapidly.

There was a certain amount of Victorian paternalism in church life. Fathers of industry often saw themselves as spiritual fathers, expecting to see their workers in the pews on Sunday and at the factory bench on Monday morning. Generous support from the silk manufacturers and professions enabled much substantial building work to be carried out.

The Primitive Methodist movement which had such effect in the industrial Potteries did not have quite the same impact in Leek. There was a P.M. chapel in Fountain Street and a few in the villages but the Wesleyans were much stronger and several silk manufactureres were Methodists - John Hall, a partner in the firm of Brough, Nicholson and Hall, to name but one.

Churches of all denominations made a significant contribution to education. with church schools teaching the great majority of Leek children, a system which would prevail well into the 20th century.

With so much going on, there was certainly no shortage of something to do in Victorian and Edwardian Leek.

And of course there were those memorable days when the town was en fete, when the ordinary folk donned their Sunday best and turned out in their hundreds to become, if not quite Spirits of their age, most certainly Faces in the Crowd.

262 LEEK TIME OFF & THE CROWDS

Leek Cricket Club 1890 (MH Miller back row, left)

Leek Harriers, 1895. Front: S Goldstraw, R Hardy, H Peach, G Moores, W Trafford.
Middle: F Hilton, E Hambleton, G Mayers, G McKinsey, E Bull.
Back: J Taylor, E Goldstraw, J Fisher, J Lowe, J Wardle, W Peach, G Gyte, A Rex,
F Pearson, S Taylor, W Hilton, H Walters.

Leek's Golden Years

Top Row: E. HASSALL, F. BYRNE, W. KNOWLES, H. STONEHEWER, W. ALLEN.
Bottom Row: W. VICKERSTAFF, H. E. WHITTLES, A. BASKERVILLE, G. TUDOR, J. BRENTNALL, M. RIDER.

The Leek FC team that reached the third round of the English Cup (fore-runner of the FA Cup) in January 1885.

A Nithsdale photograph.

Ball Haye Green FC 1901-2.
COMMITTEE: H Wilson, J Cottam, J Perry, J Smith, H Biddulph, TS Myatt, D Porter, C Rhead, A Green, G Rider, G Burnett, J Day (secretary)
PLAYERS Back: E Tatton, F Whitter, S Ratcliffe, E Shenton, J Burnett, C Ball, A Naden
Front: F Dale, A Brown, R Green, S Pickford, E Sherratt.

Leek St Marys 1906-7
PLAYERS: Front: CE Goodwin, J Graham, J Alsop, H Hill, M Conway,
Second row: H Cope, H Trafford, H Fitch, AL Kidd, Jim Moss
OFFICIALS: J Moss, W Cope, J Morgan, C Gell, S Mitchell, SW Bailey, J Furby, J Drury, A Moss, P Birch, G Fisher

**A memorable day.
Trades Demonstration 22 June 1909**

Christmas 1906 in New Zealand, a party of 22 Leek men who have travelled to visit their host, Mr Rod, a Leek emigrant - some exchange visit!
E Bullen, G Bailey, H Meakin, R Bailey, T Wood, T Hambleton, G Stanyer, A Simpson
Middle: W Heath, T Plant, J Baxter, J Heath, A Dale, H Porter, F Hassall, E Amson.
Front: C Bonsall, E Brough, J Rod, J Rod jnr, W Newall, F Brooks, E Goodwin, G Ball.

A typical Club Day gathering in the Market Place.

Club Day - in the yard of the Brunswick Methodist Sunday School, Regent Street.

Leek's Golden Years 267

Club Day 1906

Parade to celebrate the wedding of Princess May to the Duke of York, 6 July 1893.

268   Leek's Golden Years

A celebration in the Market Place

Band of Hope, 25th June 1907.

Parade to a military funeral at Leek Cemetery.

Brough Park was opened to the public - note the bandstand.

Colonel Heath, Conservative, is returned 1910.

Robert Pearce, successful liberal candidate later the same year.

BELOW: A group of Leek Liberals, 1895, promoting Pearce when he first stood for election.

Leek's Golden Years 271

Robert Pearce (Lib.) addressing a meeting outside the Coffee Tavern 1910 Election.

Col. Heath (Cons.) addressing a meeting outside the Coffee Tavern 1910 Election.

LEEK AMATEUR MUSICAL SOCIETY.

THE FIRST CONCERT

OF THIS SOCIETY WILL BE GIVEN

ON TUESDAY EVENING, MAY 8th, 1866,

IN THE TEMPERANCE HALL, UNION STREET,

When, in addition to the Vocal Music by the members,

THE REV. DR. ARMSTRONG, Rector of Burslem,
SOLO FLUTE,

THE REV. C. A. BARKER, Curate of Chesterton,
SOLO PIANOFORTE,

AND

MR. J. F. CADMAN,
SOLO VIOLIN,

Have very kindly consented to give their valuable aid to the Society.

THE PROGRAMME WILL INCLUDE

Two Solos on the Flute.
One of Dr. Beriot's Grand Solos for the Violin, and a Duet Concertante for Violin and Pianoforte.
Two Pianoforte Solos by the Rev. C. A. Barker, on Themes arranged by himself.
Bishop's celebrated Solo and Chorus, "Now Tramp."
Three of Mendelssohn's finest Part Songs.
Handel's Laughing Song and Chorus, "Haste thee Nymph."
Bishop's Quintett, "Blow gentle gales."
Several ancient MADRIGALS & modern CHORAL GLEES, with SONGS & DUETS by various Members of the Society.

The Body of the Hall will be reserved for Members and for those Friends who purchase a 5s. Ticket, which will admit to all the Concerts of the Society during the year.

THE GALLERY WILL BE THROWN OPEN TO THE PUBLIC.
TICKETS 1s. each, to be obtained of Mr. Rider.

DOORS OPEN at 7.30, THE CONCERT TO COMMENCE AT 8 PRECISELY.
There will be a Cloak Room for Ladies on the right hand of the Entrance Hall.
BOOKS OF WORDS MAY BE OBTAINED IN THE HALL, PRICE 1d.

Leek Amateur Musical Society - programme for the first concert 1866.

Leek's Golden Years 273

A typical play bill for the travelling theatre.

Celebrating Queen Victoria's Golden Jubilee, 21 June 1887 in the Cattle Market (later Memorial site). A brief account appeared later in the Leek News (1932):

It was one of the hottest days of that glorious summer, and the scholars, bands Volunteers, friendly societies, etc began to assemble in the Cattle Market at 1.30pm. At 1.55 the Blue Ribbon Army Band struck up 'Rule, Britannia' and at 2 o'clock the first hymn was sung. Then the Earl of Shrewsbury's Band played 'God Bless the Prince of Wales', after which the second hymn was sung. followed by the bugle call for silence and the Volunteers fired a 'Feu de Joie'. Then while the bands played the whole assembly sung the National Anthem.

The procession formed in this order: Superintendent of police (mounted). No 1 Company 1st Volunteer Batt. North Staffs Regt (Leek Detachment) headed by their band, the Magistrates, the Commissioners, Ministers of Religion, female scholars and children, the Blue ribbon Army Band, male scholars and children, the Earl of Shrewsbury's Band, the friendly societies: Pride of the Moorlands United Sisters, Leek Independent Male Humane Society, Foresters Court 545, Oddfellows Manchester Unity, Foresters - Court Pacific, Gardeners, Druids, Provident Society, Oddfellows - Prince Albert Lodge, Moorlands Lodge, Victoria Lodge, then the Fire Brigade and Police.

The route was anti-clockwise round the town then up to the Pickwood Recreation Ground where Mr Challinor formally handed the Deed of Conveyance to the Chairman of Commissioners . The children received a commemorative mug and tea followed by sports and amusements concluding with a grand fireworks display, bonfire and torchlight procession.

Sixteen
FACES IN THE CROWD

Most English towns have a tradition of parades to celebrate great occasions and local customs. Leek is no exception and the townsfolk of Leek have always taken a great delight in public occasions, and have needed little encouragement to pull out all the stops in support of the grand show. Such gatherings have usually seen the entire spectrum of the social classes in the town turning out to take part, or just to watch.

Royal occasions, visits and anniversaries, proclamations, peace celebrations, trade demonstrations, grand openings, local historical events, civic occasions, religious gatherings, carnivals, galas and fetes have always seen the Leek crowds. To see the streets around the town centre thronged with people, standing up to twelve deep on the pavements was a glorious sight indeed. Young and old, rich and poor, worker and manager were drawn together in a common desire to witness the civic pride in the town or to demonstrate their religious or political beliefs - or just to bring some fun into their otherwise hard lives and feel, for a little while, one of the crowd.

Take, for example, the great event that took place on 21 June 1897, when William Challinor presented the Pickwood Recreation Ground to the town. Many civic dignitaries were present, dressed in their finery - the Leek Improvement Commissioners, the silk manufacturers and professional men, with Challinor himself basking in the glory of the accolades lauded upon him. And all this excitement was taking place literally in his own back garden, as it were, for Pickwood Hall, his home, was just on the edge of the land designated for the recreation ground.

By far the most excited and animated members of the crowd were the children, some from the better-off families dressed in their Sunday best, others of more humble stock in their ragged trousers and pinafore dresses.

On this red-letter day, to celebrate Queen Victoria's Jubilee, commemorative mugs were presented to 5000 local school children assembled at 'the Rec'. How many of these mugs would be smashed before they left the scene? But many would be carried lovingly and carefully back home, like a crock of gold, perhaps only to be commandeered for father's beer. Others would languish on dusty sideboards or in cupboards, to re-emerge many years later on the antiques market, commanding prices way beyond their original value.

Among the 5000 children present were several of the offspring of Lewis Fisher and Harriet Peach. Their marriage had produced no less than 15 children. Several had already left school, and were too old to qualify for a mug. Clara Fisher was then aged 18, and working as a silk winder. She had yet to meet Arthur Poole, who she would marry, for he was then only 14 years old. Arthur's sisters, Emily (13), Eliza (9) and Amelia (7) would no doubt be present to receive their mugs. Several of the younger Fishers were also present: Lewis (11), Ashley (10), Robert (7), Mary Ann (6), Charles (5) and Arthur (4) were all in line for mugs. Occasions like this would enliven their mundane lives. and we can guess the impact these events had on their young minds. Treats were rare and very special when they came along.

The great annual treat for many Leek children was the Club Day procession, another event which brought the different social classes together. Originally called 'Cap Sunday' this celebration brought together the Leek Sunday Schools. The Sunday School movement in Leek had gone from strength to strength since it was founded in 1797. By the early 19th century churches of every denomination had established Sunday Schools which, besides teaching the fundamentals of Christianity, were bringing a rudimentary education to working class children. The tradition of a procession around the town culminating in a singing of hymns in the Market Place began.

Some measure of paternalism led many of Leek's leading citizens - silk manufacturers, shop keepers and business men - to lend their support to the Sunday Schools. But they did this in a spirit of real generosity, and subscription lists on appeal days were headed by well-known names. They would often be seen heading the Club Day procession, with the children following behind. Their generosity usually also provided tea and some entertainment for the children after the procession, by which time they could retire to the comfort of their fine houses.

The annual event, the Band of Hope Demonstration, was yet another excuse for a grand parade around the town. Born out of the temperance movement, the Band of Hope was strongly supported by the churches, and the heart of its message was the danger of strong drink. It was another opportunity for the upper classes to be seen supporting moral causes, and they did so strongly. The procession brought together young and old, rich and poor. The Fishers and the Pooles, not wanting to miss anything, would again be here, for again the people of Leek - teetotallers and drinkers alike - turned out in great numbers to watch the parade.

These public demonstrations were non-political, but Leek people have also never been shy at making a visual display of their allegiances. Perhaps working class folk were looking for ways to make their voices heard and reinforce the work of the local trade unions. In 1907 an initiative was launched in Leek to increase trade union membership, placing the emphasis on women members. A great trades demonstration was held in the town - involving, of course, a parade. A series of photographs of the event, taken by WH Nithsdale, show crowded streets thronged with demonstrators and spectators, as over 3000 people took part.

It was a peaceful demonstration, but with so many faces in the crowd its impact was significant, especially since the parade marched along St Edward Street, passing close to the front windows of the local gentry in their fine houses on the western side of the street.

One of the grand houses of the gentry was Spout Hall in St Edward Street. Designed by the great architect Richard Norman Shaw in a fine Tudor style it stands proudly on the western side, asserting itself alongside other fine gentlemen's residences, a monument to Victorian munificence. The Sleigh, Wardle and Allen families were among the residents of Victorian St Edward Street, and their fine houses looked out across the street to the more humble properties on the eastern side.

The small shops which fronted the eastern side of St Edward Street were punctuated by the odd court or alley leading into a very different world. For here, hidden from the view of the fine houses opposite, were the courts which housed the tiny cottages of working-class folk. The epitome of the typical English market town, you may say, retaining something of the spirit of Elizabethan England. Gentility and squalor side by side. The higgledy-piggledy nature of St Edward Street, both in its buildings and its people, is part of its glory.

Did the gentry peep through their lace curtains to observe the townsfolk coming and going about their daily business? Here were the silk workers, road sweepers, washerwomen, labourers, gardeners, errand boys, servants, ragged-trousered children and ladies of the night, vigorously striving to retain their pride and independence in spite of the squalor in which so many of them lived. These folk embodied the spirit of Leek which has always been unique, and has always been an important reason for the creative nature of the town.

Old-time elections were usually high-profile affairs, and lots of fun. The hustings of yesterday were fought over with great vigour, very much in the public eye. Candidates addressed crowded meetings, very often in the open air. At the 1895 election the local Liberals used a group of cyclists, with election posters emblazoned on their bikes, to tour the constituency.

1910 was a particularly exciting year - there were TWO General Elections. At the first one, the Conservative candidate, Colonel Heath, spoke to a large gathering, a crowd of bowler hats and cloth caps, assembled in front of the Coffee Tavern, near the old cattle market. His platform was a cart belonging to a local trader. The result of this election was a very narrow victory by a mere 10 votes for the Conservative Heath over the Liberal Robert Pearce. This was Pearce's fourth attempt to get elected. His luck was to change at his fifth attempt later in 1910, when he won by 590 votes over Colonel Bromley Davenport. Scenes of wild excitement were witnessed in the streets when the result was announced, with crowds of electors celebrating this famous victory.

The Pooles and the Fishers, always politically motivated, would no doubt be amongst the crowd, alongside their silk working colleagues. One eyewitness, the late Mrs Barbara Priest (nee Allen, daughter of William Allen, living in St Edward Street) recalled seeing a great crowd of people rushing down the street and shouting that Pearce was elected. What a shock that must have been to her solid Conservative parents!

Leek has always been a town where just a few, the forgers of Leek's destiny, stand above the many, but the many, the faces in the crowd, are strong and independent, the wroughters of the town's creativity. Even today, on Club Day, St Georges Day, at Christmas - whenever an excuse can be found - the crowds are there, Leek faces acknowledging their fellow townsfolk.

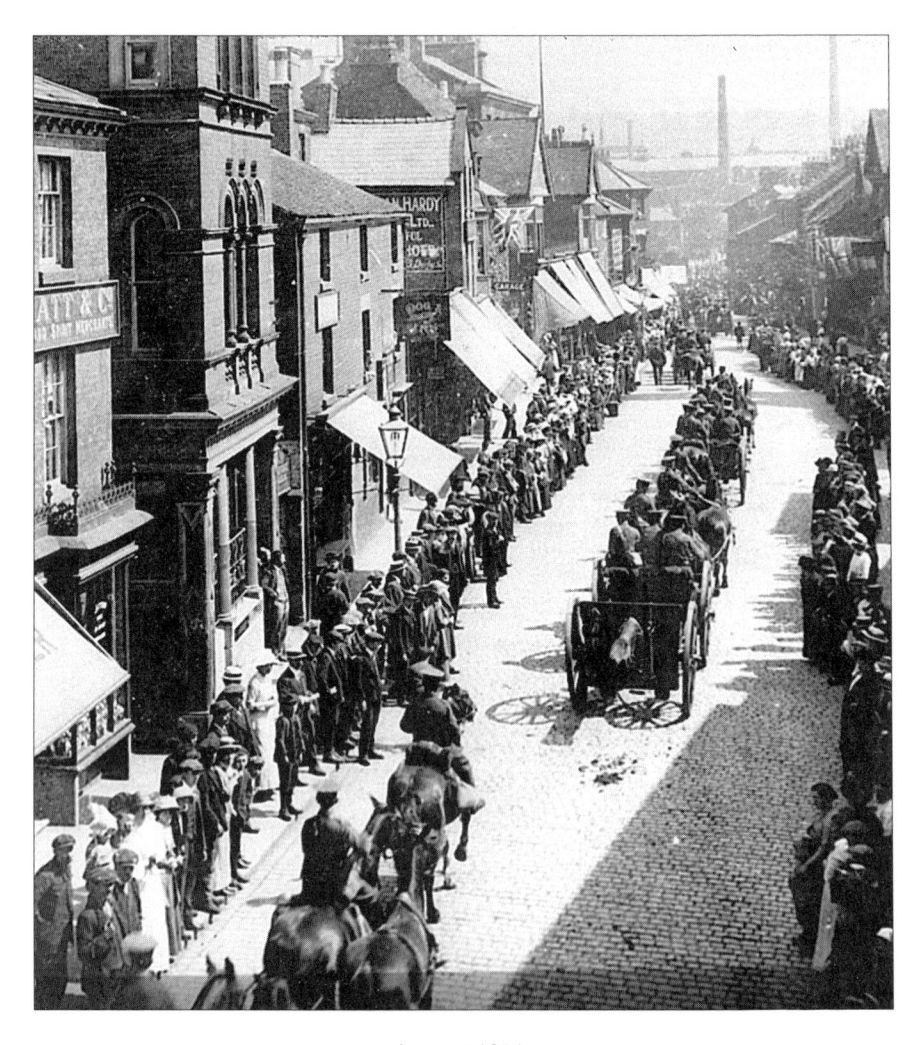

August 1914.
The Leek Battery marches off to war,
and the end of the 'Edwardian Summer'.

POSTSCRIPT

In the company of our leading players we have explored many aspects of life in this ancient town as it developed through the Victorian years into the Edwardian era. They commanded respect and admiration, but none was exactly a saint. The dubious Victorian virtues of imperialism and paternalism were apparent in them all, and most of them had an eye to the main chance. This is not to say that they abused their positions, but they certainly exploited the opportunities of the growing town to the full. As a result, Leek became during this period a centre of excellence in industry, art and culture. This continued into the 20th century, but the march of Victorian imperialism was over and the long Edwardian summer was drawing to a close. The events of 1914 would change things for ever.

The working-class folk of Leek put in long hours at the mill, singing in the church and chapel choirs, playing in the various sports teams, drinking in the pubs and procreating large families to keep the whole thing going. George Fisher and his family were typical of this, and out of his descendents came a long line of fifteen siblings, one of whom was my paternal grandmother, a silk winder who herself worked half time in the mill when she was a girl. Such families were the mainstay of the silk industry, and tragically also fed the guns of the Great War. Few escaped the impact of the conflict in some way or other. George Fisher's great-grandson, my uncle George Henry Poole, survived the Great War. He served with the 2nd Battalion Royal Fusiliers in their attack on the Hawthorn Redout on the first day of the Battle of the Somme, where he was wounded. Like many of the survivors he refused to speak about his experiences - and I never remember him doing so.

And what became of the silk industry? By the latter quarter of the 20th century things were in decline. The old 'family firms' were gone, many of them the subject of take-over bids from the textile giants. The advent of man-made fibres meant that real silk goods could not compete, and whilst this led to a mini renaissance in the industry, this did not last. And with the growing import trade in cheaper garments from abroad, the writing was on the wall. Closure followed closure, some of them hastened by the ever-present tragedy of factory fires, and a once-proud industry drew to a close. Although many of the fine old factory buildings have survived and been converted into dwellings or places of commercial or cultural use.

So what of the future? The early years of the 21st century have seen a growth in tourism. Leek stands at the edge of the Peak District National Park, close to the major theme park of Alton Towers and with a steam railway and canal nearby. It is a noted centre for antiques, and home to two major Building Societies, each of which enjoys national recognition.

Its people still sing in choirs, and take part in musical and dramatic productions, with a high level of success and support. It has entered into a twinning arrangement with the Italian town of Este and cultural exchanges take place between the two. In sport it has produced individuals who have gone on to achieve fame at a higher level, and boasts many good football, cricket, rugby and hockey teams, athletics, the cyclists, and of course two medallists in the Bejing Olympics, to name but a few.

Leek has avoided major schemes of urbanisation and has not been carved up by road schemes. It has retained its essential character as the old market town which enjoyed such great prosperity in the golden years of the silk industry. Much of its Victorian architecture still remains, studied with much interest by visitors and students alike.

So what would our emminent Victorians make of 21st century Leek? They would surely applaud the town's continued development, in food production, agricultural engineering, building societies, the antiques trade, as well as a flourishing arts scene. History is a continuing process, from cottage button-makers to steam-driven factories, from small savings to multi-million pound societies, from Commissioners to District Councillors - and it is the lessons of history which will shape the future.

Appendices

THE WORKS OF SUGDEN & SON, LEEK'S VICTORIAN ARCHITECTS

The following is a list, in chronological order, of the known main buildings of William and Larner Sugden, in the Leek town area. This does not take into account smaller house schemes, renovations and furniture design projects which the firm undertook from time to time.

c.1850	New Black's Head (Market Place)
1852	Savings Bank, 7 Stockwell Street
1854	West Street School
1856	Brunswick Wesleyan Chapel, Market Street (Builders J & J Matthews) 3 Houses: 49, 51 and 53 Queen Street (for George Salt) Bermingham's Factory, Compton (warehouse and shade) Alterations to Butcher's Arms, Queen Street (for Charles Wilson) Richard Cutting Tomb (St Edward's Churchyard)
1857	Rosebank House (for James Johnson) House on Ball Haye Green (for T Shenton) 2 Houses in Brunswick Street (for Joseph Hall)
1858	4 Houses: 4, 6, 8 and 10 Queen Street (for W B Nixon) Cemetery Chapel
1859	6 Houses in Park Road (for Isaac Middleton) House in Westwood Terrace (for Mr Needham) Shopfront, 57 Derby Street (for Henry Haynes)
1860	Big Mill, Mill Street (for Lovatt and Gould) House, later Park Tavern (for T Gell)
1862	Cemetery Chapel (extensive repairs following storm damage) Mechanics Institute, Russell Street
1863	Congregational Church, Derby Street/Russell Street Roman Catholic School, King Street
1864	Alexandra Mill, Earl Street (for Davidson & Myatt) Shop for H G Carr, 7 Derby Street
1865	Warehouse, offices and shade, Cross Street/Well Street (for Brough's) Alterations to Butcher's Arms, 12 Derby Street
1866	Work on The Angel, Market Place (for Platt's) Shop for Wooliscroft,s, 12 Derby Street (formerly Butcher's Arms) Alterations to Howard's shop, Market Place Extension at Leek Foundry, Newcastle Road Alterations to shade, Weston Street Mill

1867	Alterations to Stockwell House (for Joshua Nicholson) Shade in Bath Street (for Price and Fynney)
1868	Frontage to Peter Magnier's shop, 15 Derby Street
1869	Sutton's shop, Market Place Carding's Corn Stores, 59 Derby Street 4 Houses: 25, 27, 29 and 31 Bath Street (for Richard Lovatt) 2 Houses: 76 and 78 Broad Street
1870	Methodist Chapel and Ragged School, Mill Street St John's Mission Church, Mill Street Stables for Charles Carr, Buxton Road Further work on Cemetery Chapel 4 Houses in Grosvenor Street (for Isaac Heath) Alterations to Compton House (for Joseph Challinor)
1871	Cottage Hospital St Luke's School, Earl Street Additions to Temperance Hall, Union Street Boiler house for Walker's Brewery, Broad Street Extensions to Roman Catholic School, King Street
1872	Lecture Hall and School, Congregational Church, Russell Street Roofing work on The Angel, Market Place (for J N Platt)
1875	Shirley's Buildings, St Edward Street/Sheepmarket
1876	Haywood Mill, Haywood Street (for H D Bailey, agricultural engineer)
1877	Restoration and enlargement, Mount Pleasant Methodist Chapel Sugden Houses, 29, 29A and 29B Queen Street
1879	2 Houses in Portland Street North (for John Naden)
1880	2 Houses: 33 and 35 Bath Street (for Mr Rider) Littlehales, Buxton Road (for W S Brough) 2 Houses: 6 and 8 Hugo Street (for Mr Tillotson)
1881	Extension to West Street School Work on Fynney's Mill, Market Street (Leek Times offices)
1882	Manchester and Liverpool District Bank, Derby Street Commencement of work on Nicholson Institute
1884	Nicholson Institute completed and opened Primitive Methodist Chapel, Fountain Street
1885	Alterations to Magnier's shop, 17 Derby Street
1886	Extensions to Leek Foundry, Newcastle Road
1887	Plans for extension to Leek Town Hall, Market Street

1890	Improvements to Brunswick Methodist Chapel
1891	Police Station, Leonard Street Plans for extensions to Woodcroft Hall (for Henry Davenport)

WILLIAM SUGDEN DIED IN 1892. ALL SUBSEQUENT WORK IS LARNER'S.

1893	Cottage Hospital gateway
1894	Sander's Buildings, Derby Street/Haywood Street Tombstone for Sgt Major Allen, Leek Cemetery
1895	Overfield's Furniture Warehouse, Russell Street Picton Street Co-op. Plans for Buttermarket and Fire Station (unsuccessful)
1896	Additions to Pickwood House (for W E Challinor)
1897	8 Houses: 45 to 61 Barngate Street (for Heath and Lowe) 2 Houses in Portland Street North (for Robert Brindley)
1898	Alterations to Central Liberal Club, Market Street
1899	Co-op Central Premises, hall and bakery, Ashbourne Road
1900	Leek Technical Schools (completed)
1901	Carr Gymnasium Conversion of Sugden Offices, 13 and 13A Derby Street, to shops

OTHER SUGDEN BUILDINGS IN NORTH STAFFORDSHIRE:

Tabernacle Church, Hanley (1882)
New Mixon Hay plans, for J W Phillips (1882)
Bagnall Hall extensions for John Keats (1885)
Town Hall and Library, Cheadle, plans (1893)
County Asylum, Cheddleton, plans (1893)
Heybridge, Tean extensions for J W Phillips
Moor Court, Oakamoor (1862) and extensions (1878) for A S Bolton
Swythamley Hall alterations for P L Brocklehurst
Basford Hurst for W H Rider
Davenport's Boat-house, Rudyard Lake (1893)
Workers' houses in Cheadle for J and N Phillips & Co.
Tatton's Dye Works, Upperhulme
Argyll House, Roches for Captain Byrom
Hanley Mechanics Institute improvements (1892)
Abbotsholme School developments
Sewage Scheme, Bucknall

St John's Roman Catholic School, Kidsgrove (1892)
Primitive Methodist Chapel, Cheadle, extensions (1881)
Dresden Congregational Church (1883)
Alstonefield School extensions
Wetton Church repairs (1894)
Horton Church, chancel
Butterton Church, spire only (1879)
Kingsley Schools
Woodhead Hall, Cheadle for W Allen (1881)
Churnet Grange for Captain Colville
Highfield Hall Lodge
Model farm at Lower Tean for J W Phillips (1863)
Newcastle-under-Lyme Public Buildings (1885)

SUGDEN BUILDINGS ELSEWHERE:

Keighley Free Church (1868)
Strong Close House, Keighley (1869)
Dalton Mill, Keighley for J and N Craven & Co. (1871)
Laurel Mount, Keighley
St Barnabas Church, Keighley
Keighley Technical Institute extensions
Cavendish Street United Methodist Church, Keighley
Congregational Church, Congleton (1877)
Congleton Town Hall alterations (1892)
Secular Society Hall, Leicester (1879)
House for Mr Brough, Scarborough (1885)
Red House, 'Maison Rouge', Buxton (1897)
Tannery at Burton for R S Elliot
One Ash, Woodthorpe, near Loughborough (1894)
Elmhurst, Mr Hunter's residence, Rugby (1895)
Ashbourne Town Hall alterations (1895)
Hillmorton House, Rugby (1895)
Newport Cemetery Chapel (1864)
Sheffield Municipal Buildings (1864)
Stafford County Council Buildings (1892)
People's Hall, Framlingham, altered and adapted (1868)
Hartley's Model Village, Aintree (1888)
Liverpool Zoological Gardens: entrance lodge, monkey house and tea rooms (1883)

OTHER ARCHITECTS AT WORK IN VICTORIAN AND EDWARDIAN LEEK

Other architects, local and national, made significant contributions to the growing town. The following list shows examples of the wealth of talent which Leek enjoyed when design and quality were paramount.

JOHN BREALEY 1 Stockwell Street, surveyor
1859 Bakehouse in Deansgate
1863 Two houses in Bath Street, Nos. 37 and 39
1868 Two houses in Portland Street
1869 Several houses in Grosvenor Street and Moorhouse Street
1875 Cattle Market Inn (alterations)

JOHN THOMAS BREALEY 15 Stockwell St, Leek & Hanley, surveyor, son of above
1893 Workshops in Shoobridge Street, for James Heath, builder
1894 Houses in Cruso Street, Nos. 19 to 31
1896/97 Butter Market and Fire Station
1898 Two houses in Daintry Street
1899 Three houses in Spencer Avenue, Nos. 2,4 and 6
1900 28 houses in Langford Street
1900 Houses in Barngate Street
1901 22 houses and shop in James Street
1902 27 houses in Osborne Street
1902 Foxlowe (alterations and additions)
1903 Two houses in Cheddleton Heath
1904 Workshop in Brunswick Street, for A J Worthington
1904 Several houses in Junction Road

JAMES GOSLING SMITH 26 (later 43) St Edward Street, surveyor
1886 Britannia Street School (St Edward's day school)
1891 Victoria Buildings, Broad Street, for Henry Bermingham
1894 Waterloo Mill, Waterloo Street, for William Broster
1894 Ten houses in Barngate Street, for J Broster and A Bowcock
1897 Four houses in Westwood Road, Nos. 11 to 17
1897 Four houses in Spring Gardens, Nos. 2 to 8

URIAH HUDSON London Road (Ashbourne Road) and York Street, surveyor
1857 House in West Street
1864 Stables at Talbot Inn
1865 Two houses in Ford Street
1866 One house in York Street and two houses in Novi Lane
1866 Three houses in York Street, Nos~ 25 to 29
1867 Nine houses in Grosvenor Street and Moorhouse Street
1867 Three houses on Ball Haye Green, Nos. 47, 49 and 49a
1867 Two houses and joiner's shop in Bath Street, for J and J Hudson
1867 Cawdry House
1867 Two houses in Queen Street
1867 Bakehouse on Compton
1867 Cattle Market Inn

1871 Bakehouse and stable in Haywood Street, for Henry Davenport
1871 Shop-front for John Sutton, Stanley Street

JOHN TAYLOR, Macclesfield

1878 Five houses in Britannia Street
1880 Brunswick School, Regent Street/Ball Haye Street

ROBERT EDGAR, Stoke-on-Trent

1863 All Saints Day School, Compton/Southbank Street

W OWEN, Warrington

1885 Parr's Bank, St Edward Street (now Bank House)

ELIJAH JONES, Hanley

1895 Smithfield House, Leonard Street

GEORGE CHAPPELL

1900 Offices and warehouse, Belle Vue Mill, for Wardle & Davenport

RICHARD NORMAN SHAW, London

1871 Spout Hall, St Edward Street, for Hugh Sleigh
1887 All Saints Church, Leek
1868 St Matthew's Church, Meerbrook, nave
1873 Also at St Matthew's Church, chancel and tower
       Possibly Condlyffe Alms Houses, Cemetery Road

GERALD HORSLEY, London

1894 All Saints School, Compton, cloakroom and other work
1914 St Luke's Church, Leek, vestry
1905 St Chad's Church, Longsdon

H and F FRANCIS, London

1847 St Luke's Church, Leek
Possible other work for local authority, including Public Baths

ALBERT VICARS

1887 St Mary's Roman Catholic Church, Compton

GEORGE EDMUND STREET, London

1865/67 St Edward's Church, Leek, new chancel

AND INTO THE TWENTIETH CENTURY:

REGINALD LONGDEN, 43 St Edward Street

1910 Leek & Moorlands Co-operative Society, shopping emporium, High St, Leek
1911 High Barn, Fynney Street, for himself
1912 London Mills, extensions, for Watson & Co
1913 Two houses in Hartington Street, Nos. 2 and 4
1914 Moorhill, Buxton Road, house and preparatory school for G J Worthington
1915 Square Croft, Fynney Street
1915 & 1918 London Mills, further extensions, for Watson & Co
1921 Prenton, Buxton Road